Six Who Changed the World

Six Who Changed the World

Moses   •   Jesus   •   Paul
Marx   •   Freud   •   Einstein

by Henry Enoch Kagan

New York • Thomas Yoseloff, Publisher • London

Thomas Yoseloff, *Publisher*
8 East 36th Street
New York 16, N. Y.

Thomas Yoseloff Ltd.
18 Charing Cross Road
London W.C.2, England

First printing September 1963
Second printing February 1964

6015
Printed in the United States of America

Contents

Six Who Changed the World

Introduction: The Genius and the Group

A genius is like all other men; like some other men; and like no other man. Moses, Jesus, Paul, Marx, Freud and Einstein were geniuses, unique in that each one radically changed the course of history. The most vital forces in our modern world originated in the lives of these six Jews. Their contributions were all in the field of thought and their ideas have become part of our daily thinking profoundly influencing our lives and our future. To fully realize what they did we must understand how much they differed from all men; but to appreciate this difference we must not be afraid to see how much they were like all men. Furthermore, by observing not only how much they differed but also how much they were the same as all men we might become more objective and for our own good consciously determine what to reject and what to accept in their ideas.

A complete portrait of a person will depict him in four dimensions. First, it will show the biological make-up basic to every individual. When a biographer looks for the unusual in his subject, he is apt to overlook the fact that all men hold in common characteristics that produce tension such as hunger and sex which need to be appeased. Second, it will reveal how the person came to be like other members of the group into which he was born and unlike those of other groups to which he did not belong. Third, the biography will define the role the person played in society, whether this be a selected or an assigned role. Now, so many combinations can be made out of these three dimensions that they might seem sufficient in themselves to portray fully any individual. Yet, no matter how completely a person may be differentiated by these three dimensions it is a fourth dimension which makes him a distinct individual.

Every person is like all or some others physically, socially and even psychologically; but there is something different about each person. Every situation in which the three determinants of physique, group and role combine to make up the individual is a unique situation. Even in a genetic sense, no two children have exactly the same parents. The variations of the nucleo-proteins in the genes are infinite. Furthermore, the parents of the second child are not the same parents they were when they had their first child. Their emotional attitudes toward a child have been changed by their relations with their first child. Finally, things simply happen to persons that are never exactly the same for any two individuals. The unpredictable or a traumatic experience, which in each case has a certain absolutely unique feature, must be included to complete the portrait of a person. Plutarch, the father of biography, made his accounts of great men come alive because he looked for that unique feature in them even if it was only to be found in some small detail. He said: "A light occasion, a word or a short saying make a man's disposition appear more plainly than the famous battles wherein are slain a thousand men."

Every person is the product of this complex process of individuation. To many persons such an idea is annoying. Most persons want a simple explanation of personality, preferably one which will match their own temperament.

Because so many factors must be considered including especially the unpredictable, emotional preference can easily inject itself even into the scientific study of the development of personality. Whether it is primarily heredity or environment which determines the potential of an individual has long been debated. The debate has produced more partisan opinion than objective fact because the scientists are also persons who bring to their study their own personal feelings. A liberal humanitarian who advocates social reforms therefore will present the cheerful, reassuring findings that environment (which can be changed) is more important than heredity in developing a person. On the other hand, a conservative authoritarian who wants to maintain the status quo will therefore insist that heredity cannot be altered by changing the environment. The fact is that hereditary and environment cannot be artificially separated to satisfy the emotional preferences of the investigator. Feeblemindedness and intelligence are both related to family inheritance; but whether intelligence will be mothered or smothered is the result of family environment, social opportunity and cultural stimulation.

False distinctions in the analysis of personality are also perpetuated unwittingly by specialized scientists who present a particular emphasis to satisfy their interests. Anthropologists emphasize, in their studies, the structure of society and the patterns of culture. Since their goal is a description of group life, they are interested in noting the similarities of the members of a group. Psychiatrists, on the other hand, direct their attention to the factors within the individual which make him different from his group. Yet, one cannot be defined without the other since a person is an individual but only so in society.

The complex interaction of the individual in his culture

applies no less to the genius. It can apply even more to the genius than to the ordinary man. There have been a number of studies of what makes a genius but they should be read with caution because these writers also injected their personal feelings or reflected the dominant views of the culture of their day. Sir Francis Galton, who made the first scientific study of genius one hundred years ago, represented the view of the aristocracy. He therefore examined the family trees of eminent British men and concluded that genius was simply a matter of heredity though it should have been obvious that one does not have to possess even talent let alone genius to become eminent for eminence is often only the result of good fortune. Cesare Lombroso, who specialized in criminology, seems to have had a cynical if not envious attitude toward genius and therefore concluded that genius was closely allied to insanity. Lewis M. Terman, the American psychologist, put an entirely different light on genius because he reflected American practicality and optimism and wanted the school systems in America to pay more attention to the gifted child. Therefore, he found that contrary to the general opinion the highly gifted were often not only more intelligent but also healthier and more sociable than the average child.

There is still another reason why these studies are not adequate for although they claim to have studied genius they really were only studying the gifted. There is a difference between the gifted and the genius. Is the difference a difference in degree or in kind? Does the genius simply have more of the same physical, mental and emotional stuff which makes up the gifted? Is the difference qualitative rather than quantitative?

We are inclined to believe that the genius is a person of a peculiar kind. We accept dramatic and poetic definitions

of the genius. Genius is a mystery. The genius is gifted
with something semi-divine. The word itself is derived
from the Latin and the Arabic. A *genius* in Roman pagan
religion was a private tutelary deity who was supposed to
accompany and guide special persons. A *jinni* in Arabian
folklore was a kind of nature daemon who could be called
upon by magic to perform great things for a person.
Accordingly, the genius both controls and is controlled by
a power. This mystical notion of the dual nature of the
genius has been perpetuated by the poets. James Russell
Lowell declared: "Talent is that which is in a man's
power. Genius is that in whose power man is." Owen
Meredith said: "Genius does what it must and talent does
what it can." The genius is not merely one who possesses
talent; he is possessed by his talent.

For daemonic possession which the poet uses to explain
genius the psychologist substitutes his own term. The
psychologist says the genius is subject to the same unconscious motivations that move the gifted and the ordinary
man. Therefore, the genius as well as the gifted and the
ordinary man can be subjected to psychological testing.
Could such a measurement be verified? Since there are
very few geniuses and many highly gifted persons, only
from the latter can there be a sampling large enough for
statistical comparisons. Modern statistical studies of the
psychology of the highly gifted are now being conducted.
From the findings about the motivations of these talented
persons some light is coming forth which helps us pene-
trate the veil of mystery that cloaks the genius.

A study of the highly gifted person has been going on
for a number of years at the Institute of Personality
Assessment and Research at the University of California.
There a variety of living creative personalities are being
studied in depth. Their attitudes, interests, and life styles

are being compared with those of the average person. It may be surprising, but it has been discovered that what distinguishes the most highly creative from the less gifted is not so much a difference in intelligence or skill. The creative personalities differ most from the average person in that they are much more aware than the average of the struggle between opposing emotional forces within themselves. Whether the materials are colors used by the painters, lines used by the architects, chemicals used by the scientists, figures used by the mathematicians, sounds used by the musicians or words used by the poets, all these creative persons have one thing in common—an awareness of inner conflict.

The most creative persons are more sensitive to their own need for reconciling opposing inner forces. They are very much less interested than the average in practical, concrete details because tangible or simple interests have little emotional conflict in them. Rather are they attracted by the contradictions between details. This stimulates their search for a unifying principle. Concerned with finding an over-all meaning, the creative persons try to discover symbolic equivalents for things and ideas. The symbols of words, sounds, colors, numbers are more maneuverable than concrete things. The creative persons may achieve with these symbols a total configuration and not be limited to a partial picture of what they seek. Therefore, the creative persons prefer intuitive perception to sense perception. This simply means that they are not satisfied with copying what they see, hear or feel. They are not content with merely becoming aware of what is. They want what could be. The conflict between what is and what could be awakens the curiosity and arouses the imagination of the creative.

Compared to the average, the talented also demonstrate the opposition of conflicting forces in a number of other areas. The highly gifted person places as great a value on aesthetic experience as he does on theoretical thinking. This is a contradiction. The aesthetic deals with beauty visualized while the theoretical deals with ideas in the abstract. A more striking evidence of opposites lies in the finding that while the creative person reveals masculine traits, feminine traits in him are also stronger than those found in the average male. The highly gifted male is assertive, dominant and self-confident. He is not effeminate but he is "feminine" in the psychological sense of that term. He is more "open to feeling" than the average male. The language describing the productivity of the genius has feminine analogies. The genius is "inspired" which means "taking in." The genius is "pregnant" with an idea and experiences pain in giving birth to it.

More openly receptive to experience, the gifted person prefers the complex and abstract to the simple and well-defined. He is less disturbed by disorder. The average person is actually afraid of disorder. He quickly tries to put everything he experiences into a form he can readily define. The creative person is much more adventurous. He is more like the great men Nietzche described who "would fain give multiformity and disorder definite shape: it stimulates them to behold chaos." Witness the creative person who welcomes disorder by taking his own good time experimenting with it. He does not force immediate solutions. This patience of the gifted has been compared to the action of water, which in quietly freezing can burst granite that no sledge hammer can crack. The highly talented person becomes exhilarated by a problem—in fact, he tends to become a part of it. He follows where its forces lead as though he were letting the problem "solve itself." Only then does creativity burst through and finish off the extended process into a new pattern of order.

According to popular opinion, the highly talented are

supposed to be non-conformists. This is true, but according to the findings, they do not conform to the stereotype of the artificial, Bohemian, non-conformist. The creative person does not conform because reconciling the opposites within himself is more important than social approval. He is not the adjusted person, who being "well-rounded" easily rolls downhill with the crowd. He develops the "sharp edges" needed to climb a mountain. If the creative person is out of step it is because, as Thoreau put it, "he hears a different drummer. Let him step to the music he hears however measured or far away."

The highly creative persons reveal another characteristic which indicates that they are more aware of inner tension than the average. They claim more than do other persons that their childhood was not very happy. Unhappy childhood is not unusual for the average person but the creative person is more likely to report it because he is more apt to retain a vivid consciousness of unhappy childhood. The creative person acknowledges what the average person represses. The average person cannot tolerate an open awareness of the opposing forces between passion and reason, between the irrational and the rational, between the unconscious and the conscious within himself. And the more the average person represses these tensions the more do they break into anxiety. The average person is not creative because this anxiety inhibits creativity. The creative person does not seek comfort or desire "peace of mind." Yet his uncertainties do not make him insecure. The creative person has the good fortune of possessing what I would call a higher tolerance for tension.

These psychological findings about the creative person might be applied to the genius. A genius has a tolerance for tension very much higher than that of the talented. Because he can take it better than anyone else he does something with tension which is unique. Tensions which may make the average man psychotic make the genius creative. This fact about the genius may account for his being associated in the past with the madman.

Many who have theorized about the genius have described his very high threshold for enduring opposites, his very high tolerance for tension. The psychoanalyst, Ernest Jones, held that the genius is conscious of conflicting forces in him. The genius deeply feels the breach of incompleteness until suddenly the breach is bridged. After a long fructifying process in his unconscious, like a flash a new insight springs forth. This happens after the most intense concentration during which the genius, as if in a hypnotic trance, listens to nothing but his own thinking no matter how fanciful it may be. This is how Coleridge said he composed his esoteric poem, *Kubla Khan*. This exhausting mental process is as true for the scientific genius as it is for the mystic poet. When asked by what method of thinking he had formulated his world shaking new laws of physics, Einstein answered that after days of conscious but fruitless effort to find his way out of the dark labyrinth of his problem, the discovery came upon him like the surprise of a sudden illumination.

In the genius the productivity of his creative powers is in direct proportion to the intensity of the opposing forces within him. The fact that most impressed Ernest Jones, the biographer of Sigmund Freud, was that the genius was a person of extreme opposites. He could be simultaneously the most skeptical and the most credulous person. Sir Isaac Newton, one of the greatest geniuses of all time, was so skeptical and doubted every scientific hypothesis that he hesitated to make any of his own. Yet he was so sure that the dates in the Bible were true that he believed one could predict the end of the world from them.

The genius is the most critical doubter and the most naive believer. Because these opposites characterized the emotional nature of Darwin, he made an original discovery while his contemporary scientist, Huxley, despite similar interest and superior intellect, did not. All doubting blocks the flow of incoming new ideas. There exists no emotional current between the opposite poles of doubt and belief through which these ideas can pass. The emotional drive of the genius is analogous to the electric current between positive and negative poles. "Passionate emotions develop," according to E. Kretschmer's study, *The Psychology of Genius,* "which drive their thought constantly in the same direction producing the utmost tension until at last a short circuit occurs: somewhere a spark leaps to a new spot where up till then no human thought had ever passed." Our definition of the genius as being the result of a superb effort to reconcile the conflict of the most profound opposites was best summarized by Pascal. Pascal wrote, "greatness is never at one extreme but consists of the union between two extremes."

The six men whose biographies compose this book meet these psychological qualifications for genius. In Moses, Jesus, Paul, Karl Marx, Sigmund Freud and Albert Einstein we shall find the highest possible tolerance for reconciling opposites. They differed widely. They are separated from each other by a thousand or even by two and three thousand years of history. Moses lived in the thirteenth century before the common era; Jesus from the year 4 B.C.E. to the year 30; Paul from the year 6 to the year 67; Marx from 1818 to 1883; Freud from 1856 to 1939; Einstein from 1879 to 1955. Moses was supposed to have been 120 when he died; Jesus was 33; Paul 60; Marx 65; Freud 83; and Einstein 76.

Their cultural backgrounds differed widely. During

the lifetime of Moses, the dominant culture was that of ancient Egypt. During the lifetime of Jesus and Paul it was Hellenistic Greco-Roman culture. During the lifetime of Marx, Freud, and Einstein, the dominant culture was Western European, and especially Germanic. They differed widely as to the fields in which their genius created new concepts. The first three were religious personalities. As founders of new religions they dealt with spiritual values. The second three were intellectual personalities. As founders of new approaches in science they dealt with material things.

Despite these vast differences in time, culture and subject, all six men have one profoundly significant thing in common. Each throughout his lifetime had to deal with a social experience of conflict which became an inextricable part of his personality. That experience was a necessary agent for generating those polar emotional forces which were to become the seedbed for fructifying each man's genius. Each of the six was born a Jew and struggled with the fact all his life. This battle of emotions was not only an inner individual struggle. It had its social external counterpart in the culture conflict—between the Hebraic and the Egyptian for Moses, between the Hebraic and the Hellenistic for Jesus and Paul, and between the Hebraic and the Germanic for Marx, Freud and Einstein.

Obviously, being a Jew does not make a man a genius. A Jew is also like all other men, like some other men, and like no other man. Among Jews are persons below average, above average, talented, highly creative—and a few geniuses. Whether that which differentiates the Jew is culturally determined or biologically inherited is a subject as fruitless to debate as it is in regard to anyone else. In the cases of Moses, Jesus, Paul, Marx, Freud and Einstein, we do know that each had a Jewish father and mother.

The descent of each could be traced back through a long direct line of Jewish ancestors. This is well known about Moses, Jesus and Paul; but Marx, Freud and Einstein also had centuries of Jewish forebearers, including a long line of rabbis. However, we have found that the most significant characteristic which differentiates the genius is not inheritance but the presence within him of a deep awareness of opposites. This conflict of extreme opposites is so intense that only the highest tolerance can absorb it and reconcile the conflicting emotions into something new. This emotional phenomenon is peculiarly intensified in the genius who is a Jew.

His awareness of being a Jew was profoundly involved in the emotional turmoil of Moses, Jesus, Paul, Marx, Freud and Einstein. The psychic tension was the same, however differently each defined the Jewish group in which he originated. They differed as to whether the Jews should be considered a people, a religious group, a nation, a race or merely an economic fallacy. But each struggled throughout his entire life with his own particular identification with Jews. With five the identification became positive; only with Marx did it become negative—an outcome which, of course, did not reduce but may in fact have increased his antagonism to this identification.

The suggestion that relatedness to Jews will condition the creativity of a genius would appear to ascribe a special group character to the Jews. However, to attribute a special personality to a group is as dangerously one-sided as to maintain that any one factor, such as heredity, is the sole cause of individual ability. Defining the traits of a group is good breeding-ground for prejudices either for or against that group. One biographer who wrote the lives of the elder Dumas, Balzac and George Sand exposed his own racial prejudice by attributing the numerous amorous affairs of the partly negro Dumas to "the natural out-croppings of African blood." Since, however, he could not find "negro blood" in Balzac or Sand, he was at a loss to account for their sexual nonconformity.

There are no single traits unique to any one group. Nevertheless, modern anthropologists have come to accept a concept of a group character, developed by its members in their sharing of motives which are derived from their particular set of values. One group does not differ from another group in behavior which satisfies basic physical needs. However, every group has made emotional invest-ments in certain values. These emotional values cannot be given mechanical, logical explanations, such as their being used to satisfy hunger or sex. Some of these emotional values may even appear to be irrational. A good example of this is the Salt Expedition of the Hopi Indians. The Hopis make a highly ceremonious annual journey to get salt. The pilgrimage is over difficult and dangerous terrain. A Mexican trader once offered to sell salt to the Hopis when they were about to start on this journey. This offer to relieve them of the hardship of the trip was ridiculous to the Hopis, because they were not just going to get salt needed for their bodies or to season their dishes. That difficult journey was a part of the involvement of their religion in corn-growing. Maintaining relations which they think will keep them in harmony with nature is for the Hopis a way of life based on a set of values they think are divine.

Geoffrey Gorer, an anthropologist who has written extensively on the question of whether there exists a national personality, has attempted to describe the national character of the Japanese, the Burmese, the Greeks and the Russians. Gorer does not believe that anthropological science has advanced far enough to predict any person's behavior from the character of the group in which he belongs. But where a group is a sufficiently stable homogeneous entity, living for a considerable span of time in a given location, the motives and the values shared by its members can be structured—and this will give that group a unique character.

It has always been difficult to define what is unique about the character of the Jewish group. The main difficulty lies in the constant movement of the Jewish group in history. For three thousand years, the Jews have moved about in many different cultures. The Jews' very mobility may be the key to their uniqueness and to the mystery of their power of survival.

The Jewish group first appears on the scene of history as a nomadic family on the move. The Hebrew patriarch Abraham, once he left his birthplace in Ur of the Chaldees, traveled over Asia Minor from the valley of Mesopotamia to Egypt, and then back to Palestine. Abraham lived among fellow Semites, so we know he was not compelled to move by anti-Semitism. Movement was the first Jew's self-chosen, positive way of life. Soil and settlement on the land constitute a necessary stabilizing factor in the character of a people. But from the beginning the peculiarity of the Jewish people was their independence from the soil. Even when the tribes of Israel were united under a covenant at Sinai and accepted a constitution as a nation, they were still without a land. They were identified not with a place but with each other. Strong family ties, strong group cohesiveness has thus always been characteristic of the Jews.

The land of Israel was always the "Promised Land." It was the place to which the Jews were moving. It was always a *goal*. Three times in their 3000-year history—under Joshua, under Zerubbabel and under Ben-Gurion — the land became a reality. But the important thing is that it was always a psychological goal—a destination. If the land were denied as a national goal, then another goal, a universal destiny, would have to replace it. Israel adopted a universal mission among the nations of the world. A people having both a national and a universal mission — this became the second characteristic of the Jewish people.

The nomad was distinguished from the farmer. The ancient worker who settled on the soil was usually enslaved. The unattached, free-moving nomad had a much greater self-reliance, spirit of independence and desire for freedom. The Jews, originally nomads, developed libertarianism as a third group characteristic. This libertarianism was so strong that it developed into a tradition that a Jew had the right to challenge God Himself if things were not right and just. The figure of an Abraham demanding of God that He practice justice became the prototype of this tradition. Family cohesion, manifest destiny and libertarianism were the leading group values which combined to give the Jewish group its unique character.

Anything that moves encounters resistance. Movement means overcoming the resistance of gravity, which may hold things fixed. The way in which the Jewish people overcame the manifold social forces that resisted their movement in the world has been called a miracle. Their original self-chosen mobility, with the resultant group-character values of family cohesion, manifest destiny and libertarianism, may help explain the miracle. By these positive assets the Jews were able to survive, for they were thus provided with both stubbornness and flexibility—the ability to adapt to the new without losing their identity, which is the way of the nomad. The Jews had a built-in cultural response to challenge.

Response to challenge is the hypothesis favored by the

historian Arnold Toynbee to explain both the survival of a group and the creativity of its culture. Toynbee has said that the Jewish people possessed this vital responsiveness, up until their Judaism fathered Christianity. Thereafter, Toynbee held, the Jews ceased to be creative and became merely an unimportant fossilized sect. He reduced them to the status of a kind of educated gypsies. However, the gypsies, who have nomadic origins, move without any goal and therefore they have never been creative. The Jew moved in search of a destiny defined in a Book. The major goal which that Book describes was initiated and clarified by Moses. It was to find a way that would reconcile opposing forces in life, bringing order out of chaos.

An ideal goal, stamped with the genius of Moses, made the mobile Jew different from the gypsy. He carried with him a vital religious culture. It continued to keep the Jew without a land creative, for wherever he moved, his vital culture made contact with a different vital culture, and the resulting ferment between these opposing cultures stimulated the Jew's creativity anew. Recently, Toynbee has come to recognize this fact. His patently prejudiced original thesis of Jewish fossilization—if not anti-Jewish, then certainly pro-Christian—proved to be awkward, for it failed to account for the striking fact that of the four men who have most influenced the entire world in the last hundred years—Marx, Darwin, Freud and Einstein—three were Jews. Indeed, Toynbee now finds qualities in Judaism so uniquely adapted for lifting the modern technological, disoriented world out of its present despair that he places Judaism among the significantly vital religions. Now, Toynbee even urges Jews to overcome their exclusiveness and begin to proselytize others.

Toynbee could be right, for the ceremonial enhancement of the sanctity of family life in Judaism could counterbalance the invasion of the state on the privacy of man;

second, the optimistic faith in the future which Judaism holds forth as man's divine destiny could counterbalance the pessimistic feeling of doom which pervades our nuclear age; and the liberty-loving spirit, the third unique characteristic of the religion of the Jews, could counterbalance those forces of mass organization which threaten man with the loss of his identity. Ability to counterbalance such opposites requires a high tolerance for tension. It is this characteristic of the Jews which has enabled them to survive three millennia of persecution and, despite an anti-Semitism more virulent than any before, to be creative in our time that has impressed Toynbee and others with the remarkable response of the Jews to challenge.

It was in this Jewish group with a high tolerance for tension that our six geniuses developed their creative powers. Their own unique talents were stimulated by the cultural character of their group. They were sharpened by the friction produced by the conflicts this group experienced throughout its history. Both the tensions within themselves and their very high tolerance for them were heightened by their consciousness of their Jewishness.

The unhappy childhood in the case of each was related to some severe form of rejection caused by his being a Jew. The births of Moses and Jesus involved being saved from an anti-Jewish tyrant. As a Greek-born Jew, Paul was always fearful of being considered inferior to Palestinian Jews. When Marx was six years old, his father had him baptized a Protestant in a vain effort to escape discrimination. When Freud and Einstein were children, both their families were forced to move because of anti-Semitism. Because of their Jewishness both had the bitter experience of being rejected during their school years. Throughout their lives all six continued to endure the turmoil of this rejection in their childhood.

Because each keenly felt he was outside the dominant

culture, each was better able to view more objectively the conflict between the opposing social forces of his day. Each then became a catalyst, fermenting and reformulating those social conflicts into something new. Out of the conflict between an undisciplined, nomadic Hebrew individualism and a tyrannical monolithic Egyptian society, Moses fashioned a new discipline under a new God of freedom. Out of the conflict between the nationalistic and the universalistic forces in Judaism, Jesus fashioned a new emphasis on the salvation of the individual. Out of the conflict between Hellenism and Hebraism, Paul fashioned a new religion, Christianity. Out of the ideological conflict between a metaphysical and a materialistic definition of man, Marx fashioned a new economic plan for society. Out of the conflict in science which separated body from mind, Freud fashioned a new form of healing, psychoanalysis. Out of the conflict between the tangible forms of matter and the intangible forces of energy, Einstein fashioned a new symbolic mathematical language which united chemistry with physics and revealed the correspondence between matter and energy.

As the rejected, as outsiders, as catalysts in society, each of the six willingly chose nonconformity. As Jews they were accustomed to it. Their individual condition and their social situation made them skeptical doubters. But since genius is the "union of two extremes," each replaced his great doubt with a greater belief. The mental process by which each achieved this greater belief also fits the definition of genius. After long contemplation and experimentation with complex disorder, each was suddenly inspired with an idea he considered to be the plain, simple truth. The doubting of Moses was produced by the chaotic array of competing pagan gods. Moses resolved his doubts with an intense belief in the simple concept of the one and only God. The doubting of Jesus was produced by the contradictions within the many moral and ritual Jewish laws. Jesus resolved his doubts with the simple conviction that only messiahship and two commandments counted. The doubting of Paul was produced by the confusion over the status of Diaspora Jews as compared with Palestinian Jews, and by the debate over whether non-Jewish converts to Christianity must keep Jewish ceremonial laws. Paul resolved his doubts with his simple plan of salvation—all could be saved through one person, Jesus, the Risen Lord Christ. The doubting of Marx was produced by the disorderly, warring competitiveness of the new industrialism and by a skepticism concerning whether a peaceful evolution of society was possible. Marx resolved his doubts with a fanatic belief in one simple solution to all social problems—the ascendancy by revolution of the proletariat who would end the class struggle. The doubting of Freud was produced by the fruitless, disordered methods practiced by neurological medicine in his day and by the separation of the organic from the psychological in healing. Freud resolved his doubts with a positive certainty about the unconscious as the simple key to unlock the mystery of neurotic illness and of all human motivation. The doubting of Einstein was produced by the lack of any unified order in the scientific thinking of his day. Einstein resolved his doubts by a firm belief in a theory of the relatedness of all things which could be expressed through a simple formula—that energy is equal to matter multiplied by the velocity of light squared. Each one of these six Jews, conditioned by a group having a high tolerance for extreme opposites, was at one and the same time a great doubter and a greater believer.

In addition to the extreme tolerance for opposing forces related to their Jewishness that characterized Moses, Jesus,

Paul, Marx, Freud and Einstein, it is of considerable interest to note certain parallels between them. There is a parallel between the first and the last of the six. Moses revealed the nature of God to be one—a single creative force which governs all men alike by ethical laws. Einstein discovered the nature of the natural world to be one, and found it to be governed also by a single physical principle. There is a parallel between Jesus and Freud. Jesus searched for the salvation of the individual from the burden of sin and guilt through the forgiveness of God; and Jesus was a healer. Freud explored the deep unconscious in the mind as a way to help man forgive himself of sin and guilt; and Freud was a healer. As a religious missionary, Paul brought the mysticism of an Oriental religion into the Western world, thus leading to the Christianization of Europe; and Paul left Judaism. As a political missionary, Marx brought the materialism of Western thought into the Eastern world, thus leading to the industrial and political mechanization of the once mystical Orient. And Marx also left Judaism.

It is significant to note that a period of two thousand years separates the first three of these Jewish geniuses from the second three. During the lifetimes of Moses, Jesus and Paul and again during the lifetimes of Marx, Freud and Einstein the ideologies of opposing cultures were in their most intense and most direct conflict with the Jew. These men lived at a time in ancient and modern history when the intermingling between the Hebraic and a non-Hebraic culture was most active. There was free access between the Hebraic and the Egyptian cultures in the days of Moses and between the Hebraic and the Hellenistic cultures in the days of Jesus and Paul. There was free access between the Hebraic and the Germanic cultures in the time of Marx, Freud and Einstein. Despite anti-Jewish persecution this free access existed. However, from the time of the establishment of Christianity as a state religion under Constantine to the French and American revolutions, with the exception of one brief period, the Jews were ghettoized and isolated. Further, after the destruction of the second State of Israel in the year 70, the spiritual leaders among the Jews preferred segregation and resisted the influence of conflicting cultures in order to preserve the Judaic heritage. Even during the one period which was an exception—when Jews and Arabs coexisted on friendly terms during the Golden Age of Arabic Spain—the great Jewish figures who arose (including some, such as Maimonides and Gabirol, who would fit our definition of genius) confined their talents to Jewish thought. Therefore, although between Paul and Marx, from the first century to the nineteenth, significant Jewish figures appeared, none appeared who was to equal the six I have named. For each of these six was not only a genius. Each concerned himself not only with Jews. Each one changed the world.

The universal change which each of these six wrought was not limited to the lifetime or the century of the man himself. In each instance, that change created a radical revolution in all human thought and behavior which has continued as a dynamic force, constantly altering and shaping the lives of tens of millions even now. These six Jews wrought changes which affect non-Jews and Jews alike, and which continue to influence them whether or not they are conscious of—even when they try to resist—that influence.

The achievement which distinguishes these six from other notable Jewish thinkers is the universality of their contributions. Out of the most intense inner conflict regarding their own Jewishness they succeeded in projecting themselves into the non-Jewish world which resisted them. Frustration may turn one inward upon oneself and thus make one more particularistic. But Moses, Jesus, Paul, Marx, Freud and Einstein—each, in his own way, triumphed over the personal defeats profoundly associated with his Jewishness. Each became not simply a great figure in a parochial world but a greater one in a universal world.

This book is based on the conviction that in order to understand our world today it is essential to know how these six Jews changed that world. We should have an understanding which is as close to the truth about them as is possible. As the author of these six biographies, I hope the reader may feel as close to these men as I did while I wrote of them. It is impossible to feel as close to them as James Boswell was close to Samuel Johnson. Boswell lived with Johnson and knew him so intimately that he identified himself with him. He cherished Johnson's frailties as well as his virtues. When Boswell was writing his biography of Johnson, one of Johnson's lady friends cautioned Boswell in a friendly manner not to dwell on Johnson's follies. Boswell replied: "I will not make my tiger a cat to please anybody." In reading the lives of these geniuses—Moses, Jesus, Paul, Marx, Freud and Einstein—you will recognize that each one was like all other men, like some other men, and like no other man.

I: Moses

Moses was more than a founder of one of the world's religions. He was the first of humanity's heroes. History records the existence of political liberators, moral legislators, military leaders, mystical prophets, makers of nations and fashioners of religion before Moses; but in him all these roles were combined for the first time. The stature of this uniquely many-sided heroic figure has not diminished through the ages. In literature, sculpture, painting and music each age has tried to recapture the significance of his life. Each age has turned back to the life of Moses as a foreshadowing of some of its own dynamic values. Therefore, the picture each age has had of Moses more nearly reflects the spirit of that age than it represents the real image of Moses.

In most of the Bible, written long after Moses died, and largely under the influence of the later prophets of Israel, Moses is proclaimed the greatest of the prophets; in the New Testament, Moses is the precursor of Jesus; in the Koran, Moses is the model for Mohammed; in Canon Law, juridical systems and in the courts, Moses is the legislator and judge par excellence, the giver of the Tablets of the Law; in Renaissance art — notably in the sculpture of Michelangelo—Moses is a tower of humanistic strength; for the writers of the seventeenth- and eighteenth-century utopias, Moses is the architect of a new social order; for socialists, Moses is a revolutionary; for mystics, Moses is the one who talked with God "face to face."

This composite portrait of Moses is constantly being added to by those who emphasize features they wish to see, or erase features they do not wish to see. As a result, the worked-over image of Moses is now, after three thousand years, too imaginative and complex to correspond to the man behind the image. The extreme modernists have found an easy way to evaluate the portrait of Moses. They repaint it into an abstraction. Moses is a myth, they say. He is only a mythological abstract of the drama of real people in ancient times. Moses is supposed to be a poetic person-ification of the history of the Hebrew people and their religious cult. However, unlike other mythological heroes of antiquity, in the historical record of this people, Moses, the Hebrew hero, is never portrayed as divine. Neither in his birth nor in his death is there any divinity. Moses is born, lives and dies a man. The Book of Exodus refers to him as "the man Moses." He cannot be a projection of the Hebrew people because this people fights against him. He seems superhuman in his constant search for spiritual communication; yet he is all too human in his own loves and angers. Moses is too real to be a myth.

When we try to get a picture of the real Moses, we find the difficulties of removing the unreal almost insuperable. The Biblical legend says the face of Moses shone so brilliantly with the radiance of a divine afflatus that he had to wear a veil in order for the people to look upon him. The distance of three millennia, the distractions of com-peting theologies and the distillations of conflicting Bibli-cal scholarship have added a thousand more veils. Not only has the divine radiance been obscured, but the human face of Moses seems to have become almost lifeless. Where can Moses be seen as a living person? The only place is still the Bible, for there is no other authentic record of his life. The Bible contains the elements of at least four biographies of Moses, although they contradict each other in various details. And in that Bible there is Moses' autobiography!

According to the orthodox tradition of both the Jews and Christians, the first five books of the Bible were actually written by Moses. As such, they still are the constitutional foundation of Judaism and Christianity. And indeed, the figure of Moses dominates all five books. He does not appear in the Book of Genesis, which is an account of the hero patriarchs—Abraham, Isaac and Jacob or Israel—and of the latter's sons, particularly Joseph, who brought the tribe of Israel to Egypt. The Genesis stories about the beginning of the semi-nomadic Hebrew tribes and their arrival in Egypt is the preparation for the birth of Moses and his career in Egypt, which are described in the Book of Exodus. In Leviticus there is a further development of the laws Moses had promulgated at Sinai. In Numbers, the long march of the freed slaves under the leadership of Moses through the peninsula of Sinai is described. In Deuteronomy are portrayed the last will and testament and the death of Moses, just before the Israelites crossed over the Jordan to settle in the land of Canaan.

How much of these five books is the work of Moses? A scientific study of the text of the Bible has been going on for the past three hundred years. Up until the twentieth century, critics of the Bible had all arrived at the conclusion that either nothing or very little in the Bible had been written by Moses. It was assumed either that Moses never lived or that if he did, he had not been able to write. Furthermore, the so-called Books of Moses were said to contain ideas so far in advance of the times when Moses might have lived that he could never have conceived all of them. According to the general theory developed by these Bible scholars, the Five Books of Moses were a collection of works by at least four different schools of authors in ancient Israel, writing in different centuries. In one school the word used for God had four Hebrew consonants, *JHWH*. In early Hebrew writings, words were written down without their vowels, and therefore the original pronunciation of *JHWH* is unknown. It certainly was not pronounced *JeHoWaH* or Jehovah — a pronunciation which a medieval church scholar deduced from a misreading of the Hebrew text of the Bible. Modern Bible scholars have labeled the text in which the ancient school used the letters *JHWH* for God the "J" code. In another school, the word for God was *Elohim;* this, therefore, was named the "E" code. In a third school, the function and supreme importance of the Jewish priests was emphasized; it therefore became the "P" code. The fourth school was interested in a policy of centralizing worship in the Temple at Jerusalem, and since its text was mostly to be found in the book of Deuteronomy, the scholars labeled it the "D" code. Each of these four schools not only wrote in a different century but also represented either the Southern Kingdom or the Northern Kingdom of Israel, as it was later divided, or a school advanced its own special religious ideas. Therefore, there are varying and contradictory accounts of the life of Moses in the Bible.

After hundreds of years of editing, these four codes were finally joined together in what is now the text of the Five Books of Moses. The final editing was completed almost one thousand years after Moses is supposed to have lived. The result of this editing further complicated things. According to the modern Bible analysts, many sentences in the Bible appear to have been pieced together out of phrases and even single words from all four—that is, out of the J, E, P and D codes. As a result of this kind of critical analysis of the text of the Five Books of Moses, up until the twentieth century it seemed absolutely hopeless to arrive at any real, authentic figure of Moses.

In the twentieth century, the scholars who studied the text of the Bible began to receive assistance from another branch of knowledge, archeology. By the beginning of the twentieth century, digging to recover the remains of ancient societies had developed into a much sounder science. In the nineteenth century, the amateur enthusiast Schliemann became wealthy and world famous by his excavations of the city of Troy—excavations which made Homer's saga of the Iliad real. In the early nineteen-hun-dreds, Sir Flinders Petrie inaugurated the kind of scientific archeological expedition that flourishes today. Not until expert excavators and reconstructors of ancient remains joined with historians and anthropologists, and especially with linguists, to make up archeological teams, did we begin to have a clearer picture of ancient civilizations. When the hieroglyphic writings on Egyptian monuments and papyri, the cuneiform inscriptions on Assyrian and Babylonian monuments and pottery, and the ancient Hebrew writings on findings in Palestine and Sinai were deciphered, an entirely new history of Bible times had to be written.

Many important books report these findings in the last sixty years from Flinders Petrie's *Researches in Sinai* and James Breasted's *Ancient Records of Egypt* in 1906 to Nelson Glueck's *The River Jordan* (1946) and W. F. Albright's *Archeology and the Religion of Israel* (1953). The more popular treatments can be read in H. H. Rowley's *Old Testament and Modern Study* (1952), John Wilson's *The Culture of Ancient Egypt* (1960) and Werner Keller's *The Bible as History* (1956). In such books a whole new light has been brought to bear on the historic reality of the Five Books of Moses. The records of Egypt now reveal the truth of the Bible insofar as these records correspond to the Bible story about the enslavement of the Hebrew tribes and their eventual liberation in the Exodus. Findings in the Sinai Peninsula confirm the wanderings of these tribes to the Jordan River. Many of the so-called miracles turn out to be poetic elaborations of real occurrences which Biblical critics before these new discoveries had dismissed as fictional.

It must be pointed out, however, that in all these dramatic and exciting new discoveries, any reference to the actual figure of Moses has yet to be found. The modern archeologists believe such a find will yet be made. Until that time, the Five Books of the Bible attributed to him will remain the only record of Moses. Although modern archeology shows these books of the Bible to be more history than legend, reconstructing the life of Moses from them still presents a problem. This is the problem which applies to the records of any people which in ancient times were written in the form of a saga. Sagas are not like ordinary historical records. They begin by being handed down by word of mouth and are therefore preserved in poetic or rhythmic forms, which are easier to remember. Furthermore, the saga not only relates the important event in the history of a tribe, it also sings of the emotional reaction of the tribe to that event. As Martin Buber reminds us, the saga may be the most inclusive kind of historical writing just because in the saga we get both the history of and the psychology of the group. The dialogues between God and Moses in the Bible can best be understood in this light. In them the saga writers describe the emotional torment of Moses.

The cause-and-effect principle for explaining events, if not wholly unknown, was certainly undeveloped among the ancients. Significant events in their lives appeared as wonders explainable only by being attributed to supernatural intervention. We now know these events did take place, and if a fact sounds like a myth in the Bible, it is so only because of the overenthusiastic description of that fact by the saga poets. Indeed, it may be easier to distinguish between fact and myth in the Biblical saga than in the Greek sagas of Homer just because the Greek heroes are mixtures of human beings and god-figures. The Bible completely separates God from the hero. It glorifies God as the author of events, but the human beings who act out these events are human indeed. Finally, the truth of the Biblical account of Moses cannot be denied on the premise that the Bible deals with religious ideas and not solely with political history. In the days of Moses, people believed in their beliefs; what they thought was sacred was real to them, not merely legendary. Therefore, to know what they considered sacred is as important as to know the events that happened if we would have a true picture of their times.

Before we can describe the time of Moses, it is logical that we first determine when he was born. Can we rely upon the chronology of the Bible, our only record? The only specific date given in the Bible account to which we can relate something in the life of Moses is the statement that between the time of the settlement of the tribes of Israel in Egypt and the day they left to begin their famous exodus under the leadership of Moses, a period of 430 years elapsed. The Bible also says that Moses was eighty years old when he made his first appearance before Pharaoh; that at that age he began his stupendous task of leading a new nation for forty years through desert and wilderness, and that when he died at the age of 120, "his eye was not dim nor his natural force abated." Is the

settlement period of 430 years any more believable than
the statement that the leadership of Moses took place
between the 80th and 120th year of his life? All that can
be said is that the tribes of Israel must have lived for some
four hundred years in Egypt. But *when?* There is another
statement in the Book of Exodus that helps to establish
the time. Tnere we are told that the Pharaoh who made
slave-laborers of the tribes of Israel "knew not Joseph."
This is strange, since Joseph is not only recorded in the
Bible. There are reliable Egyptian references to him as
having been a powerful and successful Grand vizier to a
Pharaoh. Now, the Egyptians were very meticulous in
keeping exact records of their rulers, which go back to at
least the year 3000 before the common era. How could an
Egyptian Pharaoh be unaware of this important vizier,
Joseph?

There is a very good reason why an Egyptian king could
be described as not having known Joseph, a Semite. The
rabbis, several thousand years later, attempted to interpret
this statement in the Book of Exodus. They commented
that this Pharaoh only pretended he had never heard of
the great administrative work of Joseph which had saved
Egypt from famine. These rabbis intuitively hit upon the
true historical explanation. There was a period in Egyptian history about which there is hardly any mention at
all in Egyptian records. When one views the careful records
the Egyptians kept uninterrupted for a thousand years and
then suddenly finds a break of complete silence, the conclusion is that the Egyptian annalists intended deliberately
to blot out of memory what had really happened during
that period—and for good reason. Egypt was invaded by a
nomadic Semitic horde from the east. These Semites
dethroned the Egyptian Pharaohs and set themselves up as
Pharaohs who ruled Egypt for 160 years, from 1730 to

1570 B.C.E. It must be remembered that the Egyptian Pharaohs were not mere kings, they were worshiped as gods. It is galling enough to be a defeated king. It is the very depth of humiliation to be a conquered god. This is what the Egyptian Pharaohs, indeed, did not want to remember.

For fifteen hundred years before this temporary replacement of the Egyptian Pharaohs, Egyptian civilization had been developing under a succession of no less than eighteen dynasties. This civilization had made a remarkable advance in culture. As early as 1800 years before the common era, the progress of Egypt was already very much greater than that of the other peoples in the ancient Near East and the Mediterranean world. Thanks to its great natural resource, the Nile River, Egypt had the advantage of developing more rapidly into a settled agricultural society. The majority of the other peoples were still in those days nomadic or semi-nomadic tribes, ever on the move. From the south beyond the cataracts of the Nile, Egypt was threatened by the black tribes of Ethiopia, which she called the land of Kush. From the west, the black men of Libya approached her borders. From islands in the Mediterranean and along the coast of Asia Minor came sea raiders; Egypt called them the Sea Peoples. From the east came Egypt's most dangerous enemies. These were the Semitic nomadic tribes whose domain extended through present-day Israel, Syria, Turkey and Iraq all the way up to the Black Sea. Through the centuries these Semitic tribes had banded together at various times to form mighty marauding hordes.

Seeking fresh grazing pasture for their flocks, these nomadic tribes found it useful to join with each other in building powerful mobile armies, either to occupy new pasture lands or to rob the farm and city settlements of the fruits of their labors. The Egyptian records are filled with descriptions of defensive battles against, or peace treaties through royal marriage alliances with these nomadic peoples who were constantly descending upon Egypt. The wealth and food of the Nile Valley—the breadbasket of Asia Minor—became a magnet for all these foreign peoples.

One of these Semitic groups was more successful than previous hordes because it had invented a new weapon— the horse-drawn chariot. The blades attached to the wheels cut down troops on the battlefield whose ranks had already been thinned by this group's superior bow power; for the Semites had also designed a composite bow which had a greater striking range than the simple bow of the Egyptian foot soldier. In the Egyptian records, these Semites of the east were called the Hyksos—which means "ruler of foreign lands." By the year 1750 B.C.E., the invincible Hyksos had reached the Nile. After conquering the land, they settled on the Delta in Lower Egypt, the richest part of the Nile for grazing flocks. They built a new fortified capital and garrisoned it with a huge army of occupation. They allowed the conquered Egyptian Pharaohs to remain in their old capital at Thebes in upper Egypt, three hundred miles farther up the Nile, and received rich tribute from them. As the new overlords, the Semitic Hyksos kings assumed the title of Pharaoh.

It was one of these Semitic Pharaohs who was lucky enough to find a Semite from another tribe already living in Egypt, Joseph by name. As a slave administrator for an Egyptian nobleman, Potiphar, Joseph had gained a wide knowledge of the Egyptian economy. The Semitic Hyksos Pharaoh emancipated Joseph and made him his chief counselor. Chapter 47 of Genesis records how well Joseph had served his master, helping him to get control of all the lands of Egyptian farmers excepting only the lands of the priests—apparently in order to persuade the powerful Egyptian priesthood to support the new regime of the Semitic conquerors. For good reason the Egyptian hated these nomadic Hyksos. The Hyksos Pharaoh was aware of this hate when he gave Joseph permission to bring his small band of fellow tribesmen of Israel down from Canaan to pasture their herds in Egypt. To protect these Israelite shepherds from the Egyptian farmers, the Semitic Pharaoh allotted them a segregated section along the Delta called Goshen. Such an allotment was made because, to quote the Bible, "every shepherd is an abomination to the Egyptian." This attitude of superiority toward the shepherd is frequently found in Egyptian records. It was not merely the ancient competitive enmity between the farmer and the herdsman. To compensate for their defeat by them and their fear of them, the conquered Egyptian farmers looked down upon the Semitic nomads as their inferiors. Certainly they wished to expunge their defeat by them from historical memory. It took the Egyptians a century and a half to regain sufficient power to take revenge and drive the Hyksos out of their land.

The difference between the Semitic nomads of West Asia and the Egyptians of the Nile included more than economic competition. As N. Thomas has observed, the herder, who takes from and denudes the soil, is the natural enemy of the farmer, who gives seed to the soil. There was also the basic psychological difference between the life of the wandering nomad which made for independence of spirit, and the life of the settled farmer who submitted to rigid controls. This was especially true of the Egyptian farmer, subject as he was to the flooding of the Nile River. There being no rainfall in the Egyptian desert oasis, plenty or famine was determined by the rise or fall of the Nile and by the ability of the Egyptians, through a system of

sluices and dykes, to make use of the only water they had
to irrigate as much as possible of the desert on both sides of
the Nile.

Conquering the desert with its threat of death was a
ceaseless effort. No civilization was ever so conscious of
death itself as the Egyptian. The effort had both a political
and a religious effect. The systems for controlling the Nile
required rigid state authority and relied on the king and
his administrators for the devising and supervision of that
control. It called for constant use of hand or, more exactly,
foot labor, for pumping the water, and thus meant the
virtual enslavement of farm labor. The peculiar situation
influenced Egyptian religion, making its major concept
the assurance of eternal life against the threat of death.
This assurance was vested in the god-king, Pharaoh. So
long as the Pharaoh lived his subjects were secure, for he
represented the god of Egypt who ruled over the Nile.
Therefore, the Pharaoh was kept alive even after death,
in the form of a mummy. Buried with his household in the
tomb and equipped with the magical text of the Book of
the Dead—the Bible of Egypt—the mummified Pharaoh
continued to rule along with his living, divine successor.
Politically and religiously the pyramid symbolized Egypt.
The pyramid, with its summit resting on the broad base
of slave labor, represented a king. It also was the tomb in
which the deathless king resided.

In contrast, the nomadic shepherd tribes were loosely
banded together. The free-moving behavior of the auton-
omous clans made for individualism. Compared to the
rigidity of the Egyptian farmer the life of the nomad was
fluid. An ancient Semitic record from Sumeria describes
the shepherd as one "who knows no submission, who has
no house in his lifetime, who does not bury his dead—he
battles, he does not conquer and is not conquered." In

that record the writer looks down upon "the peasant tied
to his clods, the cowardly townsfolk who seek to protect
themselves behind walls and who serve the lord as a slave."
Whereas the leadership of the Egyptian was vested in a
continuing dynasty by inheritance, the leaders of the
nomad tribes won their roles by means of their special
gifts. This was especially true in the religious cult of the
nomadic tribesmen. The gods of Egypt were fixed in one
place on the Nil, and belonged to a hierarchy; the
nomads' gods wandered with them. Nomadic religious
leadership was charismatic and not dynastic. This was
typical and continued among the nomads as late as the
time of Mohammed. The religious leader rose by suddenly
demonstrating divine gifts, or charisma.

These nomadic characteristics belonged also to the
Semitic tribes from Canaan who came into Egypt in the
wake of the Hyksos conquest, and who were known as the
Habiru. *Habiru,* whence *Hebrew,* means either "unsettled
rovers" or "those yonder"—that is, from the other side of
the Euphrates River. Under the charismatic leadership of
Abraham described in the introductory chapter, they had
traveled from Ur of the Chaldees to Canaan where their
single god had accompanied them. This god was easier to
take along because he was not an idol that needed to be
carried. Their god was invisible. The ancient farmer who
lived in the flatlands needed some visible idol of great
size and height to answer his spiritual aspirations. The
shepherd who took his flock to graze even on the sparse
pastures of the uplands found his aspirations fulfilled by
"looking unto the mountains whence cometh my help."
Thus in the Biblical sagas of the origins of the Semitic
tribe of the Habiru, the "voice of God" is heard by its
charismatic leaders—Abraham, Isaac and Jacob—from the
top of the mountain.

Into the tribe of the Hebrews Moses was born at a time
when there rose a Pharaoh who "knew not Joseph." The
Bible text does not give this Egyptian Pharaoh a name,
but it does specify that he was the great Pharaoh who built
the city of Rameses, for which much slave labor was
needed. According to Egyptian records, the Pharaoh who
built the city of Rameses was Rameses II (1290—1224
B.C.E.). Two hundred and fifty years after his predecessors
had succeeded in driving out the Semitic Hyksos invaders,
Rameses II became the god-king of Egypt. During that
interval of almost three centuries, covering the eighteenth
and nineteenth dynasties and a succession of sixteen Egyptian Pharaohs, Egyptian civilization under Rameses II
reached its Golden Age. The wall of isolation with which
the old Egyptian culture had surrounded itself at the
capital of Thebes in Upper Egypt had been breached by
the Semitic conquerors. Communications between the
newly arrived Semitic culture in Lower Egypt, with its
capital of Tanis on the Nile Delta, and the old Egyptian
culture in the south developed. The records show a com-
mingling of Semites and Egyptians all over that area and
up into Palestine. This process of interchange included an
assimilation of each other's gods. As a slave administrator
to an Egyptian overlord, the Semite Joseph had become so
Egyptianized that he married the daughter of the priest
of On—the Biblical name for the Egyptian god Re. However, when the Semites lived under the Semitic Pharaohs
they resisted becoming Egyptianized. Among the learned
on both sides a kind of international language developed,
called Akkadian.

When the Egyptians learned the superior Semitic art of
war and adopted the chariot and multiple bow, they finally
were able to march north from Thebes, storm and destroy
the Hyksos capital of Tanis. The Semitic settlers in that

area who escaped slaughter were made slaves. Among the enslaved were the Hebrew Semites. This took place under the regime of Ahmose I, who reconquered the Delta in 1570 B.C.E. Ahmose I was the Pharaoh who "knew not Joseph," because he wanted to forget the Semitic humiliation of his gods.

To protect their new position and to prevent the return of the Semitic invaders from Asia, the Egyptian Pharaohs adopted a new policy of imperialism. They pursued the retreating enemy and established Egyptian garrisons from across the Nile into Canaan and northward. In Egyptian records these forts are referred to as the "Wall of the Ruler" to keep out "foreign hordes from coming down again to Egypt so that they could beg after their fashion for their flocks to drink." Eventually the Egyptians' military strategy required moving their capital from the south to the Delta, and they began to rebuild the Hyksos capital. Their imperialist policy led in turn to a change of religion. The new empire extending beyond the borders of the Nile required a more universal god-idea. The god Amun, the chief of the pantheon at the old isolated capital of Thebes, amalgamated into himself the lesser gods such as Re and became Amun-Re, the father of all the gods. The priests of Amun-Re became the most vigorous proponents of conquest and expansion. After each expedition into Asia, more Semitic Bedouins were brought back to fill the harems or to work in slave labor.

But about eighty years before Rameses II became Pharaoh, another young Pharaoh, Amenhotep IV, had temporarily interrupted this expansionism. The frontiers of Egypt were now far-flung. This was the time to enjoy the fruits of conquest by luxurious, peaceful living at home—such was the philosophy of Amenhotep IV. He was happily married to one of the most beautiful of queens, Nefertiti; and his mother, the dowager Queen Tiy, was an unusually brilliant woman. His father had married her even though she was an Egyptian commoner. The old conservative Egyptian folkways had given way to urbane and cosmopolitan living.

Amenhotep was a brooding, introspective iconoclast. To dramatize his policy of opposition to expansionist war, he broke away from tradition in doing two things. First he built a new, beautiful quasi-rural capital, Tell-el-Amarna, where he and his family and courtiers lived much less formally than his god-king predecessors. This change is illustrated in the superb naturalism of the Amarna period in Egyptian art: human beings and animals were no longer portrayed in rigid stylized positions but in humanistic forms magnificently caught in motion. Second, to dramatize his idea of a peaceful reign over all Egypt's conquered peoples he invented a new religion—new in that it envisioned a god who reigned with Pharaoh over all, and not only over the Egyptians. As his emblem he chose the sun disk, for which the word in Egyptian is *aton*. Aton replaced the mysterious god Amun of the old powerful priesthood. Amun—the word means "hidden"—had been concealed mysteriously in the temples. He was now replaced by a new, warm, open-air sun god, Aton. To complete this heretical religious revolution, this Pharaoh changed his name from Amenhotep, meaning "Amun is satisfied with me," to Akhenaton, "he who is serviceable to Aton."

Some have assumed that the monotheism which Moses brought to the tribes of Israel was merely a copy of Atonism. This hypothesis cannot be supported. Although Egyptian hymns to Aton include such statements as that he was a god "like whom there is no other," Atonism did not eliminate all other gods on the premise that there were no other gods besides the one. Although Aton is defined as a kind of universal god, intimacy with him was the privilege only of the Pharaoh Akhenaton and his immediate family. All others worshiped the Pharaoh as a god, as Aton's representative. Furthermore, Atonism lacked all ethical content. It did not declare that all men were equal because there was one God who demanded justice for all. Therefore, Atonism did not produce either ethics or law. Atonism was the sentimental personal religion of one Pharaoh, Akhenaton, a heretic against the traditional Egyptian religion. Therefore, Atonism completely collapsed and disappeared with Akhenaton's death. Some of its beautiful hymns, which spoke of bringing the sun-god out into the open as a creative and kindly deity who offers the gifts of life to all, continued as models of poetic form. The literary style of Atonism did have an influence centuries later, even in Palestine, as may be seen in the parallels between Psalm 104 in the Bible and Akhenaton's famous hymn to his private personal sun-god.

Whether any of the ideas of Atonism, with their intimations of monotheism, were transmitted to Moses is questionable. Moses was born some seventy-five years after the complete collapse of this personal religion of one heretical Pharaoh. When Akhenaton died, the reaction against that religion was violent. The priests of Amun, restored to power, systematically destroyed all Akhenaton's followers and expunged his name and his god from the monuments. Howard Fast's biography, *The Prince of Moses,* is based on the entirely fictional assumption that Moses was secretly taught Atonism in an underground movement. There is no evidence at all that this momentary heretical movement survived even secretly among Egyptians. It was only a private religion of one Pharaoh which died with him. Akhenaton's dynasty was replaced by an army commander who re-established the expansionist policy of conquest and abandoned his predecessor's rural capital. Thebes once again became the religious capital of the restored priesthood of Amun-Re. To establish a stronger military center, a new capital nearer to Asia and the Mediterranean was instituted. In the process of re-winning the empire, this capital was finally completed by Rameses II, who named it after himself. The records describe it as a large, beautiful garden city with palaces, temples to the gods and barracks for soldiers, chariots and horses, and with many warships moored on the Nile.

Rameses ushered in the period of greatest glory in Egypt's long history. He ruled for sixty years. His was an era of continuous military conquest in Palestine and Assyria. He brought back literally tens of thousands of captives, who supplied slave labor for his building program. The ruins at Luxor and Karnak and Abu Simbel still bear mute testimony to the glory of Rameses. It was the remains of a colossal statue of the ruler himself that inspired Shelley's poem *Ozymandias:*

> "My name is Ozymandias, King of Kings;
> Look on my works, ye mighty, and despair!"
> Nothing beside remains. Round the decay
> Of that colossal wreck, boundless and bare,
> The lone and level sands stretch far away.

Though now covered by the sands of time, the reign of Rameses was so glorious that during the next thousand years, no less than nine of his successors assumed the name of Rameses. Since of his more than one hundred sons the first twelve had died, Rameses II was succeeded by his thirteenth son, Merneptah.

Merneptah was not at all like his father. Nevertheless, he tried to continue the same policy of conquest and of bringing back more and more slaves to supply manpower for the empire. His weakness is indicated by the fact that his reign was threatened by the first serious attempt to invade Egypt in the 350 years since the Hyksos had been driven out. The invaders came from Libya in the west and were eventually repulsed. However, this was the beginning of increasing threats of invasion, especially from the Sea Peoples and the nomadic Philistines of the Asiatic coast. Within seventy-five years, Egypt had to withdraw from Palestine and Syria.

The renewed pressure of Semitic invaders posed a new threat to Egypt. That danger came from the Semitic peoples Egypt kept as slave laborers within its own borders. Slave labor was the lifeblood of Egypt's imperial economy, but there was ever present the danger that the slaves might be incited to rebel by the news of an approaching invader. This was especially true of the nomadic shepherds of Israel who had been enslaved in Egypt. They still had memories of their former independence. It was Rameses who used enslaved Israelites to extend his city, but it was Merneptah whom the Bible quotes as having said, "Let us deal wisely with them lest they join the enemy." The Israelites were a minority among the many slaves held captive in Egypt. Merneptah's policy regarding them was simple. He would get rid of them by two methods: First, he would increase the severity of their forced labor, thus benefiting himself economically and at the same time bringing about the rapid death of the adults. Second, he would kill all male children. This is the first record in human history of an official governmental policy of genocide. Merneptah also tried to destroy any possible base of operations among their nearest Semitic relatives in Palestine. He boasted of his success in one of his monuments, where we read, "Israel is laid waste, his seed is not; Palestine has become a widow for Egypt! All lands together, they are pacified. Everyone who was restless has been bound by Merneptah." The year of this monument was around 1230 B.C.E.

"Everyone who was restless" was not bound, however, by a Merneptah boasting in order to cover up his weakness. One, in particular, proved how empty was Merneptah's self-glorification. He was the most restless and the least bound of the Israelites, even though he bore the Egyptian name of Moses. In Egyptian, *Moses* simply means "son of." Pharaohs were named Kahmose, Ahmose or Thutmose, meaning sons of particular gods. Had the name Moses been detached from some prefix consisting of the name of an Egyptian god after he had been taught to believe in the God of his own Semitic tribe? The nomadic Israelites called their God *Shaddai,* meaning "Mighty One of the Mountain." Because of their long enslavement, among the majority of the Israelites the memory of their God had become dim and indistinct. There was one exception—the tribe of Levi. The Levites were responsible for the religious cult of the nomadic Israelite tribesmen. Amram and Jochebed, the father and mother of Moses, were of this tribe. Indeed, the Levite family of Moses seems to have had a special relation to the religious cult, for later Aaron, his older brother, easily assumed the role of a priest and his sister Miriam assumed the function of a prophetess. Among the nomadic Arab tribes, even in much later times, it was not uncommon for a whole family to claim the clairvoyance of seers, whom the Berber Arabs called *Kahin.* Mohammed doubted whether he himself was anything but a possessed Kahin until he had become convinced that an angel had spoken to him.

How could Moses have been taught anything about his own nomadic religious Israelite background if, according to the Bible record, he was brought up by an Egyptian princess who had adopted him soon after he was weaned?

Literally hundreds of sons and daughters were born to the voluptuary Pharaoh, Rameses II. Just as one of his sons married a non-Egyptian commoner, daughter of a Syrian ship captain, so it would not have been extraordinary for one of his daughters to have adopted a Hebrew child such as Moses. In the Biblical saga, this Egyptian princess is supposed to have found the baby Moses in a reed box sealed with pitch floating down the Nile, from which she "drew him." She then had him nursed by a Hebrew woman who, unknown to her, was the child's mother. This idyllic tale has always charmed the Bible reader.

However, the picture is only an exact duplicate of an ancient Semitic legend already popular for fourteen hundred years before Moses was born. This original legend was about the great King Sargon, who ruled around 2300 B.C.E. and was the founder of the Semitic dynasty of Akkad. In that legend, Sargon's mother is said to have been a temple prostitute. Since his father was unknown, his mother bore her son in secret to avoid public shame, and then put him in a reed box sealed with pitch and placed it in the river where he was eventually found by a gardener. Later the goddess Ishtar loved Sargon and made him a king. This legend, well known to the Semites of Asia Minor, was woven into the biography of Moses by the later Israel saga writers for two reasons. First, through this legend they could account for the strange fact that the child Moses had been able to escape Merneptah's policy of genocide. Second, the legend explained what was equally strange to the Bible saga writers—how this Israelite Moses, particularly since he was a Levite, could have become so Egyptianized.

The Bible biographers writing in Hebrew tried to mitigate their embarrassment at the Egyptianization of

Moses by giving his name a Hebrew interpretation. The
Bible states that the Egyptian princess gave him a Hebrew
name—*Moses,* which in Hebrew means "to draw out."
However, the Bible saga leaves no doubt that Moses was
reared as an Egyptian. His royal adoptive mother gave
him a name meaning merely "son of" because to her his
father was unknown. The Bible record tells us absolutely
nothing of how Moses was brought up or educated in the
Egyptian court. It follows the idyllic picture of the rescue
of the infant Moses with the sentence, "And it came to
pass in those days, when Moses was grown up, that he
went out unto his brethren, and looked on their burdens;
and he saw an Egyptian smiting a Hebrew, one of his
brethren."

The absence of any Biblical information about the life
of Moses from his infancy to grown manhood is striking.
The Bible saga writers may have deliberately omitted all
such information in order to minimize how much Moses
had assimilated Egyptian culture. It may also be that they
no longer considered the Egyptian background of Moses
significant. By the time the saga poets were writing their
biographies of Moses, Egypt had already declined—had
become, to quote the later prophet Isaiah, "a broken reed."
(Because the marshlands along the Nile were filled with
reeds from which the papyrus documents were made,
Egypt is referred to in the Bible as the land of the reeds.)

Jewish thinkers after the writing of the Bible had been
completed were always puzzled by the hiatus in the record
of Moses' upbringing. The formative period of his life
became a subject for speculation by Jewish commentators
for a thousand years. In the first century, the widely known
Jewish philosopher Philo wrote a *Life of Moses.* Philo
lived in the Hellenized Egyptian city of Alexandria and
wrote in Greek. He defended Judaism against Greek intel-

lectual attacks upon it. In his role as a Jewish polemicist who lived in Egypt, Philo may have indulged in some exaggerations to demonstrate how Moses had been thoroughly schooled in the advanced Egyptian culture of his day. Philo says Moses studied mathematics, astronomy and philosophy in Egypt. Though Philo wrote some twelve hundred years after Moses lived, there would be good reason to assume that Moses, living in the Egyptian court, had had a wide knowledge of Egyptian religious culture. There is also the ancient Jewish legend that Moses received military training as the adopted son of the princess, and even led an Egyptian expedition into Ethiopia. This legend may also have a factual basis, for the Bible does record that Moses had married an Ethiopian negress, "the Cushite woman" (Numbers 12:1). She is the excuse used by his priest brother and prophetess sister for their rebellion against the authority of Moses and for insisting that they had as much right to speak for God as Moses did. It would appear only natural that Moses should have had a thorough training in the arts of government, Egyptian religion and military science before he became the lawgiver, the founder of a religion and the military strategist who planned the battles his freed fellow tribesmen had to fight against other nomads who blocked their march across the Sinai Peninsula on the way to Canaan.

The most significant of the legends about the period that formed the character of Moses are those that deal with his inner emotional struggle over whether he should be a loyal Egyptian or a loyal Hebrew. In the Louis Ginzberg collection of these ancient post-Biblical legends about the youth and early manhood of Moses, there is the legend which describes the first meeting of Moses with Zipporah, the daughter of Jethro, the priest in the land of Midian, where Moses lived for many years after he fled from Egypt.

"Moses had allowed Jethro's daughter to describe him as an Egyptian to her father, without protesting or asserting his Hebrew birth. For this, God punished him by causing him to die outside of the Promised Land. Joseph, who had proclaimed in public that he was a Hebrew when he was in Egypt, found his last resting place, when his bones were removed, in the land of the Hebrews; but Moses who apparently had no objection to being considered an Egyptian had to live and die outside of that land."

That Moses was confronted with a great emotional struggle early in his life is confirmed by all the modern findings about the psychology of the assimilationist. What an opportunity for the disappearance of a Hebrew, one of the persecuted, must have been dangling before the eyes of Moses in the Egyptian court! He had had a bad start in life. He had been born into a slave family oppressed with such fear and anxiety that, according to a legend, his older sister bore the name Miriam because in Hebrew this meant "bitterness," and his brother was named Aaron because in Hebrew the word meant, "woe unto this pregnancy." Moses must have spent at least three years in this family—the usual period for weaning in those days—before he was returned to the princess. Even though the intent of his family in giving him up was to save him, the childhood memories that Moses had of being the adopted child of an unwed Egyptian princess must have involved the feeling of having been rejected by his own family.

It must have been a tremendous struggle for Moses to reach the point which the Bible records so casually—that when he was grown Moses "went out to his brethren." This decision itself demonstrates the outstanding quality of his personality. Moses was a man with a will of iron. Here, too, the legends confirm this fact. One legend relates the story of a king of Arabia who heard of the thrilling success of Moses against their common enemy, the mighty Egyptian empire. He sent one of his court artists to meet Moses in the Sinai Peninsula in order to paint a portrait of him. The king was indignant at the painting the artist brought back, for in it the face of Moses appeared "covetous, haughty, sensual, in short, disfigured by all possible ugly traits." The king's counselors declared the portrait was a picture of a villain, and the king charged his artist with incompetency. Since the artist defended himself, the king went in person to see Moses. True enough, the Moses on the canvas was an exact copy of the real Moses. Then, continues this ancient Jewish legend, Moses said, "Thy artist and thy counselors alike are masters each in their own line. If my fine qualities were a product of nature, I were no better than a log of wood which remains forever as nature produced it at first. Unashamed, I make the confession to thee that by nature I possess all the reprehensible traits thy wisemen read in my picture and ascribe to me, perhaps to a greater degree than they think. But I mastered my evil impulses with my strong will and the character I acquired through severe discipline has become the opposite of the disposition with which I was born. Through this change wrought in me by my own efforts, I have earned honor and the commendation upon Earth as well as in Heaven."

Legends are not purely fictional; they reveal the drama of the psyche in the individuals they describe. In the case of Moses, the initial emotional struggle was to conquer a feeling of rejection. To side with his Hebrew brethren meant also overcoming the feeling that the Hebrews too had rejected him. At the very beginning they disdained him as a lucky but renegade assimilationist. This is clearly implied in the Bible account of Moses' defense of a

Hebrew slave and his attempt to pacify two Hebrews
quarreling with one another. The Bible verses read:

... and he saw an Egyptian smiting a Hebrew, one of his
brethren. And he looked this way and that way, and when he
saw that there was no man, he smote the Egyptian, and hid
him in the sand. And he went out the second day, and, behold,
two men of the Hebrews were striving together; and he said to
him that did the wrong, "Wherefore smitest thou thy fellow?"
And he said: "Who made thee a ruler and a judge over us?
Thinkest thou to kill me as thou did kill the Egyptian?"

The very boldness of the guilty Hebrew slave reflects his
disdain toward Moses for being an assimilated, Egyptianized Hebrew. That Moses knew little about the behavior
of his own people is reflected in his dismay at seeing two
Hebrews quarrel with each other. He projected his own
sympathies for their persecution into the assumption that
the Hebrews would be united with each another by reason
of their common fate. With such confused, ambivalent
feelings, what then did move Moses to slay the Egyptian
taskmaster for beating a Hebrew slave?

Just as Moses willed to conquer his rejection, so now he
allowed himself to be moved by his intuitive sensitivity to
injustice. Moses was repelled by the ruthless cruelty upon
which the structure of Egyptian society was built. The
scenes on Egyptian monuments and the writings in
preserved Egyptian papyrus documents show that this
society was divided into three classes—the royal, military,
religious and administrative upper class; the Egyptian
farming and laboring class; and finally the captive slave
class. Scenes show Egyptian farmers lying prone while
being beaten by the tax-collectors. Papyri are remarkable in
their realistic description of the depressed Egyptian crafts-
men and labor class. One of the scribes put in the mouth

of an Egyptian workman the words, "I am putrefying with hunger." This same privileged scribe says of the working classes, "Plebeians stink." Sometimes the situation became so desperate that the Egyptian records actually describe strikes by working men and peasant revolts in the fields. Such privileges could be entertained only by the Egyptian workers, who in the records are described as being at least human—"They have hearts"—whereas the records describe the captive slaves as inhuman beasts—"They have no hearts." The difference between the Egyptian workman and the slave worker is also evident in the scenes on the monuments. Egyptian workers are depicted as individuals; there are spaces between the figures. On the other hand, non-Egyptian slave laborers are depicted massed together in monotonous repetition, without any spaces between.

In rebelling against this totalitarian slave state, Moses became profoundly conscious of the fact that he was not an Egyptian but a Hebrew. It was his sense of justice that led to this awareness. Such a reaction was natural and human. It reminds one of the reaction of a modern assimilated Jew from Vienna who became aware of his Jewishness when he too first saw the miscarriage of justice against a fellow Jew. His name was Theodor Herzl. In the early 1900's a Jewish captain in the French army by the name of Dreyfus had become the innocent victim of a false charge of treason inspired by anti-Semitism. To conceal their own conspiracy with the German military, corrupt French officers accused Dreyfus of a traitorous crime actually committed by one of themselves. As a journalist, Herzl had come to Paris to report the trial for his Viennese newspaper. The anti-semitic hysteria so shocked him that as a reaction, literally overnight, he became a conscious Jew. The very next day he began to write *The Jewish State,* the book upon which the modern

nationalist emancipation of European Jews and the establishment of the new State of Israel was to be based. Simi-
larly, Moses overnight became aware of his loyalty to the
Israelites when he first saw the cruelty of their enslavement. The very next day he went out to appeal to two
quarreling Hebrews. It took Herzl only three days to write
out his program, for he had the advantage of a 3000-year
heritage as well as the example of Moses. As the pioneer
who was the first to conceive of the people of Israel as a
special nation, it took Moses many years to arrive at his
own unique concept.

Moses alone created his concept of a specially chosen
religious people, and only after he had completed the
struggle to resolve his own personal conflict. Should he
choose the highly advanced Egyptian culture or the seemingly primitive nomadic cult of his own people? When he
chose his own people, he had to reject Egyptian civilization
entirely. This is the major reason why the Bible saga
writers found it superfluous to describe the Egyptian
training of Moses. That training influenced the formation
of the ideas of Moses only in so far as his thinking completely repudiated Egypt and replaced the culture of Egypt
with an entirely new concept of God and of man.

The originality of Moses grew out of a reflective process,
during which his mind was able to draw upon the religious
cult of his Semitic nomadic brethren in exposing the
decadence of the greatest tyrannical power of his day. This
reflection took place away from Egypt, in the mountainous
region of the Sinai Peninsula to which Moses had fled after
his slaying of the taskmaster and this rebellious act against
Egypt had become known. Sinai was a natural hiding place
because no Egyptian garrisons were stationed there. However, Moses deliberately chose to flee to a special region
around Mount Sinai called Midian. In that region lived

nomadic Semitic tribesmen who were half-cousins of Moses.

According to the Bible genealogy, the patriarch Abraham had married Keturah after the death of his first wife Sarah. One of the sons of this marriage was Midian, who therefore was the half-brother of Isaac, Sarah's son. Isaac was the grandfather of Levi, who originated the tribe into which Moses was born. It may well have been that at the time of his flight, Moses sought out his own family and was advised by his priest brother Aaron to find refuge among the Midianites. Being responsible for the religious cult of the Israelites, the Levites kept the ancient tribal traditions alive. A Levite cult-priest could well have had special contact with his half-cousin in Midian—a man named Jethro—because the latter too was a priest. In this role, Jethro also could have kept alive the ancient traditions of the family and tribal cult. It was in the home of this Jethro that Moses found protection and refuge. Here he married Jethro's daughter Zipporah, who bore his two sons Gershom and Eliezer.

Since Jethro was a priest, it is natural to expect that Moses must have learned from his father-in-law something about the religious cult of this blood-related tribe in Midian. These tribesmen settled in the south-central part of the Sinai Peninsula were not only shepherds, they were also coppersmiths. The mountain range in this area is rich in copper, and the archeologist Nelson Glueck has discovered the remains of extensive smelting operations carried on there in ancient times. The Semitic word for "smith" is *Kein*. The Bible refers also to Jethro's Midianites as Kenites (Numbers 24:21).

Certain Bible critics used to entertain what was called the Kenite theory, which held that Moses was taught by his father-in-law to believe in the fire-god of these Kenite

smelters. This, according to those critics, explained the
Bible's saga legends about the revelation of God to Moses
in a burning bush or on a volcanic mountain. There is
no basis in the Bible for this Kenite hypothesis. In the
Bible, Jethro was not introduced to Moses as the priest
of a god by any such name as Moses himself later used to
describe his own God. Jethro was introduced only as a
priest of the Midian Kenites. Moses came unwittingly,
while shepherding his father-in-law's flock, to the "Mountain of God" where the revelation of the burning bush
was supposed to have occurred. Jethro did not tell him
previously that it was holy ground sacred to his fire-god.
There was no cult altar to a fire-god on Sinai. In the
legend of the burning bush, Moses had to ask the name of
the God who was speaking to him. Nothing about Mount
Sinai had been told Moses by Jethro.

The difference between Moses and Jethro is the same
as the difference between Moses and Akhenaton. To
Jethro, the Kenite fire-god was a tribal god, one among
other gods. The God of Moses' unique conception was
the one and only God. Later, when Moses returned to
Midian victorious over Egypt, his father-in-law, according
to the Bible record, came to meet him and was then converted to the God-idea of Moses at a typical nomad meal
and sacrifice for the purpose. The Kenites did not join
up with Moses, though Moses suggested the alliance to
his brother-in-law Hobab. Nevertheless, Jethro was convinced of the new God-idea of Moses because of Moses'
victory over the tyrannical common enemy, Egypt. Jethro
expressed this new conviction by himself using, for the
first time, Moses' name for God, saying, "Now I know that
the Lord is greater than all gods."

The uniqueness of the genius of Moses lay in his being
the very first to conceive of an invisible God who was

everywhere, Who ruled all and Who demanded just law for all. In this concept one might find evidence of the earlier invisible God of Abraham. Since this god wandered with this nomadic chief, he was not limited to one place. One might even find elements of revulsion against the gods of Egypt just because they were devoid of justice and law. There still remains the unsolved mystery of how the thought of Moses put these elements together as he shepherded the flock of his father-in-law over the mountain ranges of Sinai. This was also a mystery to the saga writers, who sang of its glory in the Biblical legend of the burning bush.

The first theophany or appearance of God to Moses has been given a naturalistic explanation. One botanist has even purported to have identified the burning bush as a Fraxinella, a three-foot plant with purple blossoms covered with tiny combustible oil glands which in strong sunshine may suddenly burst into flame. Another scholar has suggested that it was a thornbush, called the *Seneh,* which is still found in the mountain regions of Sinai. When the blossoms of the mistletoe growing on this bush are in full bloom, their flaming color makes the bush look as if it were on fire. Either of these naturalistic explanations of the burning bush may be true, and may thus explain the Bible text which says, ". . . behold, the bush burned with fire, and the bush was not consumed." The sight must have been familiar to the native shepherds in that district who knew the bush was not literally on fire. However, it was a new and surprising experience to Moses when first he shepherded his father-in-law's flock on that mountain range—one that aroused his curiosity to investigate "this great sight" and to reflect on "why the bush is not burnt."

The Bible saga writers tried to re-create the "drama of the psyche" involved in the transformation which took place in Moses himself. They took their cue from the resistance which Moses put up to the call of his conscience to duty. This resistance of Moses recalled to the saga writers the written confession of Jeremiah, one of the later literary prophets of Israel, who followed the example of Moses. Jeremiah also at first resisted the call to a dangerous duty, but his conscience would not let him alone. Jeremiah was doubtful whether his fellow Israelites would respond to his warning that they should mend their ways and follow the path of justice. He complained bitterly, for he had already been rejected by them. Jeremiah cried out: "O Lord, Thou hast enticed me, and I was enticed, Thou hast overcome me, and hast prevailed; I am become a laughing-stock all the day, every one mocketh me. For as often as I speak, I cry out, I cry, 'Violence and spoil'; because the word of the Lord is made a reproach unto me and a derision, all the day. And if I say: 'I will not make mention of Him, nor speak any more in His name,' then there is in my heart as it were a *burning fire* shut up in my bones, and I weary myself to hold it in, but cannot."

The desire to free the Israelites from Egyptian slavery had become a "burning fire" shut up in the bones of Moses, who also wearied himself in attempting to hold it in but could not. This raging conflict within Moses was dramatized by the saga writers of the Bible in their dialogue between Moses and the voice of God speaking from the burning bush. A natural phenomenon, perfectly ordinary to the uninspired shepherd on Sinai, became extraordinary to the shepherd Moses because it reflected the "burning fire" within him. This fight with conscience is brilliantly described in the saga dialogue in the Book of Exodus. God orders Moses to free His people Israel because He has seen their oppression and heard their cries. Moses resists by saying he is an unknown and is unable to perform the mission. From the burning bush the voice of God says that God will equip Moses with the magic of turning a rod into a serpent, or his own hand into a leprous one and back again, or water into blood. Moses, unconvinced, declines because, he says, he is "slow of speech." When God replies that He will speak for him, Moses still urges that another person be sent. Whereupon God becomes angry with Moses and commands him to accept the mission, with the assurance that his brother Aaron will speak for him.

It is most significant to note in this Bible account that Moses was not impressed with magic. In fact, the Bible saga later turned over the whole business of performing magic in Egypt to Aaron. To Moses the "burning fire" of desire for freedom could not be satisfied with a god of magic, for such a god of magic was employed by the priests of Pharaoh to support slavery. Freedom was not to be won by magic. For the winning of freedom even the old god of his nomadic ancestors, who wandered with them as their benevolent protector, would need a much greater power than that possessed by a god confined to tribal traditions. To the ancients what a god was really like was contained in his name. A god's character was revealed in that name. To the patriarchal Israelites Abraham, Isaac and Jacob, says the Bible saga, God was known by the name *Shaddai,* meaning "Mighty One of the Mountain." Now to achieve freedom for his people, Moses in the saga gave his God a new name. God would no longer need to be conjured up by magic, nor would He be limited to the movement of free-moving nomads. God would have to be present not sometimes but all the time. Therefore Moses took the Hebrew verb *hoyo,* which means "being" or "existence," and named his God *JHWH,* or "He who is always present." The saga of the Bible declares that by this name God was not known previously to the patriarchs.

Moses was the first to conceive of a universal God of freedom who works not through magic but through justice and whose justice is demonstrated everywhere throughout human history. Supported by this faith, Moses set forth on his mission to free Israel from Egyptian slavery. His success would prove not only to the Israelites but also to the Egyptians that his JHWH was the one and only God. Revelation of the new is repudiation of the old. In the burning bush Moses repudiated the guilt feeling that had stemmed from his ambivalence over whether he should be an Egyptian or a Hebrew. He had made up his mind to be on the side of freedom.

Although the saga writers of the Bible decorate the emancipation of Israel by Moses in Egypt with "signs and wonders," this magic is not consistent with the character of Moses. What did really happen under his inspired leadership is realistically described in the Bible text. By penetrating beneath the magical, the factual can be found. As has been said, every new threat of an invader against the declining Egyptian empire stimulated rebellion among the captive slaves. Desperate though they were, the Israelite slaves were still cowed and disorganized. The first task Moses undertook was to build up a following from among them and the Bible records the resistance to this effort on the part of these fear-ridden slaves. They simply refused to believe or to risk rebellion. Patiently Moses worked to convince them that a God of freedom was on their side, reminding them that they once had been freedom-loving nomads like their forefathers. Moses declared that his JHWH was the same God who protected the patriarchal nomads.

The original settlement of the Israelite slaves in their segregated section on the Delta bordering the desert had become a slave colony, from which the slaves were dragged daily to the building places. Moses worked among them and when he felt he had prepared them, he first tried a ruse. He requested permission for the Israelites to go for a three days' journey eastward into the desert, ostensibly for a tribal religious festival. With this head start they might be able to escape. This was considered acceptable to the Pharaoh as one way of possibly mollifying the increasing rebelliousness of the slaves. However, suspecting a ruse, Pharaoh granted permission only on condition that the women and children remain in Goshen as hostages. His ruse having failed, Moses reluctantly undertook a more drastic measure. He instituted a period of terror.

Terroristic methods employed by the desperately oppressed to liberate themselves have been repeated frequently in the history of many peoples. Among the Israelites we are reminded that twelve hundred years after Moses a party known as the Zealots fought as assassins and guerrilla terrorists in hopes that they could frighten the Romans out of the land. Two of the twelve apostles of Jesus, the Zebedee brothers, were members of this terroristic group. In more recent times, the Irgun employed similar tactics of assassination in order to terrorize the British forces of occupation and thus to hasten the day of independence of the new State of Israel. In his own young manhood, Moses had killed an Egyptian taskmaster. He knew the results had been inconclusive, and indeed negative, because he had had to flee. He was now wiser and older, and therefore it could have been only sheer desperation that made Moses now resort to terrorism.

Moses put off the extreme measure of killing Egyptians for as long as he could. The delay is evident in the very elaborate Biblical account of the ten plagues. These famous plagues were supposed to have preceded the bloody night of assassination. In each miraculous plague the saga writers could have had in mind a real occurrence in Egypt. These plagues may well have been coincidental with the development of the rebellion of the Hebrew slaves. The Nile River can suddenly take on a dark reddish color, so that it indeed looks like blood, owing to the deposits of red silt coming down from the mountain headwaters during unusual flood times. The floods could carry frogs with them onto the land. Flies, lice and parasites of cattle regularly plague the area. Skin diseases, including boils, are prevalent in Egypt. They have been described in ancient Egyptian records and even by the later writers in Israel, who refer to them as "the Nile itch" or "the botch of Egypt." Swarms of locusts still threaten crops in that area, and sudden sandstorms swept by the Khamsin winds blot out the sun and turn the daylight into darkness. Only one plague, the killing of the first-born, has no natural parallel.

One of the Bible biographies makes no reference at all to the other nine plagues. It attributes the emancipation of the Israelites entirely to the panic created by the shock of the killing of the Egyptians. Even in the account in which ten plagues are enumerated, none of the first nine softened "the hardened heart" of Pharaoh. Only after the assassination of the Egyptians did Pharaoh let the people go. If the saga writers could attribute to God such use of terror, according to our modern concepts it should be less radical to attribute having ordered killing the first-born to Moses. Since the Bible text says that when the Hebrews left they "went up armed out of the land of Egypt," it appears that the Hebrew slaves had the knives to carry out the order of Moses. The sudden attack at midnight by the Hebrew terrorists threw the Egyptian countryside and capital into panic. "There was a great cry in Egypt; for there was not a house where there was not one dead." The Bible text gives evidence of this panic in the statement that Egyptians gave the terrorists jewels for ransom. Pharaoh, who had thus far hardened his heart against releasing the Hebrew slaves, was finally convinced by his own people to let them go. The saga writers dramatized a whole series of audiences between Pharaoh and Moses. It would seem that this oft-sung story of the boldness of Moses never happened. It is more realistic to surmise that the formerly Egyptianized Moses, returning as a revolutionist, had kept himself incognito. After the night of terror he led his followers out of Goshen and when the panic subsided Pharaoh tried to recapture them.

It stands to reason that Moses had made careful plans for the sudden midnight act of rebellion by the armed slaves. As he had appealed to their nomadic memories of once having been free men, so he now revived a nomadic ceremony which their forefathers had practiced to solemnize an agreement either to unite tribes in peace or as a preparation for making war. This old ceremony was the shepherd's holy meal before the chief's tent. A firstling of the flock was slaughtered and the blood of the animal smeared on the tent to keep the demons of misfortune away. Then the contracting parties ate the roasted meat at a common meal. If the tribe was to follow this pact with war, then the youths wearing masks of goats would engage in a mimetic war dance to imitate the forthcoming victory. The Hebrew word for a hopping dance is *Pesach*, and the Hebrew for dancing in a circle is *Hag*. Moses revived the nomadic communion meal and the *Hag Pesach* to usher in the night of killing. That terroristic act did require the unity of the Hebrew slaves which this meal symbolized. The meal was followed by a kind of dance whose postures imitated the act of leaving slavery. In the

Bible text, Moses ordered this combined ceremony of meal and imitative dance with these words: "And so thus shall ye eat it: with your loins girded, your shoes on your feet, and your staff in your hand, and ye shall eat it in haste— it is the Lord's passover."

The ceremony was carried out secretly by each family, and the blood of the slaughtered lamb was smeared on each doorpost. Every family did it at the same time, just before midnight, to symbolize dramatically the unification of the Hebrews for the great moment of liberation. The saga writers of the Bible, no longer conversant with this ancient Hebrew nomadic ceremony, adorned it with later accretions in the annual celebration of this great event of liberty once the Hebrews were settled in Canaan. There the Hebrews became farmers and incorporated the local agricultural festivals of the unleavened bread and the sacrifice of the first of the flock into the annual historical festival celebrating their liberty. The *Pesach* was then reinterpreted to mean passover, because death had "passed over" the houses of the Hebrews in Egypt when they "passed out" of the land of Egypt.

Moses had repudiated magic, yet the single never-to-be-forgotten event in this great liberation that must have appeared to be a miracle even to Moses was the crossing of the Red Sea. No other event so convinced Moses that his JHWH was truly the only God of justice, Who demonstrated His will in the act of history. On the basis of his own Egyptian military career, Moses was aware that Egypt had garrisoned forts on the main direct route to Canaan. It was one thing for Hebrew terrorists in the cover of the night to create panic in an Egyptian town. It was quite another for Hebrews marching together, even though armed, to be a match for the Egyptian war chariots in the open field. Moses decided, therefore, to lead them from

Goshen southeastward toward the Sinai area where he himself had once taken refuge among his half-cousins, the Kenite semi-nomads, in Midian.

The Bible states that slaves from other captive groups, "a mixed multitude," risked joining the rebelling Hebrews and gives a round figure of six hundred thousand footmen as having been freed, not including their families. This is a highly exaggerated figure. Were it accurate, these armed men would have had no trouble defeating one of the Sinai nomadic tribes, the Amalekites, who blocked their path. What ensued was the famous battle fought in the Sinai Peninsula, in which Israel prevailed only as long as Moses had held his hand aloft during the battle. In that area some six thousand nomads live today. Since this battle in the Bible was so evenly matched, it is suggested that the figure of the fleeing slaves was probably closer to six thousand. Had there been six hundred thousand, Pharaoh would have needed more than the six hundred chariots the Bible said he assigned to bring the escaping Hebrews back. Regardless of the numbers of Egyptians engaged in the pursuit to recapture the Hebrews, this effort turned out to be a complete fiasco for the weak and boastful Pharaoh Merneptah.

To avoid the main caravan and military route, the approach from the Nile Delta to southeast Sinai lies across the marshland known as the Sea of Reeds. The Sea of Reeds is at the north end of the Gulf of Suez which leads southward into the Red Sea. This upper marshland comprised the area dredged in modern times to make the Suez Canal. The famous song of Miriam celebrating the victory of Israel against Egypt at the crossing at this place is clearly a very old one, since in the Bible it is given in a poetic, rhythmic form (Exodus 15). In that song of Miriam, the place where the Israelites crossed is called Yam Suf. *Yam* means "sea" and *suf* means "reeds"—a word easily confused with the English word *red*. The Israelites could not have crossed the very wide Red Sea. However, they could have crossed the marshland or Sea of Reeds, particularly during the night—when, to quote the Bible, "a strong east wind" kept back the tides of the adjacent Gulf of Suez. The captains of Pharaoh's chariots had hoped to recapture the slaves just at the point where they would be "entangled in the land" of the marshes. Instead, their own chariot wheels sank in the marshland, "which made them to drive heavily," and there they were overwhelmed.

That Moses did not wait for a miracle is implied in the Bible passage in which the voice of JHWH answers Moses' complaint about this crisis with these words: "Wherefore criest thou unto Me? Speak unto the children of Israel that they go forward." The ancient poem of Miriam gives an exact picture of what happened in the marshland when it says of the Egyptians that "they sank as lead" and that "the earth swallowed them." It was only by the later saga writers, in their over-enthusiastic account of the great victory which the strategy of Moses achieved, that the crossing is described as a miraculous separating of the Red Sea, making a path of dry land between two walls of water through which the Israelites marched to freedom. It was the crossing of the Sea of Reeds that was forever sung by the singers and prophets of Israel as being a sign of the greatness of Moses' JHWH. *JHWH* is the only word used for God in Miriam's poem, whose major theme is, "Who is like unto thee, JHWH, among the mighty!"

With the liberation of the Hebrew slaves, Moses had arrived at his outstanding political achievement. So far as military and political leadership is concerned, the remainder of his career was an anticlimax. It was marked by the slow, painstaking effort to take the Israelites through the Sinai mountain ranges and steppes back to the farming and grazing pastures of Canaan, back to the land of "milk and honey" where the founders of these nomadic tribes once had lived. Furthermore, it required consolidating these nomads, who had lost their tribal traditions during four hundred years of enslavement, into a newly organized, disciplined fighting group. Leading the emancipated Hebrew tribes through Sinai was easier than disciplining them. Moses, who had been his father-in-law's shepherd in that region for many years, was thoroughly familiar with the terrain. His first objective was to reach the safe refuge of the Kenites, the half-cousins of the Israelites. The guideposts for this area that Moses remembered best were the copper smelting pots which have been described by the archeologist Nelson Glueck, who excavated them, as the Pittsburgh of the ancient Near East. Smoke ascending from these copper smelting pots could be seen during the day and fire could be seen during the night. The Bible saga writers dramatized this natural guidepost as "a pillar of cloud by day and a pillar of fire by night," with which the God JHWH had led the children of Israel through the wilderness. The natural basis for this miracle of the Bible saga is confirmed by the saga writers, who have these pillars of God lead the Israelites only up to the time they reach the region where the fire and smoke of the Kenite smelters in the region of Mount Sinai could be seen; thereafter they are led, according to the saga, by "an angel."

Crossing the barren land of the Sinai Peninsula presented crisis after crisis. The route Moses took circumvented the desert in the center of that peninsula. The route of the "wandering of the children of Israel in the wilderness of Sin" can be traced today by following the oases still in existence along the western coast of Sinai and the Gulf of Suez. The route then crossed the upland steppes and passed through the narrow valleys in the Sinai mountain ranges in the south of the peninsula. It then proceeded to the other side of the peninsula, which borders on the Gulf of Aquaba. It next went northward to the oasis named by the Bible Eziongeber—the present thriving seaport of Elath at the southern tip of the Negev in the new State of Israel. Although semi-nomads like the related Kenites extended hospitality to the marching Israelites, others like the Amalekites blocked their path and had to be fought. This part of the trek, covering some three or four hundred miles, took two years. However, a good part of this time was spent with the Kenites. Among them the Israelites pitched their tents in the valley at the foot of Sinai, a mountain which rises more than eight thousand feet.

From Eziongeber the route led northward through the present Negev to the southern border of Canaan, where entrance into the promised land of their forefathers could have easily been made had it not been for the opposition of the semi-nomadic Amorites who were settled there and who repulsed the advance of the Israelites. Defeated in that battle, Moses retreated to a large oasis area which in the Bible is called Kadesh. That name has survived to this day in the oasis of Ain Quedeis, which still has an ample water supply. The Israelites remained at Kadesh for thirty-eight years before the final push into Canaan.

During the thirty-eight years of the temporary settlement at Kadesh, Moses finally consolidated the disorganized slaves into a determined people. There he had disciplined them by means of a new moral code, a new legal system, a new religion with a new ceremonial cult, and by a new idealism which replaced the tribal traditions with a new concept of a united nation with a historic destiny. This not only required the superb leadership of Moses; it needed an entire new generation. That generation did not make the revolution but was born into it, was reared by it, and knew only its spirit of freedom. This generation reared in Kadesh could be compared to the present-day Sabra born in the new State of Israel, whose psychology differs from that of the western-born assimilated Jew who may settle there. It needed such a new generation, which did not know the old life as it had been known by its parents who still looked back on the false security of Egypt to which even slaves become accustomed or inured. This old generation had to die off.

It was fortunate that Moses had those thirty-eight years at Kadesh to teach a new generation his ideas, because the old generation had given him constant trouble all along the route of the long journey. There was always the problem of water and food. After the miraculous crossing of the marshland of the Reed Sea, there were fully three days before the Israelites came upon the first oasis, at Marah. Its waters even today are sulphurous and taste bitter. Immediately the slaves who had been freed only a few days ago began to complain. When the food gave out, they yearned for "the fleshpots of Egypt." Moses, familiar with the country from his shepherd days, taught them how to gather manna.

One of the most popular miracles associated with Moses is the story of manna from heaven. The saga writers at one place implied it was bread which JHWH let fall from heaven; yet at the same time a very realistic and elaborate description of this food is retained in the Bible text. In the morning the Israelites found lying among the underbrush "a small round thing, as small as the hoarfrost on the ground." Moses had to tell them that it was manna; "and it was like coriander seed, white; and the taste of it was like wafers made with honey." This manna from heaven is a product exported even today from the Sinai Peninsula.

Monks have been gathering manna for food during the past sixteen hundred years, ever since they first occupied a church at the foot of Jebal Musa or the mountain of Moses. This church was fortified in the reign of the first Christian Emperor, Constantine. Recently, two botanists from the Hebrew University photographed manna on an organized expedition. Manna is nothing more than a secretion exuded by the tamarisk, a bush indigenous to Sinai, when pierced by a certain plant insect. The secretion, which falls to the ground, is about the size of a seed and tastes like honey. It must be gathered quickly in the morning; otherwise it is eaten up by the ants. After a good rainy season, one Bedouin even now can collect four pounds in a day. It is today made into a soup or into honey cakes. This is exactly what Moses in the Bible text instructed his followers to do: "every man according to his eating" was to prepare manna, in a pot or in cakes; "but if some left it over the morning it bred worms."

A natural phenomenon also explains the miracle of the quails that "came up, and covered the camp" and were caught for food. The exodus began in the spring, at the time of the migration of the birds. Today quails leaving the hot regions of Africa to spend a cooler summer in Europe, fly over the Red Sea. Exhausted by this long flight, they alight on the shores of the Sinai Peninsula to rest before resuming their journey over the mountains to the Mediterranean. Even today Bedouins in that area catch the exhausted quails by hand in the springtime and also in the autumn on their return migration.

During his exile among the Kenites of Midian, Moses became familiar not only with these natural supplies of food but also with the local methods for finding water. Large porous limestone rocks are found in the beds of the streams, or "wadis," which dry up during summer periods.

These rocks absorb a great deal of water. When the encrusted limestone is split open, the rocks give up the water they have absorbed. This method of striking water is practiced today even as it was in the time when, according to the Bible, "Moses lifted up his hand, and smote the rock with his rod twice; and the water came forth abundantly, and the congregation drank, and their cattle."

The complaints about the hardships on the trek were in some instances petty annoyances like missing "the fish which we were wont to eat in Egypt for nought; the cucumbers, and the melons, and the leeks, and the onions, and the garlic." More serious than the absence of these savory foods was the opposition to Moses for beginning what certainly seemed to the Israelites an endless and fruitless trek leading nowhere. Certain elements lost confidence in the leadership of Moses. It was a painful experience for Moses when Dathan and Abiram, of the frequently belligerent tribe of Reuben, led a political rebellion. Their conspiracy involved two hundred and fifty captains. It was based on the conclusion that it was bad enough to have been misled into the Sinai wilderness to die and never to reach any goal, but that matters had been made even worse because Moses had assumed a tyrannical authority. They charged Moses with the words, "But must thou also make thyself a prince over us?" Moses defended himself before JWHW by saying, "I have not taken one ass from them, neither have I hurt one of them." He had to be ruthless in putting down this conspiracy. The most distressing aspect of this bloody rebellion lay in the fact that it had been inspired and abetted by his cousin Korah, from his own tribe of the Levites. Korah was jealous of the priestly role Moses had assigned to his brother Aaron. Even more disillusioning to Moses than these rebellious setbacks was the unfair disapproval of his authority by his own brother

Aaron and his sister Miriam on the grounds that Moses had a negress for a concubine. They, too, had to be severely disciplined.

More challenging than the rebellions of these minority groups was the anxiety of the majority. At least the rebels had spirit. But the frightened behavior of the majority brought Moses to such a point of despair that he was ready to face the possibility of final defeat by his own people and of a complete fiasco for his great adventure. This defection occurred at Kadesh after Moses had sent the twelve spies, selected to represent each of the tribes, to reconnoiter the land of Canaan. The huge cluster of grapes brought back gave proof of the fruitfulness of the land, but the spies also sadly reported that a severe battle lay ahead, for the land was covered with fortified towns. The fears of the tribesmen became so hysterical that they cried out, "Let us make a captain, and let us return into Egypt." Two of the spies tried to reassure the mob. Joshua and Caleb chided them for their defeatism by saying so long as they looked upon themselves as nothing but "grasshoppers" the enemy would also look upon them as nothing more. The mob threatened to stone Joshua and Caleb to death. It was this anxiety of the majority which the rebellious conspirators had unsuccessfully tried to exploit. It was because of the people's fear that Moses decided to remain in Kadesh to consolidate his forces. There he would inspire a new generation with a self-confidence like that of Caleb, whom Moses called "a man who had another spirit with him."

To imbue the people with "another spirit," to change a frightened tribe wandering without a goal into a people filled with a fighting courage because they had a destiny, became the supreme task of Moses. Within himself Moses waged a tremendous psychological battle between determination and vacillation as he made his supreme effort to

change a tribe of "stiffnecked" but frightened individual-
ists into a people. This personal conflict is the theme of all
the private prayers of Moses with which the Bible saga
writers interspersed their account of these conspiracies,
rebellions and fears among the tribes. In one of these
prayers, Moses boldly reproves JHWH for "laying the
burden of all this people upon me." He pleads for death:
". . . let me no longer look upon my wretchedness." In a
dialogue between God and Moses, the saga writers imply
that Moses even thought of abandoning these weakling
slaves altogether and finding a new group to carry out his
vision. However, in the most moving of all saga dialogues,
Moses is shown conquering his doubts by reaffirming his
faith in the God of justice and freedom he had discovered
at Sinai, in the God who had originally strengthened his
burning desire to free the slaves. In this dialogue, JHWH
tells Moses He is so angered at the tribes' rebelliousness
that He desires to kill them all. It is Moses who defends the
Israelites by reminding God that failure to establish them
as a free people would be interpreted by the world as
God's failure, since it is God who has inspired the entire
march to freedom. Before the emancipation of the slaves,
Moses had appealed to his God's sense of justice; now he
appeals to his God's forgiving love. He prays, ". . . let the
power of the Lord be great. . . . The Lord is slow to anger,
and plenteous in lovingkindness . . . Pardon, I pray Thee,
the iniquity of this people according unto the greatness of
Thy lovingkindness, and according as Thou hast forgiven
this people, from Egypt even until now."

To transform the tribes into a united people with a
destiny would need more than sympathy and more than his
personal authority. Moses had some comfort in knowing
that here and there individuals like Eldad or Medad supported his policy by acting as "prophets." Not being mem-

bers of the official Aaronite family of "seers," they were less suspect and therefore had some success in influencing the people. Another group of seventy elder chieftains became a kind of public-relations group in support of Moses. According to the saga writers, God told Moses He would inspire them: "I will take the spirit which is upon thee, and will put it upon them; and they shall bear the burden of the people with thee, that thee bear it not thyself alone." However, Moses realized that he could not rely upon his own personal authority, great as it was, to hold this people together. Obviously, he could not rely upon other individuals or groups of individuals, or even the judges whom he had appointed under the advice of his father-in-law, Jethro. The tribes would require a law higher than the authority of man. With this law Moses set himself the task of thoroughly indoctrinating a new generation during the thirty-eight years at Kadesh.

The Laws of Moses are undoubtedly his greatest contribution. These laws are a combination of moral, legal, communal and religious precepts. While leaders in many generations have been inspired to emulate the role of Moses as liberator, the Laws of Moses changed the world. The historical necessity for these laws is implicit in the relation of the emancipator, Moses, to the rebellious slaves he had freed to resume their former, forgotten nomadic life. Certain types of law were already known to the highly cultured Moses. As an Egyptianized Hebrew, he had been aware that the slave state of Egypt had no concept of a legal code to which a Pharaoh was subject—not to speak of a system of law applying to all classes alike. What might be called law in ancient Egypt was the fiat pronouncement by each Pharaoh. On the other hand, during his long exile on the Sinai Peninsula the semi-nomadic Semites had acquainted Moses with the written laws the

Semite peoples in western Asia had been developing for centuries.

One of the most dramatic of archeological finds was made at the oasis of Dophka in the Sinai Peninsula. When recently deciphered the monument turned out to contain Canaanite writing on tablets of stone dating from around the year 1500 B.C.E. The Hebrew alphabet is based on these Canaanite letters. The oasis of Dophka was the place where Moses encamped just before his stop at the foot of Mount Sinai. In other words, the Semites in that area had already been writing down records on stone for a period of no less than three hundred years before Moses arrived. Moses also could write. It is after its account of his leaving this oasis that the Bible text speaks for the first time of the command of JHWH to Moses to write down laws. That he was acquainted with Semitic laws is also evident from the similarities between Moses' Ten Commandments and the code of Hammurabi, which this Semitic King of Babylon had promulgated eight centuries before, in the year 2060 B.C.E.

There is a world of difference between the basis of the Laws of Moses and the basis of the laws of Hammurabi. The prohibitions of murder, theft, adultery, false witness, and so on, are found in both codes. The novelty in the Laws of Moses is not in the content but in the way these common social laws were legalized by Moses. His code is not the command of one ruler based on this king's relation with a private god among gods, as is that of Hammurabi. The code of Moses is not even given to him as a special seer. The uniqueness of the Laws of Moses is in the method of their giving. For the first time in human history, morality is the expression of the supreme will of the only God, and for the first time this code is given directly to a whole people. The uniqueness is not in the particular laws of civilization but in the fact that a people is to bring God's will into realization by following the laws. The Laws of Moses at Sinai are accepted publicly by a group. Morality for the first time is no longer a private affair.

As it has been necessary to separate the four different narrative biographies of the life of Moses, so is it important to separate the four different bodies of law that the four schools of Bible writers had incorporated into their separate records. It is obvious that all the laws in the Five Books of Moses could not have been promulgated by him. Many of them could not have been conceived in his day, for they are based on a settled agricultural life in Canaan and upon a well-developed later monarchy, as well as upon an extensive priest-controlled religious society. In order to establish their constitutionality, the legal tradition of Israel called for all laws to be derived from Moses. However, it is less difficult to find out what laws Moses himself did promulgate than it is to separate the narrative accounts of his life. Each of the bodies of law has been recorded intact in one of the four records. Therefore it is easier to recognize their duplications as well as their contradiction. The J and the E corpus of laws both date from around the year 800, the P corpus of law from around 700 and the D from around 600 B.C.E.

It was around the year 400 B.C.E., during the period of the restoration of Israel after the Babylonian exile, that the four sets of laws in the present Five Books of Moses were incorporated into one. The Restoration was a period of penitence for the fall of the state of Judah. Therefore Nehemiah and Ezra, who were the leaders of the Restoration, insisted that the returning exiles pledge to follow all the past laws. They ignored the apparent conflicts.

Within these conflicting bodies of law the most authentic findings of modern scholarship have attributed to

Moses himself the Decalogue or Ten Commandments in
Exodus 20:2–14. To Moses are also attributed what has
been termed the Large Book of Covenant laws, in Exodus
20:14–23:19, and the smaller book of Covenant laws in
Exodus 34:10–26. The Ten Commandments were written
by Moses on tablets of stone at Sinai. The additional laws
of the Covenant were developed and written down on
papyrus in scroll form during the thirty-eight years' stay
at Kadesh. It must be emphasized, however, that the Ten
Commandments and the additional laws were preceded by
a dramatic act. This act Moses called a *Berith* or Covenant.
The *Berith* marked two things: the unification of the
tribes as a people and an agreement between this people
and JHWH, the God of Moses.

The Bible saga writers give several accounts of this act,
by which a universal God made a covenant with an especially chosen people and which became so world-shaping
an event in human history. One account may be found in
Exodus 19–24, and a second in Exodus 32–34. In their
effort to comprehend the incomprehensible mystery of the
revelation at Sinai, the saga writers seem to have become
confused. It is not clear to them which came first—the
ceremony of the agreement between the unified tribes and
JHWH or the Ten Commandments. When the coldly
objective textual analysis of the Bible critic Wellhausen is
combined with the deep, warm psychic insight of the
philosopher Martin Buber, the dramatic act can be recon-
structed both historically and psychologically. There is
no doubt that the Covenant ceremony took place *before*
the giving of the Ten Commandments.

At Sinai Moses decided to establish a covenant relationship between JHWH and Israel. The decision was made
none too soon. The liberated slaves had arrived there only
three months after leaving Egypt; yet their rebelliousness

had already become evident. The signs of distrust and the danger of the disintegration of the tribes had become unmistakable to Moses. He was reminded of his earlier personal experience at Sinai, where the event of the burning bush had removed his doubts and fortified his determination to accept his mission. As at Sinai Moses had given up his own resistance, so at Sinai the Israelites might relinquish their stubbornness. If they could be inspired as Moses had been, then they might commit themselves as he had to JHWH. A great event must make them believe in the invisible God of the Universe who had selected them in order to demonstrate through their history that there is only one God. The Israelites must learn that the will of JHWH was not to be fulfilled by Bedouin anarchy but by giving order to freedom through the establishment of justice.

Dramatically Moses prepared the tribes for the event. To the Israelites who had lived in the flatlands of the Nile for four hundred years, the 8000-foot mountain towering above them was an overwhelming and majestic sight. Moses announced to the people that he would go alone up the mountain, on whose lower pasture slopes he had once led Jethro's sheep to graze. There he would report to JHWH of the success of his mission. Thus far the mission had indeed been successful. On the same day Moses returned and announced, according to the saga writers, that JHWH had asked him to remind the Israelites, "Ye have seen what I did unto the Egyptians, and how I bore you on eagles' wings and brought you unto Myself. Now therefore, if ye will hearken unto My voice indeed, and keep My covenant, then ye shall be Mine own treasure from among all peoples; for all the earth is Mine; and ye shall be unto Me a kingdom of priests, and a holy nation." In other words, Moses said to the Israelites that the God who had freed them was now willing to make a permanent covenant to protect and guide them. With the miracle of the crossing of the marshland still fresh in their minds, the tribesmen were ready to accept this strange contract with an invisible God.

Now Moses revived the old custom of the nomadic Israelites which always preceded making a pact for a peaceful unification of several tribes. It was similar to the old custom that Moses had revived on the Night of Terror before leaving Egypt, when he had united the tribes by a common meal which had preceded the terrorism. This time the old nomadic pact was transformed by the genius of Moses into something different. Whereas the old nomadic pact had been between a tribal chief and his tribesmen, the new pact was between God as King and Israel as His "own treasure." The pact was at one and the same time political and religious—between God and a "holy nation." This was not to mean that the God was but one among many gods who also had their own favorite nations. This JHWH, explained Moses, was the God of all the earth. Like the eagle that teaches its young to fly, this God was to be the One who would teach Israel how to be a free people. The people probably did not understand the true meaning of this definition of a Universal God, but they did relish their freedom. So they agreed to submit in advance to the covenant with this JHWH.

Then to solemnize the promise and make the agreement of the Israelites to the covenant an impressive one, Moses revived the nomadic purification ceremony that had preceded a tribal peace pact. For three days sex relations were prohibited; the mountain was declared out of bounds, so that the place itself would assume a sacred character for the event. On the third day a ram's horn was blown to assemble the tribes at the base of the mountain, in order, as the saga

writers state, "to meet JHWH." Moses repeated the offer
of the covenant, and the people again agreed to submit
their fealty to JHWH. At this point, Moses symbolized the
unification of the tribes which this new commitment of
fealty required. He erected an altar made of twelve stones,
representing the twelve tribes. This was followed by the
sacrificial ritual used in the old nomadic cult to seal a
tribal covenant. Sheep were sacrificed. The blood was
sprinkled on the arms of the agreeing parties, signalizing
that they had become a clan of blood brothers. To involve
the next generation in this commitment to a new kind of
covenant, Moses assigned the youth to prepare the sacrifice
and fill the basins with the blood. Once again Moses read
the terms of the covenant which he had now written down
on a papyrus scroll (in the text called "the Book of the
Covenant"). Again, the people responded, "All that the
Lord hath spoken will we do, and obey." Then the blood
was spilled on the two contracting parties—on the altar as
a symbol of JHWH, and on each Israelite. This blood ceremony completed, Moses then announced, "Behold the
blood of the covenant, which the Lord hath made with you
in agreement with all these words."

To emphasize that the covenant was made not between
JHWH and Moses, but between JHWH and a whole people, Moses then invited the seventy elder chieftains who
had supported his leadership to ascend the mountain with
him. This time Moses did not stop below the timber line
where, herding Jethro's flocks, he had himself experienced
the inspiration of the burning bush. Moses and the chiefs
climbed to the summit above the clouds. It was an awe-
inspiring sight to the slaves, freed but yesterday from the
flatlands of Egypt. The sun's rays reflected brilliant colors
on the low-hanging clouds beneath them, and above was
the clear blue sky. The scene struck the party of nobles

with awe and wonder. One can actually see the scene in the poetic imagery with which the saga writers tried to recapture that moment. To the party on the summit, they write, it appeared as though the invisible JHWH were coming to meet them to place his signature on the agreement: "and there was under His feet the like of a paved work of sapphire stone [the sun reflected on the clouds], and the like of the very heaven for clearness."

This beautiful Biblical saga poetry is immediately followed by a simple sentence which acted out the agreement of the parties to the covenant in typical nomadic terms. JHWH and the chiefs "did eat and drink" together. Such a primitive anthropomorphic description of a deity who is supposed to be invisible may be surprising. More striking, however, is the ingenuity of Moses in utilizing the familiar to deal with the extraordinary. The old nomadic common meal that signalized the completion of a tribal agreement was transformed by Moses on the mountain top to a completion of the agreement between JHWH and the whole people represented by these seventy men. The meal completed, Moses then instructed the party to descend through the clouds and to return to the people assembled at the base of the mountain. This symbolized once again the fact that the covenant was made with the whole people. Staying behind above the clouds, Moses left instructions that his brother Aaron was temporarily to assume his authority while he was absent.

On the summit of Sinai Moses remained for forty days. There he would spell out in simple, direct language the specific terms of the covenant already agreed upon and ratified by the common meal. The Bible saga writers surrounded this great moment with a return to the fire symbolism of the burning bush. This time, since the covenant was made with the whole people and not with one

man, they wrote, "And the appearance of the glory of the
Lord was like devouring fire on the top of the mount in the
eyes of the children of Israel." So it may have seemed "in
the eyes of the children of Israel"; but to Moses it was the
first time since his long struggle to free the slaves that he
could be alone.

What had transpired in the mind of Moses during this
period of solitude was not accompanied by the thunder,
lightning and fire popularly associated with that moment.
What happened can be inferred from the Biblical account
of what had happened to a prophet when he fled to Sinai
some four hundred years later. Following the model of
Moses, the prophet Elijah had also fought injustice based
on idolatry. This time it was a Hebrew king and not a
Pharaoh who was the tyrant. King Ahab and his infamous
wife Jezebel sought to kill Elijah as Pharaoh had tried to
eliminate Moses. Again, as Moses had done before him, so
did Elijah find refuge in the Sinai region. There Elijah
climbed the now famed and sacred mountain of Sinai. In
describing that moment in the life of Elijah, the Bible saga
writers stated that the top of the mountain was surrounded
by thunder, lightning and fire, and then continued, " . . .
but the Lord was not in the fire; and after the fire a still
small voice." By this phrase they meant the voice of
conscience and thus they record Elijah's determination to
overthrow Ahab. It had been his own conscience that had
moved Elijah to declare that he had been "jealous for
JHWH" and for the covenant.

In the saga account of Moses on Sinai, not only is the
entire mountain aflame but also a flame descends from
heaven to meet it. This implies that the covenant was not
to be a commitment merely between JHWH and Moses,
such as the burning bush had symbolized. Rather it meant
an agreement between JHWH and the entire people at the

foot of the mountain. As it was later to be with Elijah, so with Moses it was not in the fire but in the "still small voice," in the silence of a long period of introspective contemplation on the mountain top, that Moses wrote down the terms of the already agreed-upon covenant.

The specific terms of the covenant which Moses spelled out and chiseled on stone tablets were what the Bible text calls "the tables of the testimony" or "the ten words." As had already been pointed out, there was no novelty in the moral prohibitions against murder, theft and adultery. The uniqueness of the Ten Commandments as set forth by Moses lay in two things—in the special form of the language and in the special definition of the contracting parties. Moses had long before repudiated the unfounded prerogatives of the divine right of a king; therefore he did not begin with "I, Moses, command you" as Hammurabi began his code. On the contrary, Moses tried to establish an intimate relationship, not between one God and himself, as Pharaoh Akhenaton did, but between this God and every Israelite. To do this he had God speaking in the first person singular: "I am the Lord who brought you out of the land of Egypt," and "You shall not." It is, as Martin Buber has so aptly pointed out, the intimate relationship of "I and Thou." Furthermore, the Ten Commandments were not meant merely to be articles of faith, a theological creed, or rules of ethical behavior. They were meant to be regulations for a particular community, considered as a whole people, who now had a God who worked not by magic but through history. Therefore, the Ten Commandments do not begin "I am JHWH, ruler of the world," but "I am the Lord, thy God, who brought thee out of the land of Egypt, out of the house of bondage." A concrete historical act of liberation stood at the beginning of this people's acceptance of the rules of the invisible, universal God.

The most revolutionary part of the Ten Commandments consists of the first three, in which Moses set forth his entirely new definition of God. There are no other gods but God. No images may be made of this invisible Deity. This God may not be conjured up by magical use of His Name; one may foolishly attempt to do so, but only "in vain." By one stroke Moses had thus demolished the entire world of polytheistic mythology, all the pagan gods who literally had controlled the minds of men.

For ages mankind had acquiesced in a blind fate to which the pagan gods were supposed to have destined it. Only by understanding the psychological effect of the pagan religion can the revolutionary impact of Moses' concept of deity be fully appreciated. By the time of Moses the concept of deity had evolved through three stages. Primitive man had invested inanimate objects with supernatural powers. This worship of trees and rocks in order to ward off evil or gain power is fetishism. The next stage was the worship of totems, or figures of animals which were supposed to possess the superhuman powers of deceased chieftains now symbolized by these animals. Civilization advanced when totemism was replaced by paganism. Now gods were depicted as human in form. Made in the image of man, there were male gods and female goddesses who cohabited with each other, loved, hated and even killed each other. They were born, lived and died, and some were reborn after death. Taking sides of a favorite person or people, the gods competed with each other in battle. To the pagan believer these gods and goddesses were real, active, living powers.

The most important aspect of paganism was the unknown, impersonally cruel force of destiny to which all the gods, including the chief Father god, were subject. Since superhuman gods were not free, how could a human

being ever hope to be free? The revolutionary concept of
Moses that there was only one God became a natural con-
comitant of his act of freeing the Hebrew slaves. Above
myth, magic and fate, JHWH was not subject to any control; and only such a God could free men. This joint
religious-political emancipation of Israel by Moses had a
phenomenally all-pervasive, continuing effect on the thinking of Israel. In one great moment, and at least a thousand
years in advance of any other group in the human race, a
whole people was freed from the pessimism of fate which
had held mankind in its grip for millennia. After Sinai,
the national disasters of the kind that blotted out other
groups from the pages of history became to the people of
Israel only challenges to be overcome. Inspired by the
teaching of Moses and emulating his example of being
unfettered by popular cult or fear of priest, an apostolic
succession of prophets would always appear to renew the
people's confidence in "the time to come" when Zion
would be restored.

The thirty-nine books of the Hebrew Bible, which
cover a thousand years after Moses, are all dedicated to
the theme that so long as Israel believes in the one God of
freedom, Israel will survive. All around the author of each
of these books there lived people who believed in the
mythological gods of Egypt, Babylon, Persia, Greece and
Rome. Yet the strangest fact about the Hebrew Bible is
that—aside from purely historical references, as to the
priests of Baal and Ashtaroth—not a single one of these
many, contemporary, very-much-alive pagan gods is
referred to in any of the books of the Bible. It cannot be
that the Bible authors had never heard of the gods of pagan
mythology, for quite a number of the myths associated
with these gods are repeated in the Bible. However, when
they are found in the Bible, the pagan myths are altered

radically. In the original pagan myth one god contends with another god over man, and both gods contend with their own fate. In the Bible version of the same myth, only one God appears and the pagan gods are reduced to mere animals. For example, in the pagan myths about a Garden of Eden a Serpent-god of evil, out of jealousy, competes with a good god by tempting this god's favorite. Although the anthropomorphic pagan way of depicting God is retained in the Bible version, the serpent is just an animal. The conflict is not between gods but between man and woman, and both are punished for the sin they commit of their own free will. Their sin is their attempt to become immortal gods.

As Yehezkel Kaufman has brilliantly demonstrated, it was not ignorance of but complete disdain for mythological gods that accounted for the fact that none of these gods living all about the people of Israel are in the Bible. They were laughed out of court as absurdities. They were simply looked upon as retentions of the most primitive type of fetishism no matter how cultivated the peoples who believed in them might have been. Whenever the people of Israel succumbed to the attractions of pagan religion, the prophets who criticized them refused to recognize any reality in quasi-human gods. They made the Israelites guilty of backsliding to pagan gods simply look ridiculous. How could any sensible people possibly believe an idol could be the image of a real, living god? Idolatry was scorned as the utter foolishness of a child's game with sticks and stones "that see not, hear not, eat not and smell not" and "must be carried because they can not walk."

With Moses the cardinal sin was idolatry precisely because it distorted the rest of the attitudes and behavior of men. This was an idea original with Moses. In all the ancient world, only among the people of Israel was idolatry a punishable sin. This fact, unique among the Israelites, is consistent with the assertion that they were the first to be given a completely monotheistic religion. Because polytheistic paganism holds many attractions, this achievement of Moses reflects all the more his commanding will power. The outstanding attraction of paganism is the association of its gods with sexuality and with death. Moses dealt a blow to these gods, in particular, in the last two acts of his life.

These two acts took place during the thirty-eight years' sojourn at Kadesh, 150 miles north of Mount Sinai. Kadesh is suited to farming as well as to the herding of sheep and goats. In that district the semi-nomadic tribes of Israel, recently freed from a long enslavement, first began to learn farming of the settled type from the Semitic farmers they found established there. This very important transition stage turned the Israelites from nomadism to settled farming, which became their main occupation once they had conquered the land of Canaan. In Kadesh they assimilated not only farming techniques but also the religious beliefs characteristic of pagan farmers. The tiller of the soil must wait for the rain to fecundate the earth before the seeds can give birth to the grain. To the pagan farmer, rain is semen and earth is the womb. In paganism, since rain comes from the sky the god of the heavens is male ("our Father who art in heaven") and the god of the earth is female ("Mother Earth"). Among the Semite farmers of western Asia the gods of the fertility of the soil all had the name *Baal*, which means "owner" (that is, of the sky and earth). In the Bible they always appear in pairs. They were symbolized by the idols of the bull and the cow. Their divine mating was looked upon as the religious foundation of the settled agricultural society.

Since imitative acts by human beings were believed to

influence the acts of the gods, the pagan farmer performed sex rites in public to stimulate the sexuality of the fertility gods. For this purpose the cult of the sacred prostitute was developed. This religious-sexual process also worked in reverse. When the gods procreated, that act was supposed to have a magic intensity, and therefore the cult imitation of the sex gods became an orgy for human beings. It was not an unbridled sexual drive but rather the mystery of the fructifying of the soil which motivated the cult of the fertility gods. In Kadesh the Israelites, copying the neighboring farmers, visited their sacred prostitutes. The Bible text refers to their worshiping Baal at Kadesh by "whoring after the daughters of Moab." It was in this context of the rivalry of the fertility gods that Moses coined the definition of his JHWH as a "jealous God" who had no tolerance for lovers faithless to Him. Moses was ruthless again in stopping this new betrayal of his one and only God.

For a god to be one, this god must be above sex, for sex requires the relation of two. God's love for the people of Israel and His concern for their welfare could have no reference to sex, for this would deny God's oneness. Moses had been forewarned of the attraction of the pagan fertility gods. When he had absented himself from the Israelites for many days on Mount Sinai, the people, still puzzled by the newness of an invisible God and afraid that Moses might not return, had rioted and demanded a visible god. This god was the golden calf or the soil-fecundating bull-god of sex which attracted them the nearer they came to sown land. Moses had come to the sad decision even then that the Israelites were not ready for an invisible God who taxed their imagination and strained their patience.

To make his JHWH more tangible Moses then changed the character of his own Tent of Meeting where he was wont to meet the chieftains and where the people came to consult him. He removed the tent from the center of the nomadic encampment and placed it outside the camp. He then announced that he and Aaron, the priest, and the Levites would go there to consult JHWH. Thus the tent of Moses became the Tabernacle. Moses ordered a portable ark to be made out of the acacia wood indigenous to Sinai, and in it he placed the two Tables of the Testimony he had chiseled on Sinai. When it rested in the Tabernacle, this ark became a symbol—the "footstool" where JHWH might rest His feet when He came to visit the Tabernacle. When the people were on the move the Ark led them, and in battle it became a standard symbolizing the presence of JHWH, whose "face" discomfited the enemy. Since he had conceived of God as invisible and also as the Lord of heaven and earth, Moses did not say that the Tabernacle housed JHWH as the temples of the pagans housed their gods. JHWH only visited the Tabernacle to meet with Israel. This was as far as Moses would go to make his invisible God visible, for he declared, "No man can see God's face and live." Thus, the Tabernacle and Ark became not even a symbol of but only a metaphor for God. From them developed the later institutions of the Temple, the Synagogue and the Church of Western civilization.

To meet the more specific challenge of the powerful influence of the fertility gods in farming, Moses revived again the old, forgotten nomadic traditions. This time it was the tribal tradition of sharing, prevalent among nomads but not among farmers. Since the JHWH of Moses "owned" heaven and earth, there could be no local nature gods. Since this God had freed the Israelites, they could be assured good crops as farmers if they would continue the nomadic custom of sharing with each other the produce of the field. By virtue of such sharing, the free Israelite nomad was assured of never again becoming a slave on a farm in order to eat. During the part time farming at Kadesh, Moses became aware of the radical contrast between the free life of the nomad and the life of the farmer threatened with enslavement. To protect the Israelites from slavery once they had settled on farms in Canaan, Moses formulated his revolutionary agricultural laws.

The fundamental agricultural law instituted by Moses was the weekly Sabbath. Among the western Semites the seventh day of the week, associated with the changing phases of the moon, was an unlucky day. Moses changed it into a day of good fortune, for on it every man, worker as well as owner, and even every animal, must be free to rest. The saga writers confirm this relation between the Sabbath and the farmer as a counter-action against farm enslavement by associating it with the very first farming act of the freed nomads of Israel. They assert that Moses had initiated the Sabbath, even before the Ten Commandments, when under his instructions the Israelites gathered the manna every day except the seventh, and that this is why in his fourth commandment Moses enjoins them to *"remember* the Sabbath day to keep it holy." Twelve hundred years later it was this Sabbath law of Moses, as incorporated into Christianity, that made the new religion so revolutionary a threat to the slave state of Rome. It formed a major attraction in the conversion of Roman slaves to Christianity, since in that religion—as in Judaism, its mother—at least once a week all were free and equal before God. The weekly Sabbath and the annual celebration of freedom, or the Passover meal, were two of the four later Jewish religious festivals which Moses himself introduced. The two others introduced by Moses were the commemoration of the Covenant agreement (Shavuoth or Pentecost) and a harvest thanksgiving festival developed at Kadesh—the Feast of Booths (Succoth).

Anticipating the economic injustices of an agricultural society by observing at Kadesh how one farmer could be so much more successful than another, thus producing a "have" and a "have not" class, Moses introduced two new acts of farm legislation—the Sabbatical year and the custom of leaving part of the field unharvested for the poor, the widow, the orphan and the stranger. Realizing how some farmers became indentured slaves in order to pay their debts, Moses established the Sabbatical year, according to which every seventh year such Hebrew slaves must be manumitted. These laws aimed at securing economic justice created many problems and aroused opposition once the Israelites were permanently settled. But in this transitional period Moses vividly saw the contrast between the free nomad and the enslaved farmer. To him these laws were not utopian but practical and necessary. His formula stemmed from his concept of God. The land belonged to JHWH, and therefore it was to be used to maintain the freedom He had won for each Israelite. Only by sharing its produce would the Israelites be assured that the land would be fruitful. Not by loving the pagan sex gods of love but only by "loving thy neighbor as thyself" could Israel enjoy a prosperous harvest. This formula became the Mosaic constitutional basis for all the remarkably progressive legislation for social justice later recorded in the Bible.

At Kadesh Moses completed his mission and prepared himself for death. He had freed the Hebrews from slavery; he had led them through the barren steppes of Sinai to the borders of a land "flowing with milk and honey"; he had transformed tribes into a united people, now called Israel; he had given them a covenant with a new invisible God, JHWH; he had lifted them out of the pessimism of paganism into the optimism of the first true monotheism in history; he had formulated for them a code of morality to distinguish between the "blessing" of life and the "curse" of death, and a set of laws to govern a community. He had instilled in them an indomitable will to live, so that for the first time in history a people as a whole possessed a sense of mission; he had even selected his successor, Joshua of the tribe of Ephraim. Indoctrinated with his teachings during the thirty-eight years at Kadesh, a new generation of Israelites was now ready to push on into Canaan. They had to circumvent the strongly fortified territories of the Edomites and Moabites, who even refused to sell them water. Thus they found themselves opposite the Jordan River facing the town of Jericho. They prepared to make their first assault on a fortified stronghold and to begin their invasion of a country which for more than three thousands year, down to this day, was to bear the name of Israel.

Moses spoke to the people of Israel for the last time as they assembled at the foot of the nearby mountain of Pisgah. As he reviewed his stewardship in his farewell address, he said he had come to them because of being *sent* by his god, JHWH. Moses was the first man in recorded history to undertake a religious mission to free an entire people. He was not moved by any divine mantic ecstasy, such as the so-called "classic prophets" were to claim for themselves. Rejecting all magic and myth, he was moved by a combination of conscience and intuition. Were he to read the saga writers in the Bible, he would approve their accounts of his life. He would agree with them that God, and not the man himself, had accomplished the great things associated with the name of Moses. The glory belonged to his invisible, universal God of freedom and justice.

Moses recognized his weaknesses—especially his temper, which could be ruthless. Yet this man of superhuman will was not arrogant for he always felt that he was only the messenger of the single Power which is superhuman. The saga writers constantly referred to the humility of Moses. Meekness is rarely associated with will power, but never had a God been so conceived by any man before Moses, and before the magnitude of that concept Moses was humble. "Oh, Lord, I am not a man of words," the saga writers had Moses reply in his first dialogue with his God. Indeed, he wanted none of the powers of the demagogic orator to deceive people with glib assurances of victory and security. He never minimized the hardships ahead. He was both a political and a military leader, but one who had an intimate sense of being a servant of that mysteriously awesome element in life which is called the holy. Moses demonstrated this unique combination of will and humility. On the one hand he boldly reproved his God's unreasonable anger and on the other hand he prostrated himself before a God who was "longsuffering and patient, forgiving thousands."

Moses, the liberator, became the willing servant of the God of his people's freedom because in his search for that God he had come to understand the meaning of his own personal suffering and to find some purpose behind the bitter conflicts of his own life. A stranger among the Egyptians who adopted him, and a stranger among his own people whom he had set free; an exile, a refugee and an immigrant himself, Moses knew from personal experience the wretched condition of loneliness. It was therefore that he taught, "And a stranger shalt thou not wrong, . . . for ye were strangers in the land of Egypt." Removed from his own parents as a child and forced to flee from his adoptive mother, Moses knew the sufferings of the broken home, and it was therefore that he taught, "Honor thy father and thy mother." Having himself killed a man and ordered the killing of others on the Night of Terror, Moses knew the guilt and the remorse that comes from taking another's life; and therefore he taught, "Thou shalt not kill." Having seen what Egypt did to captive slaves, and also how the Hebrew rebels stooped to malign his own integrity in their effort to undermine his plan for uniting the tribes, Moses taught, "Thou shalt not go up and down as a talebearer . . . Thou shalt not hate thy brother in thy heart . . . Thou shalt not take vengeance, nor bear any grudge . . . but thou shalt love thy neighbor as thyself."

The genius of Moses lay in his rare ability for joining rational thought with intuition. The extreme contrasts between the conflicting cultures he experienced—between nomadic fluidity and Egyptian rigidity — helped Moses unchain his intuition from the bonds of tradition. With this unique talent he transformed his own experience in the world of his time into a new spiritual consciousness. The undeveloped spirituality of the freed slaves made it necessary for Moses to create religious institutions and ceremonies for them to serve as tangible symbols of his invisible God. Despite this, there was implicit in the way he chose to die the faith that even they could experience in their lives what he had experienced. In his deliberate last act he hoped to show by his own example that what counts in the eyes of the invisible God is what one does with one's life.

For hundreds of years the Israelites had watched Egyptians corrupt and abuse the sacred gift of earthly life in order to prepare for an eternal existence after death. Not only the Pharaohs but every Egyptian willingly mortgaged body and soul to insure this end. To Moses, just as no magic could control life, so no magic could avert death. He had shown the Israelites how not to be afraid to fight for freedom. He would now show them how not to be afraid to die. The monumental tombs of dead Pharaohs did not perpetuate their lives. For Moses to have been buried even in a simple grave might prove dangerous; for just as the Egyptians worshiped at Pharaoh's tombs, so Israelites might come to his grave as a result of thinking of him as someone divine who could intercede for them with his invisible God. This would have been a repudiation of his whole fight against idolatry. The way he died would make impossible any future apotheosis of himself.

Only in the saga of a people who through Moses came to believe in one invisible God, and in no other saga, is there recorded the death of a hero such as the Bible records the death of Moses. On the top of Mount Pisgah, from which he could see the Promised Land that he would never enter, he remained to die unburied. He had passed his leadership on to the next generation with his final counsel: "Be strong and of good courage." Once again the aged Moses climbed a mountain: this time to die alone.

II: Jesus

Man fears the unknown. The unknowables man fears the most are the Future and Death. From the beginning of human consciousness, man has tried to prepare himself to meet these two inevitables. The less he has known about the Future and Death, the more his imagination has exaggerated their dangers, making greater his need for protection against them. Since he had yet to develop even the most modest control of his own destiny, primitive man invented superhuman powers to help his situation. These powers were to take pity on his helplessness and assist him in his grave extremity. Out of these primitive powers there eventually grew the myths of the great gods of the ancient world. There were wicked gods who hindered and harmed man. For their own cynical entertainment some gods even made a farcical play out of their tempting of man. There were also good gods. These gods were so good that they would endanger their lives and even sacrifice themselves to help man. Two such mythical gods come to mind: one god who helped man conquer the Future; the other god who helped man overcome Death.

The Greeks invented a god named Prometheus, the son of an Olympian god and goddess. He suffered torture bound to a rock because he had brought down from heaven the divine fire of the gods and had given it to man. With that fire man overcame the injustices of Zeus, the chief god, and man began to have a future. The Egyptians placed in their pantheon a god named Osiris. As the god of vegetation, Osiris aided man in planting seed. The seed, dying in the winter, has to be resown and reborn in the springtime. This good god, Osiris, was murdered by a brother god. His dismembered body was found by his wife, Isis, who buried him with elaborate mysteries. Osiris was then resurrected from the dead. A mysterious rite symbolically carrying out this burial and resurrection was performed every winter by the priests of Osiris in order to assure the return of their dead god of vegetation in the spring.

The suffering Prometheus and the resurrected Osiris were classical myths of the Greeks and the Egyptians. Both peoples believed in many gods and therefore could give their imaginations full play concerning them. They could invent good gods to counteract the evil ones. Such a self-serving, easy solution was not available for one people in the ancient world—the Jews. The members of this peculiar people were indeed peculiar to their contemporaries, precisely because they had only one God. According to their teacher, Moses, the God of the Jews was not only one, He was also invisible. Even if this God were all goodness, loving as well as just, how could He come down to earth to help man as did the gods of the Greeks and the Egyptians, since this Jewish God was invisible?

Yet according to Jewish cosmogony, man was the most precious of all creatures to the Jewish God, the Creator. Only once did God regret his handiwork and threaten to annihilate all men because of their wickedness. Because one man, Noah, was just and therefore proved man redeemable, God gave man, through Noah, a second chance after the destruction of the rest of mankind by a world-wide flood. God decided to be patient and longsuffering with man's weakness. He put His confidence in man's ability to repent and reform. Yet even God's patience could be taxed to the limit, and He would then have to punish man in order to discipline him. God would be justified in being less patient with His own favorite people, the Jews, than with any other group. The Jews should know the importance of avoiding wickedness. Were they not the first to be taught by Moses the laws, both ceremonial and ethical, which man should keep in order to enjoy God's favor? "Because I have chosen thee, therefore will I punish thee," said one of the Jewish prophets.

All the literary prophets of the Bible, from Amos to Malachi, interpreted the historical destiny of the Jews in accordance with the doctrine of a special people chosen by God. Through Moses, God had made a contract with the people of Israel. God would love and protect this people if they would keep the vows made at Sinai to obey the commandments—ceremonial commandments such as keeping the Sabbath and ethical commandments such as not committing adultery. This Sinaitic contract was frequently compared by the later prophets to a marriage contract. They spoke of God not only as the Father but also as the Husband. "For thy maker is thy husband, for the Lord has called thee to Himself as a wife." When the people were guilty of idol worship, the prophets would charge Israel with "whoring after false gods." Just as Hosea forgave his own wife for her infidelity, he defined God as also being forgiving if a faithless Israel would return to the path of righteousness.

The question was who would lead Israel back to the proper road of righteousness. God would not make a personal appearance to lead her, even though the primitive Hebrew God had once visited Adam and Eve in person in the garden of Eden. The advanced Jewish view was that the invisible God would inspire a prophet who in turn would select one of the sons of Israel to lead the people away from their unrighteousness. Election to this exalted leadership would be signalized by the anointment of this son with oil at the hands of an especially appointed Jewish prophet. When the first Jewish king, Saul, failed because he was half mad, the prophet Samuel anointed David to take Saul's place. The Hebrew word for "anointed" is *Messiah*. God's love for Israel, which was like a husband's love for his wife, would give Israel a blessed son to save her.

The original Jewish concept of a Messiah envisioned both a political and a spiritual leader. The state in Biblical times was a theocracy. Religion and politics were not separated. It was as a religio-political king that David brought the holy Ark of Moses to Jerusalem and set it on Zion's hill. Around it his royal son, King Solomon, built the famous Temple to the God of Israel. This Temple was administered by priests of hereditary families comparable to the Brahmins of India. The Temple was not merely a center of worship, it was the symbol of the nation's political security and future; as such, it was comparable to the Capitol building in Washington. As long as the Temple stood, no evil could overtake the nation. Therefore, whenever a prophet was determined to arouse the Jewish people in order to correct social injustices he would threaten them with the direst of all calamities: he would declare that unless the Jews repented and changed their ways the Temple would fall.

The Temple did fall, after a continuous 500-year reign by the kings of the Davidic dynasty. The Babylonians came, conquered the kingdom and destroyed the Temple. The despair of the people, and their utterly broken morale at that time, are epitomized in the famous lament of the Jewish poet in exile who wrote the 137th Psalm. "By the rivers of Babylon, there we sat down, yea, we wept, when we remembered Zion." The people of Israel never fully recovered from this fateful blow. Even when some of the leaders among the exiles returned and rebuilt a smaller Temple in the days of Ezra and Nehemiah, the land was still a Persian satrapy, later becoming a Greek province governed by foreign rulers.

Something had to be done to keep alive the hope of the full restoration of Israel's independence and the national glory that had been King David's. In Jewish thought there began a new development centered about a new kind of role which the Jewish Messiah was to play. In the first five hundred years before the Babylonian exile, the King-Messiah was envisioned primarily as a political leader, who concerned himself only with the nation as a whole. After the exile, the conviction that a nation might be only as strong as its individual citizens began to take firmer root. In the days of Moses the slave people were not ready for the idea of the responsibility of the idividual for the fate of his nation. In making his last testament, Moses had hoped that eventually Israel would understand this individual responsibility. It took the labors of the later prophets in the Bible, such as Jeremiah and Ezekiel, to impress upon a few of the people that responsibility was centered not in the nation but in the individual. These prophets were not entirely successful, and so this responsibility became the new role of the long-awaited Jewish Messiah. This Messiah would be a restorer of the nation entitled, as a descendant of David, to political kingship. However, to achieve that kingship this Messiah must teach personal responsibility. He would teach it by his own personal example.

The Messiah would give a demonstration of selflessness by being himself ready to suffer for the nation's salvation. Thus, there came to be three qualifications for the Jewish

Messiah who would represent God's help to the Jew. First, the Messiah must be a direct descendant of David, the greatest of all Jewish kings. Second, he must himself have experienced suffering—"the pangs of the Messiah"—as a proof of his selflessness. Third, he must succeed in conquering Israel's enemies and restore her national independence. When the Messiah had qualified in these three matters, he would then sit in judgment over the whole world.

The appearance of just such a Jewish Messiah was promised by an unnamed prophet whose writings are attached to the Book of Isaiah. This prophet, known as the Second Isaiah, tried to comfort the people during the long period of despair after the exile. In chapters 52 and 53 of Isaiah we find his description of this Jewish Messiah: "Behold, My servant shall prosper . . . so shall he startle many nations . . . He had no form nor comeliness . . . He was despised, and forsaken of men, a man of pains . . . We esteemed him not . . . We did esteem him stricken, smitten by God . . . wounded because of our transgressions . . . with his stripes we were healed. . . . For he was cut off out of the land of the living, for the transgressions of my people . . . He was oppressed, though he humbled himself, and opened not his mouth; as a lamb that is led to the slaughter, and as a sheep that before her shearers is dumb; yea, he opened not his mouth. And they made his grave with the wicked, and with the rich his tomb; although he had done no violence, neither was any deceit in his mouth. Yet it pleased the Lord to crush him . . . that the purpose of the Lord might prosper by his hand: Of the travail of his soul he shall see to the full, even My servant, who by his knowledge did justify the Righteous One to the many, and their iniquities he did bear . . . He bared his soul unto death . . . he bore the sin of many, and made intercession for the transgressors."

During this period another Jewish poet tried to imagine what the feelings of this Jewish Messiah would be. He sensed the bewilderment of a Messiah being made by God to suffer in order to deliver Israel. In Psalm 22 this poet put into the mouth of his imaginary Messiah these words: "My God, my God, why hath thou forsaken me? . . . In Thee did our fathers trust . . . But I am a worm, and no man; a reproach of men . . . All they that see me laugh me to scorn . . . [saying] 'Let God deliver him, seeing He delighteth in him.'. . . Thou art my God from my mother's womb. Be not far from me; for trouble is near; for there is none to help. . . . For dogs have encompassed me; a company of evil-doers have inclosed me; . . . they are at my hands and my feet . . . They look and gloat over me. They part my garments among them, and for my clothes they cast lots . . . But Thou, O Lord, . . . hasten to help me. . . . For He hath not despised nor abhorred the lowliness of the poor . . . All the ends of the earth shall remember and turn unto the Lord . . . For the Kingdom is the Lord's. . . ."

What could justify this extreme suffering of the Jewish Messiah? Another Jewish poet addressed himself to this question and answered it by saying that the special selection of the Messiah by God would be followed by a world-shaking wonder. This Messiah would not only restore Israel but rule all the nations of the world. This writer, in Psalm 2, put into the mouth of his Messiah these words: ". . . The rulers take counsel together, against the Lord, and against his anointed. . . . He that sitteth in heaven laugheth . . . Then will He speak to them in His wrath: 'Truly it is I that have established My king upon Zion, My holy mountain.' I will tell of the decree: The Lord said unto me: 'Thou art My son, this day have I begotten thee. Ask of Me, and I will give the nations for thine

inheritance, and the ends of the earth for thy possession." To carry this idea of world dominion for the Messiah
still further, a most imaginative writer composed that part
of the Bible called the Book of Daniel. In metaphoric
language he listed in that book the kingdoms that had
risen and fallen—Babylonia, Persia, the Greece—and still
other nations that were to exist until the Jewish Messiah
should finally take over. Thus does the writer of Daniel
describe the glorious world victory of the Jewish Messiah:
"I saw in the night visions, and, behold, there came with
the clouds of heaven one like unto a son of man, and he
came even to the Ancient of days, and he was brought near
before Him. And there was given him dominion, and
glory, and a kingdom, that all the peoples, nations, and
languages should serve him; His dominion is an everlasting
dominion, which shall not pass away, and His kingdom
that which shall not be destroyed."

All these various Jewish Messianic writings composed
between the year 500 and 160 B.C.E. became popular
much as astrology becomes popular in times of trouble
today. The popular descriptions of the Messiah in Isaiah
53, Psalms 2 and 22, and the Book of Daniel were eventually taken over almost completely and incorporated in the
New Testament passages concerning the Messiah.

Assuredly the enthronement of the Messiah as king over
Israel, who would cast down the evil kings of the world,
would be a great day of vindication and victory for conquered Israel. However, how would the people know the
Messiah who would be coming as a "son of man on a
cloud"? According to the Jewish tradition the Messiah
would have to be anointed first by an especially appointed
prophet. For several reasons Elijah was the prophet tradi-
tionally assigned to this role. Elijah, who lived in the ninth
century before the common era, had become a kind of

people's prophet, popular because he had led the people in an actual political revolution which dethroned an evil king. Furthermore, Elijah had defeated the priests who served the foreign god of Baal in the land. After his death many popular legends arose about the life of Elijah. He had performed miracles. According to one of the legends, Elijah did not actually die but ascended into heaven in a fiery chariot. Another legend declared Elijah would return and make the announcement of God's universal judgment. According to the last of the literary prophets in the Bible, Malachi, it was Elijah who was to be the announcer of the great event: "Behold, I will send you Elijah the prophet before the coming of the great and terrible day of the Lord."

No matter who was to make the announcement, the sure sign that the deliverer of the people was the Messiah would be his direct descent from King David. Members of the Maccabean family who became kings of Judea were the first to throw out the foreign overlords, in this case the Greek overlords. The Maccabeans established a completely independent nation some four hundred years after the Babylonian exile. However, Jewish religious leaders never looked upon any of the Maccabeans as a Messiah because they were not descendants of King David. It was during the 400-year period of the exile, from 586 to 160 B.C.E., that the concept of a Jewish Messiah had been developing. His character was to be the embodiment of justice and righteousness. The original Maccabeans were honored in the festival of Hannukah for their rededication of the Temple as a symbol of Israel's independence. However, the reign of this family for about one hundred years was characterized by a succession of kings as depraved and corrupted by lust for power as any of the worst of the Seleucid emperors who were their contemporaries. In fact, the Book of Daniel, which hopes for the coming of the Messiah riding on a cloud, is critical of the Maccabean kings, during whose reign of terror the book was written.

The Maccabeans, by continuous warfare, expanded their new state. By the sword they even compelled those they conquered to accept Judaism. They made Judea as large and powerful as it had been in the days of David, so that even Rome was forced to take the revived Jewish kingdom seriously. Yet the new Judea rapidly deteriorated because the sons and grandsons of the Maccabean family fought among themselves for the throne in incessant, bloody wars. One faction conspired with Rome to support its claims. By their invitation the Roman legions made their first appearance in Judea; eventually those legions were to destroy her completely. Out of this political chaos arose an unscrupulous half-Jew, an Edomite, from one of those conquered groups that had been forced into conversion. He captured the throne by marrying into the royal family and by assassinating all possible Maccabean rivals, including his own two sons. His name was Herod. Proudly he enlarged the Temple and made it one of the most magnificent structures in the Mediterranean world. However, as an ally of Rome, a traitor who had hired foreign mercenaries to control his subjects, Herod was bitterly hated by the Jews. When he died in the year 4 of the common era, the Jewish people rose in such rebellion that Rome sent cohorts of legions into the land and after a frightful bloodletting, Rome's domination of Judea was complete.

Judea was now cut up by Rome into three provinces and each of these was governed by one of Herod's three surviving sons. One son, Herod Antipas, the Tetrarch over Galilee who beheaded John the Baptist, was thoroughly despised by his Jewish subjects. One of these, a Galilean named Jesus, labeled him "The Fox." The atrocities of a

second son, Archelon, who was made governor of Jerusalem, even shocked the Roman Emperor. He had Archelon
removed and sent to Gaul as an exile, appointing a Roman
governor or Procurator in his place. Thereafter the Jewish
High Priests held their appointments by order of the
Procurator. Even the vestments they wore in the Holy of
Holies in the Temple on the Day of Atonement had to be
secured from the Procurator—a sign of Judea's complete
subjection. The Procurators terrorized this peculiar people.
They had nothing but contempt for the Jews' fanatic
belief in an invisible God—a concept which prompted the
Romans to label Jews atheists. For their rebellious dreams
about a religio-political savior called a Messiah, the Romans had nothing but ridicule. Thousands of Jews were
executed by the most cruel method then in use by the
Romans, namely crucifixion. Among the most cruel of
this succession of Procurators was Pontius Pilate. Ignoring
public feeling, Pilate deliberately incited riots by bringing
images of the Emperor on the standards of his troops into
the holy city of Jerusalem. Pilate was eventually called
back to Rome to account for his unmitigated venality and
barbarity.

When the conditions of the century into which Jesus
was born are reviewed (conditions authentically described
by Roman historians, and especially by the contemporary
Jewish historian Josephus) we see how very profound was
the desperation of the Jewish people. Their situation
seemed so hopeless that only a miracle could save them.
It is estimated that during this period of Herodian wars
and Roman terror not less than 200,000 of the Jews' finest
youth perished, an appalling number for such a compar-
atively small country. Fear and poverty stalked the land.
The Jew lived in an armed prison, spied upon by Romans
and by the Judean quislings of the house of Herod. What

a chasm lay between reality and five hundred years of dreaming about a Messiah! Instead of all nations bowing down to Judea, the people were being literally bled to death by taxes paid to tyrannical Rome. Instead of a glorious son of David, the Lion of Judah, they had to endure the dog of a Herod: instead of the songs of free men, there was the silence of frightened men.

The desperate extremity of the situation begat extremists. On the one hand, there arose utterly fanatical rebels who fought as assassins or guerrilla terrorists; on the other hand, there developed utterly despairing mystics who either withdrew from the turmoil and humbly awaited the coming of a savior or who privately and secretly preached the mystic doctrine of the suffering Messiah.

The rebels were the Zealots, the tough-minded young patriotic insurgents who were to be found especially among the Jewish peasants and fishermen of Galilee, far removed from the sophisticated society of Jerusalem. To them God alone was King in Israel—and his cause was to be defended, if need be, by force.

The very opposite of the Zealots were the aristocratic minority, the wealthy priestly families in Jerusalem, the sophisticated who collaborated with Herod and with Rome, and who intellectually did not believe either in a resurrection or in a Messiah. They were the Sadducees, named after Zadok, a High Priest.

Between the rebels and the collaborators was the majority popular party, called the Pharisees; the word meant "Separatists." The Pharisees tried to keep the Jewish religious way of life clean and unpolluted—in other words, "separated" from the corroding pressures of the pagan milieu and rulers. The Pharisee program was puritanical. It included training rabbis, establishing schools to teach Torah, developing services in synagogues, holding fast to ceremonies, fulfilling all commandments, demanding that the paganized Jewish priests be faithful to the Temple traditions and believing both in a resurrection and in a Messiah. The Pharisees, however, were moderate in their political views. The coming of the Messiah could not be hastened, they argued; for the Pharisees were practical in facing the political realities of their day. A person claiming to be a Messiah would only endanger the Jewish community by bringing on the reprisals of the Roman ruler. On the other hand, the Jew, according to the Pharisees, should prepare for the eventual appearance of the Messiah by a detached attitude toward life's pleasures, and by high ethical standards such as their greatest teacher, Hillel, had propounded. It was through the Pharisees and their isolationist philosophy of "a fence around the Torah" that Judaism as a religion survived the chaos of the first and second centuries.

The most remarkable of the Jewish extremists were the ascetic mystics called Essenes—the word is a Greek equivalent for "Hasidim" or pietists. The Essenes would not even fight under the heroic Judas Maccabeus and his priestly family in behalf of independence. The Essenes were Jewish pacifists. The most devoted withdrew to a few ascetic communities. One such Jewish monastery, recently uncovered near the Dead Sea, has become world-famous and is the subject of intense and dramatic debate among Christian and Jewish Biblical scholars today. The "Dead Sea scrolls" describe the activities and beliefs of these Essenes and shed new light on the Jewish origins of Christianity. Approximately one hundred years before Jesus was born the leader of this pietist, pacifistic group of Jews, who was called the Teacher of Righteousness, was believed by his disciples to be the Messiah. Their scrolls say he was condemned by a Sadduceean High Priest because he had announced that a day of judgment would fall on Jerusalem to atone for the wickedness of the rulers there. The Teacher of Righteousness was put to death. His followers believed their Messiah would return to judge the world.

This Jewish monastic order operated along socialistic lines. The members owned no property. They shared all things equally. They ate together at a simple common meal preceded by prayer. Their members could be married, but celibacy was preferred. To maintain their numbers they would adopt and train orphan boys. Some of their members might live alone in the desert as hermit monks and Jews in search of a new way of life might come to study with them. The great Jewish historian Josephus says he did this in his own youth. The special rites of these Jewish mystics included initiation by bathing. This baptism was symbolic of the cleansing from sin after the soul had already been purified by the person's resolution to become righteous. Repentance preceded baptism. Incidentally, for the same reason even the Orthodox Pharisaic rabbis required of proselytes not only circumcision but also baptism to make the convert a newly born Jew. The Essenes participated daily in public and private prayers. While they maintained their loyalty to the Temple in Jerusalem, their own offerings were other than animal sacrifice—which they opposed, probably because they were vegetarians. They also pledged their members to secrecy about their belief in the reappearance of the Messiah.

In order to preach to the public the imminent reappearance of the Messiah, one of this Essene group broke the pledge of secrecy and left the monastic order, which had a settlement near the desert community of Jericho. By this act this member overcame anonymity and had his name recorded for all time in the pages of history—as *the* Baptist. His name was Yochanan, or John. He wore a cloak of camel's hair with a leather girdle. He ate only clean locusts and honeycomb—food available in that isolated community. He believed he was Elijah come to announce the Messiah. Because he was looked upon by some as a madman, John concealed his belief that he was Elijah. Nonetheless, he urged the Jews to get ready for the Messiah, repeating everywhere he went, "Repent ye, for the Kingdom of Heaven is at hand." To make oneself ready for this event it was not sufficient to claim that one was a descendant of Abraham to whom God had promised eternal survival. Each Jew had his own individual responsibility for getting ready for the imminent approach of the great Day of Judgment, by himself performing good deeds of charity.

The one Jew most receptive to the warning call of John was a carpenter of Nazareth named Joshua. His Hebrew name, Yeshuah, meant "God is the Savior." He was known to his fellow Galileans by the Hebrew abbreviation for this name—"Yesu."

It was on the shores of the Jordan River that Yesu met Yochanan. He had come from his home village with other Jews in that area to hear this mystic preacher, John. Jesus was then about thirty-two years old. It was in the springtime. Twelve months later, on the eve of Passover, he was dead. What had happened in the first thirty years of his life to have made Jesus so responsive to the pronouncement of John, so committed to the Jewish idea of the immediacy of the Messiah's coming that he paid for it with his life? What happened during that short period of twelve months that made his death a necessity? And a necessity for whom? Short of the miraculous, how could a career of only one year result in the origin of a brand-new religion that was eventually to involve the lives of hundreds of millions for two thousand years?

For some scholars it has been so difficult to separate the real from the mythological in that career that they have concluded Jesus never lived. That certainly is an easy way out of any attempt to understand Jesus. To a Georg Brandes or to an Arthur Drews, Jesus is a myth woven out of the threads of previous Jewish writings about a Messiah and what he would do on the final Day of Judgment: a myth woven out of the material of so-called eschatological Jewish Books, woven together with threads from myths of the suffering Greek god and of the resurrected Egyptian god, both of whose mothers were virgin goddesses. These classical myths are the origins of the belief in the resurrection as well as in the virgin birth of Jesus in the New Testament.

To be sure, there is much that is unreal and mythological in the four major original accounts of the life of Jesus in the New Testament—the gospels of Mark, Matthew, Luke and John. They had a special purpose in writing their biographies, and made the facts fit their theories. One argument that Jesus was a myth is based on the fact that he is not mentioned in any of the authentic Jewish sources contemporary with his own life. Jesus is undoubtedly alluded to in the Talmud by rabbis who are quoted there and who lived in the second and third centuries. However, there is not a single reference to Jesus by first-century rabbis who are quoted in the Talmud and who were his contemporaries. It may be that because the career of Jesus was so short and his immediate Jewish followers so few, and because even the dramatic events about those twelve months of his life's career were so inconspicuous in the total picture, that any important notice about him, and therefore any Talmudic reference to him, seemed not to be justified. Despite the absence of any contemporary Jewish references to Jesus, the picture of him in the four

biographies of the New Testament is still too realistic to
be a myth. The gospel stories are too real, even though
not one of the four writers was an eye-witness to his short
career or knew Jesus personally. The nearest to the time of
Jesus was Mark, who wrote around the year 50; the furthest
from his lifetime was the Gospel of John, written around
the year 150.

It is difficult to arrive at a single clear picture of the
personality of Jesus from the four Gospels because these
four biographers were absolutely certain that Jesus was
the Messiah. They thus make their accounts of Jesus fit
the previous required qualifications for the Messiah. They
are more certain that Jesus was the Messiah than Jesus was
himself, because they also insist that Jesus was resurrected
three days after his death in order to continue to act in
the capacity of Messiah. The primary—if not the only—
purpose of the four Gospels was missionary. They set out
to answer the question of potential converts: "Prove to
me that your Jesus is the Messiah." Furthermore, each of
the four Gospel writers was pleading his case before a different kind of audience. Each, therefore, used different
proofs, and thus it comes about that in many respects they
contradict each other.

Mark, who accompanied the missionary Paul to Rome,
wrote a brief, 25-page account of the life of Jesus for
Roman readers. He realized they would have no interest
at all in the Jewishness of Jesus, and therefore in Mark
little of the Hebrew Bible or Torah is quoted by Jesus.
The Gospel of Mark does not even emphasize the preaching of Jesus on the great ideals of Jewish ethics; it does
not contain the Sermon on the Mount, which is mainly a
repetition of Jewish moral sayings. Although to a Jew it
would be necessary for Jesus to be a descendant of King
David in order to be an acceptable Messiah, it would not

be so to a Roman. Therefore in Mark, written for Romans, there is no genealogy tracing Jesus back to David. The major theme of Mark is the supernatural birth and the resurrection of Jesus. Romans, acquainted with their own suffering and resurrected gods, could appreciate such mythical qualifications for a savior-god.

In contrast to Mark, Matthew, a customhouse officer, a Hellenized Jew from Galilee now turned Christian, desired to convert Jews, or Gentiles living among Jews in Galilee, who knew the Jewish requirements for a Messiah. Therefore in his short account, running to thirty-four pages, Matthew invented a family tree for Jesus that goes back not merely to David but all the way back to the first Jew, Abraham. In Matthew, everything that is Jewish about Jesus is emphasized: Jesus' knowledge of Torah, Jewish ethics, Jewish ceremonies, Jewish moral sayings and parables from the rabbinic teachers of the Talmud. Indeed, in Matthew, Jesus declares the Jewish people to be superior to all other people. In one instance, in Matthew, Jesus even disdained to aid a woman appealing for help simply because she was not Jewish. Nevertheless, because Matthew, a Hellenized Jew, could not understand why all Jews did not immediately convert, there is in his writing a bitter animosity against the Jews. Matthew is especially antagonistic to the Pharisee opponents of Jesus.

In Luke we find still another motive. Luke, a physician, was a friend of Paul, the most successful Jewish missionary for the Christ Jesus. Luke had had a Greek education. His 37-page account is written in a more logical sequence, and therefore in Luke it is easier to follow the footsteps of Jesus during those fateful twelve months. The more cultivated Luke minimized the peasant Galilean background. To prove to non-Jews that Jesus was the direct son of God for the whole humanity, Luke is ingenious in inventing a family tree. He traces Jesus beyond the mere Jews, David and Abraham, back to Adam himself—to the first man, who in the Bible legend was also directly created by God.

The Gospel of John is the one furthest removed from the real events. In his twenty-seven pages, this biographer was most interested in justifying the theology of the already growing but still young official Christian Church. John, the writer, was less concerned than the other Gospel writers with the ethical teachings of Jesus and more interested in proving that Jesus was not merely divine, but was God himself. In order that his new Christianity might not be interpreted as having more than one God, John introduced the Greek idea of the *Logos,* or the Word of God, as being incarnate in the body of Jesus. According to John, since Jesus was already divine and sinless he had no need to be baptized to remove his sin. Therefore, in the Gospel of John, Jesus is not baptized by John the Baptist as in the three earlier Gospel biographies. The biographer John also wanted to prove the importance of the Eucharist, the ceremony of the wine and wafer used in the Christian rites. These were derived originally from the Passover Seder which Jesus conducted before his crucifixion by the Romans. In the Christian world this last Passover Seder conducted by Jesus is known as the Last Supper. The matzos and wine of the Passover Seder John now interpreted as being actually the body and the blood of Christ. Furthermore, John desired to prove the supernatural power of the new Church as it was exercised through the authority passed on to Peter, who was Jesus' favorite disciple. It is obvious that the Gospel writer John is interested in converting Romans and in what was to become the established authority of the early Roman Church. He thus deliberately removed all evidence from his propaganda that might be an embarrassment to the Roman Church, such as the possibility that Jesus could have been a political rebel against Rome itself. To do this, John distorted the facts, going so far as to exonerate the cruel Pontius Pilate of all guilt, trying to disassociate Jesus from the Jewish people altogether, and putting a curse on the entire Jewish people forever for rejecting Jesus as the Messiah.

Despite these propagandistic contradictions, there is a core of reality in the synopses of the life of Jesus, particularly in those of Mark, Matthew and Luke. Yet even in this core we confront difficulties. In the period of his very short public career, Jesus himself vacillated in the process of selecting from the dominant Jewish views about the Messiah a view that would finally correspond to his own special Messianic solution to the sore problems of his day. Like most Jews, Jesus rejected the priestly Sadducees. In one dramatic instance Jesus took the Zealots' position of defending God by force and in an act of violence drove the priestly money-changers from the Temple. However, at another time he rebuked the Zebedee brothers, two of his twelve followers, because of their readiness to fight. On the other hand, sometimes Jesus supported the Pharisees by insisting that all the laws of the Torah be fulfilled; but at other times he charged some Pharisees with hypocrisy because they zealously kept rituals but conveniently overlooked good deeds. Sometimes Jesus followed the example of the Essenes by withdrawing from society, by fasting and praying or by preaching the equal sharing of wealth and denouncing the rich; but at other times he contradicted this asceticism by enjoying a marriage feast or a banquet at the table of a rich Jewish tax collector, or by delighting in being perfumed and attended by such women as Mary Magdalene.

These contradictions in behavior increase the strangeness in Jesus and add to the complexity of his personality. Out of his ambivalent nature there looms a towering though sad person. He is not the simple, winsome humanitarian portrayed by the Frenchman, Ernest Renan. He is not a plain peasant of mediocre intelligence, as he was characterized by the French scholar Alfred Loisy. He is not a burning but misguided Jewish nationalist, as seen by the Israeli Jew, Joseph Klausner. Jesus is all these but something more, possessing also the heroic and tragic qualities attributed to him by Albert Schweitzer.

Any effort to re-create the real person Jesus involves the danger of subjectivity, the handicap of seeing in Jesus what one wishes to see. One Frenchman views him as a romantic, another Frenchman as an unsophisticated peasant. He is viewed by a Zionist Jew as a nationalist and by a German as a philosopher with Wagnerian tragic overtones. What impresses this writer is the variety, the conflicts in the personality of Jesus. He is winsome with little children. He is not an intellectual in debating with the rabbis, though he is sharp-witted. He does burn with zeal to save the Jewish people. He is heroic and tragic in his crucifixion. He could be so changeable because he was not rooted in a simple pattern of behavior.

It would be easier to understand Jesus as the man of thirty if we only knew all the facts of his roots, the story of his childhood. However, the period from his birth to his twelve months' career is wrapped in mystery, even as was the formative period of Moses. Only a few facts have been preserved in the record.

Jesus was born in the small village of Nazareth in Galilee —and not in Bethlehem, as was asserted in a myth added later to prove his connection with King David, who was born in Bethlehem. Jesus was the first-born son of Joseph and Mary, and had four brothers and two sisters. He learned his father's trade, carpentry, and in this simple working-class family he helped to provide for its daily needs. In the local synagogue he was taught Torah, the Prophets, the Psalms and the Book of Daniel. The beautiful and meaningful parables which Jesus related so expertly he also learned in the Synagogue, for each of his parables in the New Testament finds its parallel in the Talmud, in the parables created by rabbis who lived before Jesus.

The father of Jesus, Joseph, is seldom mentioned in the record, although his mother, Mary, appears in many places. Nonetheless, there is strong evidence that he was more attached to his father than to his mother. In his sayings, Jesus never once refers to a mother's love, although he frequently talks of fatherly love. In one of his parables, the prodigal son is welcomed home by the father. In fact, the record states that his mother, not his father, was embarrassed by this oldest son who turned away from carpentry and the support of his family to become an eccentric itinerant preacher. She and his brothers tried to dissuade Jesus by force. It was at this moment that Jesus brusquely, without any of the tenderness he showed to others, rejected his mother and family by saying, "Who is my mother or my brethren?"

After his baptism by John, Jesus began preaching around the towns, such as Capernaum, in the vicinity of the Sea of Galilee. He then returned to his native village where he preached only once on the Sabbath in his local synagogue on the subject of the coming of the Messiah. However, the villagers of Nazareth had known him as the son of a carpenter and were embarrassed for his family. Jesus was a complete failure in Nazareth. He left it in despair, never to return. This rejection by his own neighbors prompted Jesus to make his famous remark, "A prophet is not without honor, save in his own country, and among his own kin, and in his own house." This is all we do know about the facts of the family background of Jesus.

It is important to be reminded that Jesus was rejected by his own family. Alienated and frustrated in his desire to be looked up to by his fellow villagers as more than a carpenter, Jesus was driven by an overpowering desire to prove himself to be above them all. If his own kin did not appreciate or understand him, God would. If he could not be a success now, when the Kingdom of Heaven prophesied by John came Jesus would be supreme. Out of the bitterness of his rejection, isolation and rootlessness, the feeling was nurtured in this Jewish mystic that he might be the Messiah—for was he not, in the words of the Jewish prophets, already despised and rejected of men?

Jesus was not rejected by all men for he did attract the lowly and the poor among the Jewish peasants and fishermen of Galilee. They yearned for a Messiah to deliver them from the chaos and oppression of their day. As an itinerant outcast himself, Jesus was especially sympathetic with other marginal persons unpopular in the general Jewish community such as the publicans or Jewish tax-gatherers, despised because they were employed by the hated Roman-Herodian government. Jesus found the unemployed, the untutored peasants and fishermen, the wayward and widowed women and the sick responsive.

To the poor, the social outcasts, the frustrated and to the oppressed, Jesus offered more than a vague hope. He assured them an absolute victory that was imminent. That the "kingdom of heaven was nigh" Jesus proclaimed with even greater certainty than did John the Baptist. The phrase "kingdom of heaven" was well known to all Jews as referring to a utopia here on earth. According to the earlier prophets of Israel and the later writers of the apocalyptic books, a "day of judgement" would precede this utopian era. Then the evil-doers among the unscrupulous rich would be punished, the righteous among the poor would be redeemed, and the independence of Israel once again established. All this would be ushered in by a Messiah. The people could speed this great day by repenting their own sins and by living righteously. Their reward was not in another world after death; it was to be enjoyed now on this earth through economic plenty and political freedom. This is what Jesus promised and what attracted his small group of followers to him. "This generation," he asserted, "shall not pass away till all be fulfilled" and "there are some standing here that shall not taste death till they see the kingdom of God coming with power."

Jesus meant the transfer of earthly power and material well-being to his disciples when he promised them "houses and fields a hundredfold." When he said: "Therefore will I make you to inherit the kingdom of heaven that ye may eat and drink of my table in my kingdom and ye shall sit on thrones and judge the twelve tribes of Israel," his followers imagined themselves in the role of a new affluent class supplanting the old rulers. This could sound like incitement to armed rebellion were it not for the fact that Jesus did not believe in the use of force. His statement "I come not to bring peace but a sword" taken in its context was only a metaphor used by Jesus to arouse his disciples from a defeatist lethargy and to sever their ties to their routine dull life, even their ties to their families if they were to follow him.

Since he believed he was the Messiah, the changeover for the poor to a position of power was to come about not by arms but suddenly by the intervention of God on the side of the Messiah. To hasten this victory Jesus urged his followers to emphasize in their lives the ethics and the prayers of Judaism. The ceremonials and the laws of Moses were not to be abrogated; they were not to be overemphasized. To his fellow-Jews Jesus said, "Think not that I am come to destroy the law or the prophets." However, Jesus added that any Jew who followed the rituals and brought a sin offering to the altar of the Temple should "first be reconciled to thy brother and then come and offer thy gift." This, of course, was also the view Moses expressed in the book of Leviticus which the rabbis restated in the Talmud.

The preeminence of Jesus as one of the world's greatest teachers of ethics is not diminished by the fact that, with a few exceptions, his teachings like his parables were not original. They have their counterpart in the ethical teachings in the Old Testament, the Apocrypha and in the Talmud where some of the sayings attributed to Jesus are found in identical language. However, in Jesus these Jewish ethical sayings stand out because they are collected together in one place, whereas in the Talmud they are dispersed throughout its many volumes. In the New Testament the ethics of Jesus are found mainly in the book of Matthew, particularly concentrated in chapters five through seven which have come to be known as the Sermon on the Mount. Here, again, it should be noted that Jesus' audience is made up of the poor, the hungry, the thirsty, the meek, the mourners, the persecuted and those who are reviled. But, if they live ethically, mercifully and peacefully they "shall inherit the earth" when the "kingdom of heaven" will soon be established on earth.

The ethical idealism which pervades the sayings of Jesus reminds us of Hillel, the outstanding teacher among the rabbis of the Pharisees, who lived during King Herod's reign of terror just before Jesus was born. Hillel also had taken a humane, liberal position in his interpretation of

Jewish law. He issued a decision to circumvent the Biblical law of Moses which would have had all loans annulled every seventh year. Unless altered, this law would not only have brought a loss to creditors but the needy would have been refused loans for fear of loss. Hillel was a man of saintly character. His many maxims emphasizing the love of man and the love of peace are succinctly summarized in his saying "what is hateful to thee, do not unto thy fellowman: this is the whole law, the rest is mere commentary." Hillel's statement of the "golden rule" as the ethical summation of the commandments Jesus repeated. When asked "which is the greatest commandment in the law" Jesus replied the love of God, quoting Deuteronomy and the love of neighbor, quoting Leviticus. The Pharisees who, in this story as related in Matthew, approved the answer of Jesus belonged to the school of Hillel.

Hillel said, "Judge not thy neighbor till thou are come into his place" which Jesus phrased as "Judge not that ye be not judged." But, contradicting this tolerance and differing from Hillel in this respect Jesus took ethical positions on some matters which were both unrealistic and extreme. Such were his strictures against the rich man, against divorce, against taking oaths in court and especially his pacifistic views of non-resistance. Jesus taught not merely loving the enemy which is found in Judaism, but the extreme position of "turning the other cheek."

However, in his teachings about prayer Jesus followed the best Jewish practice when he warned his followers against "vain repetition as the heathen do: for they think they shall be heard by their much speaking." The prophet, Isaiah, hundreds of years before had said the same thing when he spoke against those who "draw near, with their mouth and with their lips do honour Me (God) but have removed their heart far from Me and their fear of Me is

a commandment of men learned by rote." And the rabbis
in the Talmud, some contemporaries of Jesus, were constantly concerned about the artificiality of praying without
meaning. The prayer in Matthew which Jesus suggested
his disciples recite came to be known as the "Lord's
Prayer" because Jesus was worshipped after his death as
the incarnation of God. It is a moving prayer of deep
devotion but it, too, Jesus composed by combining into
a single prayer clauses from other current Jewish prayers
well known to the Jews. One ancient Jewish prayer said
before the Scroll is placed in the Ark of the synagogue
begins "May it be Thy will, oh our Father which art in
heaven." "May Thy name be hallowed and may Thy
kingdom come" is from the *Kaddish* or mourner's prayer
universally used by Jews. When Rabbi Eliezer in the
Talmud was asked, "What is a short prayer?", he replied,
"Thy will be done, as in heaven so on earth." The phrase
in the prayer of Jesus "give us our daily bread" is a variant
of "give to everyone his needs and to every being sufficient
for his lack" which is in Rabbi Eliezer's short prayer. "Forgive us our debts" is the sixth of the eighteen benedictions
in the Jewish prayerbook and "lead us not into temptation" is in a Talmudic prayer. As a Jew, Jesus had frequently recited these separate prayers in his synagogue at
Nazareth which he incorporated into the single prayer he
taught his followers.

The relation of Jesus to the sick was particularly significant to him as his conviction grew that he must be the
Messiah. After his baptism there is no doubt that his
newly found self-assurance combined with his mystical
nature produced in Jesus a serenity and confidence. This
quiet self-confidence was so powerful that it was transferred
to others, particularly to those who were suffering from
what we today would diagnose as neurotic conversion hys-

teria, and whom his contemporaries described as being possessed by demons. By the hypnotic power of auto-suggestion inherent in exorcism, Jesus was a healer. He did not raise the dead or heal organic ailments, feats attributed to him by the myth writers to prove he was the Messiah. However, he was a healer of psychoneurotic conditions, mainly of hysteria. It seems that Jesus disliked being called upon to cure the hopelessly ill—a request which was embarrassing to him. He even hesitated to claim Messiahship on the basis that the people had begun to look upon him as a miracle-worker. Nevertheless, the unquestionable talent of Jesus in the use of faith healing for neurotics strengthened the faith of his followers in him and increased their numbers.

A special inner group of twelve became the most faithful followers of Jesus. His three favorites were Peter, an uneducated but enthusiastic man, and James and John, ambitious and angered Zealots. To these three Jews, Jesus revealed his conviction that he was the Messiah, but pledged them to secrecy. Shortly after they had met, Jesus learned that John the Baptist had been executed by Herod Antipas. John the Baptist had claimed only to be the announcer. What might be his own fate if Jesus claimed to be the actual deliverer?

Jesus was already facing difficulties with the local Jewish religious authorities, for since coming secretly to believe he was the Messiah he had begun to act like one. He stated that he could, if he wanted to, abrogate the laws of the Torah, such as those concerned with diet and the prohibition of work on the Sabbath—that he could even abrogate the Temple worship itself. Furthermore, although Judaism held that only God forgave sins, as God's secret Messiah-agent, Jesus began to declare that he possessed the power to forgive sins. Soon he was unwelcome in other Jewish Galilean towns and for a brief period unsuccessfully tried his luck in non-Jewish border towns. Embittered by his total failure, he uttered at this time the heart-rending words, "The foxes have holes, and the birds of the heaven have nests, but the Son of man hath not where to lay his head."

Welcomed only by a few followers among the fringe elements and even the outcasts, Jesus began to feel despised and rejected. He may have thought that it would be necessary to be rejected by the entire nation—the height of suffering—before the whole Jewish people would at last recognize him as their Messiáh. Already opposed by Sadducees, Herodians and some Pharisees in his local countryside, Jesus made up his mind to challenge these parties in their very seat of power, in Jerusalem. He chose a time when he was assured of the largest possible Jewish audience, namely when the entire people made the pilgrimage to Jerusalem to celebrate the Passover. It never entered his mind that he might be put to death by the occupation forces of Rome as an ordinary political revolutionist. It should always be remembered that to become a *Jewish* Messiah one did not have to die, one need only suffer rejection. When Jesus had experienced this rejection in Jerusalem, the people would assuredly then accept his Messiahship.

Peter feared the risk of arguing with Pharisees or Sadducees in Jerusalem. This was a much graver danger than debating with them in Galilee. Jesus overruled Peter by saying that his apostles must suffer with him if they wished to merit important posts in his kingdom when he had been proclaimed the ruling Messiah. Nevertheless, as this small band of Jewish pilgrims drew near Jerusalem five days before Passover, the disciples grew more frightened. On the outskirts of the holy city they encamped. Jesus recalled that one of the Jewish prophets, Zechariah, had written:

"Rejoice, . . . Jerusalem; behold, thy King cometh unto thee, he is triumphant, and victorious, lowly, and riding upon an ass." Therefore, Jesus had two of his disciples get him a young ass, on which he rode into the city. This would be the sign. Again he was disappointed and frustrated. The Jewish pilgrims converging on Jerusalem to celebrate Passover saw this Galilean Jew and his handful of disciples, and all they remarked was, "This is Jeshua, the prophet of Nazareth of Galilee." To the Jews Jesus was not even Elijah, let alone the Messiah. To his Jewish contemporaries Jesus was only another preaching prophet.

Jesus then determined that he must do something very dramatic to capture wide public attention. He performed at this juncture his only great public deed in his short career. He would purify the Temple and thus usher in the people's repentance, which was to precede the coming of the Messiah. His act was to drive out of the public courtyard of the Temple those who changed Roman coins into Temple coins in order to purchase the animals for Temple sacrifice. If a person today entered a cathedral and destroyed the collection boxes where a worshiper pays for candles used in Catholic devotions, he would be arrested for disturbing the peace. Why was not Jesus immediately arrested by the Temple police force? The priests were afraid that the arrest of Jesus for this act would incite the people assembled in the Temple courtyard to riot. The priests were hated by the general Jewish population, and were particularly resented because the animal sacrifice in the Temple was a profitable source of income to the Herodian priestly collaborators with Rome. Therefore the Jewish people actually approved this act of Jesus in driving out the money-changers. The money had to be changed because Roman coins contained images which were not admissible into the Temple courtyard. Should the priests arrest Jesus

and a riot follow, there might occur the dangerous inter-
ference of the Roman legions.

The Temple police force did not arrest Jesus. When he
reappeared the next day and was asked why he had acted
so rashly, he gave a cryptic reply in a parable which in
effect meant that though he seemed to be only a simple
Galilean carpenter-turned-preacher, he was really the
Messiah. Jesus was then in real danger, for the Herodian
priests, angered by his rebellious act of the preceding day,
tried to draw Jesus into admitting he meant he was a
political Messiah come to throw out the Romans. This
Jesus astutely denied in his reply, "Render to Caesar the
things that are Caesar's." Therefore the Herodian priests
felt they must bide their time and not arrest Jesus until
the populace had retired from Jerusalem after the Passover.

Passover fell that year on Saturday. The Seder meal
would be eaten on Friday night. This involved an important question of ritual. Could the laws of the Sabbath be
broken in order to sacrifice the Paschal lamb? The liberal
Hillel Pharisees answered in the affirmative; but the
orthodox Shammai Pharisees answered in the negative
The latter said that when Passover fell on Saturday, the
Passover sacrifice meal must be held on Thursday night
It is interesting to note that Jesus and his Galilean disciples
were more strictly orthodox than the Pharisees in this
regard, and therefore held their Seder in Jerusalem on
Thursday night. Rural folk are generally more orthodox
than city-dwellers.

After partaking of their Passover Seder in Jerusalem
Jesus and his disciples returned to their encampment in
the Garden of Gethsemane. Jesus again fell into a deep
despair, for still nothing had happened to proclaim him
Messiah. In his premonition of complete and final failure

he desperately prayed, "Father, all things are possible unto thee; remove this cup from me." That night the Sadducean police arrested Jesus, because even though he had cleverly denied being a political Messiah they now had a witness to prove that Jesus had in fact made such a claim. That witness was Judas Iscariot. Judas Iscariot had come to the conclusion that Jesus, his master, was a failure if not indeed a false Messiah. A Sicari, and a Zealot, he was the only non-Galilean Jew who had come up from the south to join the group led by Jesus, hoping for a political as well as a religious revolution. When Jesus was arrested, all his other disciples fled, including Peter. Never was a man with such a great vision of his glorious destiny left so utterly alone.

The record of the arrest, trial and execution of Jesus has been rewritten by the myth-makers in the Gospels in order to condemn the Jewish people. Such mythological accounts are no more believable than the record of the eye-witnesses to the resurrection of Jesus from his grave three days later. Among these eye-witnesses was the hysterical Mary Magdalene.

At the preliminary investigation held in the night court of the Herodian priests, Jesus openly stated he was the Messiah, but he undoubtedly had in mind a religious mission and not a political one. Nevertheless, these Herodian collaborators of Rome turned Jesus over to Pontius Pilate. Pilate alone had the authority to pass sentence leading to capital punishment.

To Pilate the innocent Jewish itinerant preacher, especially since he was from Galilee, the hotbed of insurgent Zealots, was simply a political rebel guilty of treason against the Emperor, for which the prescribed Roman penalty was crucifixion. The Roman soldiers put on the cross on which they crucified Jesus the phrase, "King of the

Jews." This was meant as a piece of mockery and derision, to show how the Romans held in contempt any Jew who claimed political ambitions against Caesar. That Friday, before sundown, the beginning of the Sabbath, a Pharisee elder, saddened by this tragedy, claimed the body of this mysteriously heroic and strangely pious orthodox Jew named Jesus, and then buried him in a tomb hewn in a rock.

What a despairing end! Among the Jewish people, to be hanged was to suffer "the curse of God." For a Jewish Messiah to be crucified was worse than hanging. His God, his Father, by whom he was a beloved as a son, had produced no miracles to save him. The short twelve-month dream of his life had utterly vanished, and with it all hope had perished. He was back where he had started, completely alienated, frustrated, defeated. As his profoundly sad and tragic last words, Jesus quoted that ancient Jewish poet whose Psalm first imagined this fate of the lonely suffering servant of God: "My God, my God, why hath thou forsaken me?" And then, "It is finished."

In this, his last moment, did Jesus change his mind? Did he finally see that he could not have been a Messiah, because there never could be a Messiah? Was his greatest contribution, as a Jew, the putting to an end once and for all the myth that Israel, and through Israel all mankind, could be saved by an especially elected son of the Jewish people?

If Jesus thought his Messiahship was "finished," then the most ironic twist of his fate was to perpetuate the Jewish idea of a Messiah among non-Jews. The non-Jewish Messiah came to be dressed up in the imagery of a suffering Prometheus and a resurrected Osiris. For the religion that grew up about Jesus is not the religion of Jesus—a Jew who never himself became a Christian. The religion that grew up about the career of Jesus used him as classical pagan men used their gods, to hide from the Future and Death.

This twisted irony is unraveled and rectified whenever a Christian sees, not in the mythical but in the real life of Jesus, a call to himself for self-sacrificing personal responsibility—a responsibility that Jesus strangely exemplified to his fellow Jews. As an orthodox Jew preaching to Jews about the needs of the poor and about becoming peacemakers, Jesus continued the Judaic appeal for individual responsibility which Moses had initiated. When asked which were the greatest laws of Judaism, Jesus was simply quoting Moses when he answered: "Thou shalt love the Lord thy God" and "thou shalt love thy neighbor as thyself." What Jesus did to change the world was an indirect contribution. It resulted from the world's symbolic transformation of Jesus' short life. As Solomon Freehof once summarized this phenomenon, "Jesus, the Jew, made the divine personal, and in gratitude myriads of non-Jews made his person divine."

III: Paul

At the tragic end of his short twelve-month career Jesus died a Jew, uncertain that he was the Messiah. Absolutely certain that Jesus was the Messiah, Paul also died as a Jew. Jesus had no notion that a new religion would be built upon his life. He remained in the fold of Judaism. Paul had a strong conviction that he was founding a new religion. However, even Paul supposed he was only extending Judaism. Today Paul is called a Christian. He deserves this title more than does Jesus. First of all, Paul spoke Greek as his native tongue, and therefore could have used the Greek word, *Christ*, for the Hebrew word *Messiah*. Jesus did not know Greek at all, and never used or even heard the word *Christ*. Even though Paul used the word, he would not have understood the application of the word *Christian* to him as it is understood today, namely to mean someone who is not a Jew.

The most successful of all missionaries, Paul converted thousands of Gentiles to belief in Jesus as Christ the Lord, and thus laid the foundations of Christianity as a separate, new religion. Nevertheless, Paul thought of his converts not as Christians but as the true Jews. Paul conceived of himself as a Jew preaching and teaching the true version of Judaism. In his letter to the Romans Paul wrote: "For he is not a Jew who is one outwardly; neither is that circumcision which is outward in the flesh; but he is a Jew

who is one inwardly; and circumcision is that of the heart."
In other words, if one accepts Paul's version of the matter,
that person is a Jew.

Paul was a Greek Jew. This will explain why he differed
in many respects from Palestinian orthodox Jews like Jesus
and his original disciples. Unlike them, Paul declared null
and void the law of Moses, including circumcision. The
laws of Moses were to be superseded by the belief that
Jesus was the Messiah, proved by the resurrection of his
body. Nonetheless, Paul was convinced that this belief was
still Jewish. He also assigned a favorite spot for Jews in
his theology and scheme of salvation. Paul felt that it was
only because of the stubbornness of his fellow Jews that
they could not see that Jesus as Christ the Lord was a continuation of God's revelation to Abraham, Moses and the
prophets who had preceded Jesus. How did it come about
that although this Jew preached what was startlingly
original from a Jewish point of view, he nevertheless
believed that his new contribution was the truest version
of Judaism? To explain this contradiction in Paul we must
understand first what it was that made Paul's teachings
startlingly new from the Jewish point of view, and second
what in his own nature made Paul find it necessary to
defend himself as the best of Jews.

The new in Paul's teaching resulted from the conflict
of ideas prevalent in his day between two great opposing
philosophies of life. This conflict was between Greek
thought and Hebrew thought, between Hellenism and
Hebraism. In Paul, who was both Greek and Jew, these
two thought systems met, and the result was a new product.
Paul was the catalyst which made of the Greek and Hebrew
mixture a new religion called Christianity. Different
though this religion was from Judaism, the inner conflict

of Paul's own personality made him nonetheless insist that this new religion was still fundamentally Jewish.

As a Jew born in a Greek city, Paul fought all his life against feeling he was inferior to the Jews born in Palestine. After he had become a member of the small group of Galilean followers of Jesus, Paul felt more keenly this feeling of inferiority to those orthodox Jews, such as Peter and James, who had known Jesus face to face. Paul never met Jesus. We can better understand the psychological origins of Christianity if we understand this dual conflict in Paul—the conflict between Greek ideology and Jewish ideology as well as the conflict within this Greek Jew himself. In this regard Paul, the Jew, is a dramatic illustration of a profound problem that has ever confronted Jews since their first Exile, down to this very day. That problem is the relation between the Diaspora Jew and the Israeli Jew. Are the obligations of Jews to Judaism in the land of Israel the same as those of Jews to Judaism outside the land of Israel?

In the first century, when Paul lived, more Jews were already living in the Greek world than in Palestine. The ratio was almost ten to one. The ratio of Jews in the Hellenized city of Alexandria in Egypt was comparable to the relation of the Jewish population of New York City to the present State of Israel. Jews lived in the entire Mediterranean area, occupying large communities in Antioch, Syria, Cyprus and Smyrna, as well as along the Black Sea and in Macedonia, down to Athens and Corinth. The migration of Jews out of Palestine had been going on for hundreds of years. This migration was further stimulated by the terrible decline in Palestine's economy after and during the Roman occupation. So many Greek-speaking Jews lived in the Greek world that the Bible had already been translated into Greek 250 years before Paul was born. This Greek translation of the Bible came to be known as the Septuagint, because it was supposed to have been translated by seventy Jewish elders—"seventy" in Greek being *septuagint*. It was as sacred to the Greek Jews as the original Hebrew had been to their forefathers. When the Greek-speaking Jewish writers of the New Testament quoted the Bible they usually quoted the Septuagint version.

Jews who lived outside of Palestine and who maintained their loyalty to the Bible and the Laws of Moses were confronted with a central problem. If all the Laws of Moses must be upheld, how could those laws be maintained which could be kept only if a Jew lived in Palestine? It should be remembered that in the days of Paul the Temple of Solomon still existed. Every Jew was duty bound to bring animal sacrifices to that Temple at least three times a year, on the pilgrim festivals of Succoth, Passover and Shavuoth. The Greek Jews found this obligation impossible. Nevertheless, all of them paid an annual tax to support the Temple in Jerusalem and its hereditary Jewish priesthood.

Difficult as his ceremonial obligations were, the ideological problems which the Jew faced in his Greek world were even more challenging. The Greeks had arrived at a highly advanced culture, which by the time of Paul had been developing over a period of one thousand years. In the first century, the Greek gods still were many; but the cultivated Greeks no longer looked upon these gods as Homer had described them seven hundred years earlier. The Greek philosophers, especially the Stoics, had long reinterpreted these gods allegorically. Each god simply mirrored a different experience in the life of each human being. Samuel Sandmel's fine summary of the contrast between Hellenism and Hebraism presents the following picture: To the Greeks the world was a place of sorrow.

Man was a mixture of bad, which came from the passions
of his body, and good, which came from his soul. Plato had
separated the soul from the body, and the soul was
superior. Life itself was a burden. The Greek plays of
Aeschylus, Sophocles and Euripides all dealt with the
tragedy of life. The goal of the Greek philosophy of Stoicism was to lighten the burden of life by escaping from
bondage to the passions of one's body. Bodily appetites
tended to drive one to impetuous and irrational acts.
Therefore to the Greek the ideal was to restrain those
appetites. Nonetheless, they did not have enough faith in
themselves to believe a man could conquer his appetite by
his own effort. Therefore, the Greeks developed mystery
religions, such as the popular Dionysian rites. At these rites
a bull made divine by the ceremony was slaughtered, and
the worshipers ate the meat of the slaughtered animal. This
ceremony has ancient origins in primitive religion. The
divine bull having been eaten, the divine then became a
part of the eater. God was now in him. The participant in
these rites became an *enthusiast* (from the Greek words *en*,
"in," and *theos*, "god"). He was "enthused" spiritually and
emotionally. His body was as dead as the dead bull's, but
his spirit was divinely reborn. He could now ignore his
own body and even his own eventual death. This is the
Greek mystical basis of Paul's theology about becoming a
part of the body of Christ to be saved from death.

The majority of the Jews resisted certain attractions in
these Greek ideas because they had been brought up for
over two thousand years with a quite different religious
philosophy. For the Jew the world was not a place of sorrow, despite all the tribulations of his people. His Bible
taught him that his God had created a world, "and, behold,
it was very good." He contended that man was the noblest
creation, made in "the image of God." Life to the Jew was

worth living. Yet like the Greek, the Jew also had to control destructive impulses and sensual appetites. To aid in self-discipline the Jew claimed a distinct advantage in having a whole set of written laws given to him by Moses. The Jew claimed that these Laws of Moses had been divinely revealed at Sinai, and that by following them the Jew could live and enjoy the good life.

The cultivated Greek Jews frequently debated their views with their Greek friends. The Greeks argued that they also had written laws, given to them by such great law-givers as Solon and even Aristotle. However, they insisted that these laws were man-made and could be changed. There was nothing divine about written laws. Only the Greek religious mystery rites were divine. The Greek Jews answered this argument by contending that although the Laws of Moses were written they were divine because they were unchangeable, like the laws of nature itself. These laws were embodied in the founders of the religion of the Hebrews—in the patriarchs Abraham, Isaac and Jacob—and Moses had simply translated them into written law. The Laws of Moses were said to be unchangeable symbols of deep human and natural principles. Keeping dietary laws symbolized the control of appetite; circumcision symbolized the control of sensuality. By such rationalizing the Greek Jew attempted to remain as orthodox as his Palestinian Jewish brethren and at the same time through these arguments to justify his position to his Greek neighbors.

Like their Palestinian brethren, the Greek Jews believed in the coming of the Messiah. For the average Palestinian Jew this meant primarily a hope that the time would come when the oppression of Rome would be removed from Jerusalem. However, Rome oppressed Greek as well as Jew in all the Mediterranean territory outside of Palestine. Rome itself was filled with Greek as well as Jewish slaves.

To the Greek Jew, therefore, belief in the coming of a
Messiah meant also hoping to be freed from Roman tyranny outside of Palestine. Thus the coming of the Jewish
Messiah would be as good for non-Jewish Greeks as for
Greek Jews. To the average Jew in Palestine, the victory of
a Messiah might be limited to the deliverance of Jews from
their national troubles. To the Greek Jew the Messiah
could also be the agent to deliver individuals, wherever
they might be, from their human troubles.

The popular Greek-Jewish philosopher Philo expounded
these Jewish views and interpreted the Bible to accom-
modate it to Greek culture. Philo lived at the time of Paul
and died only five years after Paul began his career. In
Alexandria, the center of Greek culture, where he lived,
Philo wrote the famous books in which he tried to justify
to Greek Jews the reason for remaining orthodox Jews.
Philo was quoted throughout the Greek-Jewish world by
cultivated Jews in their effort to withstand the challenge of
Greek philosophy. In his effort to explain Judaism to the
Greeks, Philo in effect declared Judaism to be the religion
that the first-century Greeks should adopt for themselves
to answer the challenge of their own ideas.

The arguments advanced by Greek-Jewish thinkers to
maintain and justify orthodoxy were, ironically, the very
arguments used by Paul to bring about a radical change in
Judaism. If kosher and circumcision were to be explained
as symbols of the control of personal character, then for one
who could practice self-control these symbols could be
abolished. If the Jewish Messiah was to save Greeks as well
as Jews from Roman tyranny, then one did not have to
become a Jew to have faith in this Messiah. This is exactly
where the joining of Greeks with Hebrew ideas led the
Greek Jew, Paul.

Unraveling the circuitous paths and retracing the way

Paul reached his revolutionary concepts is an extremely complicated undertaking. Paul was not a systematic philosopher like Philo. His writings do not indicate just how he arrived at his unique view of Judaism. Paul had a talent for dialectical logic and his writings are therefore argumentative. He was not an objective philosopher; he was a passionate propagandist. Everything Paul wrote had a definite purpose—to convert Jews, Greeks, and, as he hoped, eventually even Romans to the belief that Jesus was the Messiah risen from the dead. Paul was a missionary. After he had made converts, Paul wrote letters for the purpose of encouraging them to remain loyal despite all opposition. Everything Paul wrote was dictated to a companion in the form of a letter of encouragement to one of the Jewish or Greek communities of converts which he had made all over the Greek world. Paul generally concluded these letters with salutations and personal greetings to close friends he had made. He would end by saying, "I salute you," or "Greet ye one another with a holy kiss." The lists of Greek names found at the end of his letters are authentic. No Jew ever had as many non-Jewish friends in the world as did Paul.

The letters or epistles of Paul finally found their way into the collection of books that make up the constitution of Christianity. The canonized Bible of Christianity is called the New Testament, in order to contrast it with the so-called Old Testament of Moses. Paul was the first to use the phrase, "the New Testament," when he came to the conclusion that the Jew Jesus Christ, the Lord, had supplanted the Jew Moses, the teacher. The epistles of Paul to his Jewish and non-Jewish Greek followers comprise over one-third of the entire New Testament. Fourteen of the letters therein are assigned to Paul, though Christian scholars centuries ago agreed that the Epistle to the

Hebrews, and personal letters to young converts named Timothy and Titus, were not written by Paul. The letters of Paul which are genuine were those written to groups converted by Paul in Thessalonica, Galatia, Corinth, Colossae, Ephesus and Rome, and one letter to a personal friend, Philemon. These letters were composed in the period between the years 50 and 60.

The earliest documents of the Christian religion are the letters of Paul. This fact cannot be too strongly emphasized. The letters of Paul predate all the four biographies of Jesus called the Gospels. In fact, we shall see that the differences between the Matthew, Mark, Luke and John biographies of Jesus result in part from an effort to slant their accounts of Jesus either to support or to refute Paul's view. It is obvious that Paul's letters are earlier than that other important book in the New Testament called "The Acts of the Apostles." This book describes the activities of all of the early apostles of Jesus, the first twelve (including Matthias, who took the place of the suicide Judas) from Peter, the first follower of Jesus, through Jesus' brother James and lastly to Paul. The Book of Acts was written by the Greek-Jewish physician Luke, who wrote one biography of Jesus and who accompanied Paul on one of Paul's missionary tours. In "Acts" we find a biography of Paul. Even though Luke was closely associated with him, is his biography of Paul, the missionary, authentic? The question is asked because Luke says things about the life of Paul in the Book of Acts that Paul does not say about himself in his own letters.

The contradiction between Paul's own letters about himself and Luke's account of him in "Acts" can be understood only if we always keep in mind that Paul was a Greek Jew. Paul's views came into direct conflict with the orthodox Palestinian Jewish followers of Jesus Christ, especially with Jesus' brother James, who was a very orthodox Palestinian Jew. Paul's friend Luke tried to modify this grave conflict by writing about Paul as though he were more a Palestinian than a Greek Jew. Writing about himself, Paul never said he had studied in Jerusalem under the famous Rabbi Gamaliel. Paul never referred to himself by the Jewish name Saul. Paul never talked about giving speeches in Hebrew. Paul did not declare that he turned from preaching to Jews to preaching to Gentiles only after he had had bitter experiences with Jews. Paul did not say about himself that he began as an orthodox Jew, and was so opposed to the early Christian Jews that he insisted that the High Priest assign him the duty of arresting these Jews who had become Christians. Paul did not assert that on the road to Damascus in search of these Christianized Jews he had had a vision of Jesus and had himself been converted. All these assertions are to be found *only* in Luke's biography of Paul in the Book of Acts. Luke's account of Paul makes him a zealous Palestinian Jew who became a convert to Jesus. As such Paul should therefore have been more acceptable to the original Palestinian Jewish followers of Jesus.

Why did Luke find it necessary to invent an imaginary Palestinian Jewish upbringing for his friend Paul? Luke tried to minimize the serious conflict that had arisen between Paul and the original Palestinian followers of Jesus. At the height of his career, this Greek-Jewish convert, Paul, was in conflict with Palestinian Jews, and his ideas were causing great confusion among the Palestinian-Jewish founders of Christianity. A direct statement to this effect is made in an epistle in the New Testament which is attributed to the orthodox Palestinian Jewish Christian, Peter. In the Second Epistle of Peter we read that there are in Paul's letters "things hard to be understood, which the ignorant and unsteadfast wrest . . . to their own destruction." What was Paul teaching that was so destructive to the early Jewish Christian Church? Why, throughout his letters, did Paul always declaim that he was as good a Jew as the other Jewish apostles of Jesus? Paul in fact insisted that he was better than the other apostles. For the answer let us turn to Paul's background.

Paul was born in Tarsus, the chief city of Cilicia, which was northwest of Syria on the Mediterranean Sea. The exact date of his birth is unknown, although he must have been born very shortly after the year one. He was converted as a follower of Jesus, the Messiah, in the year 35, and thereafter worked for seventeen years, largely in the area of his birthplace. Paul did not begin his world tours until around the year 50. He was most probably executed in Rome around the year 64.

Paul speaks proudly of his birthplace as "no mean city." The pride is justifiable, for Tarsus was a rich and cosmopolitan city, active in trade and commerce, as well as a cultural center renowned for its Greek thinkers. Because the people of Tarsus had aided his invasion, the Roman general Pompey had granted them the honor of becoming Roman citizens. To protect himself from arrest and trial during his career, Paul frequently claimed privileges allotted only to Roman citizens. In Tarsus Paul had learned the trade of tentmaking, which required skill in the weaving of goats' hair and he supported himself by this trade. In fact, one of his letters tells how he was housed by a Greek tentmaker in Corinth.

The synagogue in Tarsus was the center of Paul's education. In one of his letters he says, "I advanced in the Jews' religion beyond many of mine own age among my countrymen, being more exceedingly zealous for the traditions of my fathers." More than once does Paul insist that he belonged to the Pharisee party, the strongest orthodox Jewish group for the preservation of Judaism.

In one of his most interesting letters Paul describes his own appearance. He was short of stature, defective in eyesight and ugly in countenance. He was a kind of Jewish Socrates. He was subject at times to sudden attacks of illness, which were apparently due to some form of epilepsy. This disease is substantiated by his own words, and it may be that he took Luke along with him not only as a fellow missionary but as a physician as well. Luke is the original Christian physician-missionary. Paul, who made so many speeches all over the known Mediterranean world, usually in a synagogue on a Sabbath morning, was surprisingly enough a very poor speaker. In his letters he refers twice to his poor speech and to the fact that his opponents called his speech-making "contemptible." There is a humorous incident related by Luke about Paul in the Book of Acts. Once Paul was giving a long-winded speech in the city of Homer, in Troy. The speech lasted past midnight, and was so long and dull that one of his listeners, a young man named Eutychus, fell asleep, toppled over and fell out of the window!

Long speech-making was only one indication of the tremendous vitality which Paul possessed despite his physical handicaps. His travels and adventures as a missionary over a period of thirty years, would have taxed stronger and younger men, particularly in view of the difficulties encountered in the travel of nineteen hundred years ago. From a careful examination of his letters scholars have concluded that Paul made at least three important missionary tours. During the first seventeen years of his missionary career he visited cities in Asia Minor around Tarsus. The cities listed in his letters at which he preached in the synagogues included Salamis and Paphos on the island of

Cyprus; Perga, Antioch, Attalia, Lystra and Derbe in the neighborhood of his home town of Tarsus. It was during this period that he paid his first visit to Jerusalem. There had been a famine, and he brought food to the small Jewish Christian community living there. Fourteen years later he revisited Jerusalem, this time to join Peter, the head of the first Jewish Christian Church, in a debate. The main subject was whether the new non-Jewish converts had to be circumcised. This was the burning issue between them and the Palestinian Jewish orthodox Christians, who insisted that all converts must be circumcised since Jesus also had been circumcised. Paul contended that circumcision was irrelevant to salvation. Later Paul undertook his fantastic journey through Asia Minor, crossing over from Troy to the Greek mainland, where he preached in the synagogues at Philippi, Thessalonica, Corinth and Athens before returning again to Tarsus. Paul's vivid descriptions of this journey included thrilling adventures such as being shipwrecked and attacked by robbers. During these astonishing journeys Paul founded the various churches which became the recipients of those letters that were destined to make him famous throughout the world for the next two thousand years.

Paul did make enemies among the Jews, even as Jesus did. However, it is important to observe that there were more critics of Paul among the Palestinian Jewish Christians than among Jews who were not Christians. We learn from the Book of Acts that at a court of inquiry it was only the Sadducean priestly quislings who did not approve of Paul, whom they called "Ringleader of the Nazarene." On the other hand, the majority non-Christian Jewish group, the Pharisees, saw no grounds for condemning Paul. As the Pharisees said, "We find no evil in this man." Indeed, on the basis of the testimony of the Pharisees, the Jewish King

Agrippa and Drusilla, the Jewish wife of the Roman procurator of Judea at the time, Paul would have been
acquitted. Whatever may have been his reason, Paul
insisted on his right as a Roman citizen to be tried in
Rome, and set forth on his final journey to make an appeal
to Caesar himself. The Caesar at that time was none other
than the depraved Nero. Rome looked on Jesus and Paul
alike as nothing more than two Jewish political rebels or
troublemakers. This business of a Jew claiming to be a
king anointed by the Jewish God was naught but treason to
Rome.

Rome crucified Jesus because he declared he was the
Messiah. Paul was crucified for repeating this claim about
Jesus, but Paul's view was quite different from the one
Jesus had about himself. Once again the difference lies
in the fact that Jesus was a Palestinian Jew whereas Paul
was a Greek Jew. Paul had been converted outside of Palestine before his first visit to Jerusalem. Three years later,
when he came to Jersusalem for a fifteen-day visit, bringing
relief for the famine, he met James the brother of Jesus.
In one of his letters Paul admits that he "was unknown by
face unto the churches of Judea which were in Christ."
As an outsider, Paul made special efforts to prove his Jewishness by declaring that he was "circumcised on the eighth
day, of the stock of Israel, of the tribe of Benjamin, a
Hebrew of Hebrews; as touching the law, a Pharisee." This
reference to the Pharisees may have meant only that he
was unlike the Sadducees but agreed with the Pharisees'
belief in the resurrection of the dead.

On the other hand, in order to be a successful missionary
among Jews, Paul might be accused of not only exag-
gerating his Jewishness, but even of being a hypocrite. In
one place Paul wrote that "to the Jews I became as a Jew,
that I might gain Jews," and that "I am become all things

to all men, that I might . . . save some." Paul was so profoundly convinced of the divine role of his mission that this attitude cannot be described as hypocritical. It was, rather, expedient on the part of Paul to assume one attitude toward the Greeks and another one toward the Jews. Paul realized that to require the Greeks to follow the Laws of Moses and insist that they practice circumcision, keep the dietary laws and respect Jewish holidays would only hinder his efforts to convert them.

It was the nature of Paul himself which accounted for his ambivalence toward Jews and his attraction to Greeks. The important fact is that Paul was a Greek Jew, and that as such he himself found it difficult to keep the Laws of Moses. It was not hypocrisy, expediency or salesmanship that led Paul to abrogate the Laws of Moses. Paul chose to resolve the conflict in himself by his radical abolition of the Mosaic Laws.

Well trained in those laws [of Moses], the Jew Paul nevertheless could not keep them. As he wrote, "I had not known sin, except through the law [of Moses]: for I had not known coveting, except the law had said, Thou shall not covet: but sin, finding occasion through the commandment, wrought in me all manner of coveting. . . . For that which I do, I know not: for not what I would that I do practice: but what I hate, that I do. For the good which I would, I do not: but the evil which I would not, that I practice. . . . I delight in the law of God after the inward man: but I see a different law in my members, warring against the law of my mind."

Paul had found himself unable to live up to the Laws of Moses *before* he became a Christian. His desire to conceal his guilt feelings in this regard explains why his attack on Palestinian Christian Jews, who insisted one should keep the Laws of Moses, became so vicious. In one of his letters Paul wrote, "I wish that those who unsettle you [his new converts] about circumcision would castrate themselves." In another letter he wrote, "Beware of the dogs, beware of the evil works, beware of those who mutilate the flesh." Only deep unconscious motives of guilt could account for such vitriolic hate for Palestinian Christian Jews, especially when we contrast this hating attitude of Paul with his constant plea to his own converts to love each other. In the magnificent statement to the Corinthians Paul said, "If I speak with the tongues of men and of angels, but have not love, I become sounding brass, or a clanging cymbal." It is apparent that only if you were on his side could Paul love you.

Disturbing psychological effects of disloyalty always haunt the apostate. His sense of guilt never disappears simply because the very visible presence of those still loyal to the apostate's former religion continue to aggravate his guilt. Paul was honestly aware of this fact when he wrote of himself, "Wretched man that I am!"—an admission that he found it impossible to live as an orthodox Christian Jew. Intellectually Paul might have accepted the views of a Philo and justified maintaining the Laws of Moses as a Jew, but emotionally he could not maintain these observances. To justify his own weakness, Paul—a Greek Jew—did what Jesus—a Palestinian Jew—never did, namely abrogate publicly and officially the Laws of Moses. From the emotional upheaval of this treason to Judaism Paul could escape and find peace of soul for himself only by his strong conviction that he was forgiven as a result of believing in the atoning death of a Christ.

When Paul preached the doctrine of Jesus as a god risen from the dead he became more of a Greek than a Jew. Earlier we pointed out that the Greeks did not accept the Jewish view that man could change himself. Man was helpless; only a god could change him. Man could not atone for his sinfulness, repent and then reform. Only a god could give man a new life—this was the Greek view. It was Paul who transmuted the Jewish Jesus into this type of a Greek god. This is the reason why Paul was never interested in the story of the life of Jesus as a human being. In his letters Paul says almost nothing about Jesus as a man. Paul makes few references to what Jesus said, to his ethics, his parables or his healing. Paul was converted only five years after the death of Jesus, and therefore he must have known about these things. It seems that Paul deliberately ignored the human aspects of Jesus. Furthermore Paul said nothing about the baptism of Jesus by John. He does not even refer to the virgin birth of Jesus. Even God's impregnation of Mary through the Holy Spirit was *too human* an act for Paul. Paul talked only about a Christ who was the Lord.

What Paul meant by Christ the Lord is not easy to understand bcause his theory is a complicated metaphysical notion. The brilliant Harvard mathematician and philosopher, Alfred North Whitehead, once wrote about Paul: "The man who did more than anybody else to distort and subvert Christ's teachings was Paul. I wonder what the other disciples thought of him . . . if they thought anything. . . . Probably they didn't understand what he was up to, and it may well be doubted whether he did himself." An objective analysis at least makes this much clear about Paul's thinking: To Paul, Christ was not merely the deification of a man; God had determined to become incarnate in Jesus before the creation of life itself. Therefore Jesus was not merely a mediator between God and man, as was Moses. In the situation of Moses, God revealed His word *to* Moses. In Paul's theology, Christ does not act for God; God is actually *in* Christ. Jesus is thus supposed to have supplanted Moses because God had only spoken to Moses. One can understand Moses by finding out what he said and actually did, and Paul frequently refers to the career of Moses in his writings. On the other hand, one does not have to know what Jesus actually said or did to experience him as Christ. As has been said, Paul never talked about Jesus' human life. How then can one experience Jesus as Christ? Paul contended that all one had to do was to believe that Jesus was God who had died and risen again.

The only important belief, according to Paul, was in the crucifixion and resurrection. God died in his body so that God's Holy Spirit could be freed from that body. Paul declared that he had been saved himself, and that others likewise could be saved, not by changing themselves— which they could not do—but by having this Holy Spirit poured into them, with the consequence that they could give up the passions of their own human bodies. Paul put this idea in these words: "I [Paul] have been crucified with Christ; and it is no longer I that live, but Christ liveth in me. . . . Ye are . . . in the spirit, if so be that the Spirit of God dwelleth in you. Anyone who does not have the Spirit of Christ, does not belong to him." In other words, Christ Jesus is the atonement which man cannot make for himself. If men die as Christ did then their spirit lives on with his. Therefore men must die as Christ did.

Paul did not mean that men must literally die in order to be saved. This would hardly engage the interest of his new converts. Paul did not preach suicide. Paul meant that one can participate in resurrection without dying. The convert dies only symbolically, in order to assure himself of citizenship in heaven when he does physically die. The symbolic vehicle of this immortality is the Eucharist, the eating of the wafer which makes one a part of the body of Christ. The most important sentence in all of Paul's

preaching about Christianity is, "We preach Christ crucified." This is Paul's unique message, and it is reiterated
over and over again. In the rite of the Eucharist, the
Christian eats of the body of the dead god who, risen,
will come a second time to redeem the believer from
physical death.

In Paul's theology the Jewish concept of God fades
almost completely away. In its place, grafted onto the
figure of Jesus, are the pagan gods—the suffering Prometheus, the dead and reborn Osiris—and the Dionysiac
mystery rites so familiar to the Greek converts Paul had
made. Before Paul, Christianity was a version of Judaism
with the additional belief that Jesus was God's messianic
agent, who had been destined to return and save mankind
—the true Jewish Messiah. With Paul and after him,
Christianity became an entirely new revelation by reason
of Paul's personal mystical experiences, which were based
on his Greek background. Here man is helpless in an alien
world; but, if he shares the death of Christ, he transmutes
his own body into spirit. Therefore the Laws of Moses, for
Paul, are no longer needed to interpret the way of God on
earth, because God himself is now directly available to the
individual through Christ.

Paul's theology astonished contemporary Jews, even the
first Jewish apostles of Jesus such as Peter and James. They
did not know what Paul was talking about. To Greeks
already familiar with the dying god in the Dionysiac rites
Paul made sense, but to the Jews he made no sense at all.
How, then, did Paul prove that he was preaching the true
gospel? He was obliged to prove that despite his Christian
Jewish opponents he was an authentic apostle.

The first followers of Jesus based their authority on their
claim that they were actual witnesses to the resurrection of
Jesus. They had been there. The New Testament states

that the first witness of the resurrection was one Cephas, followed by the twelve original apostles and then by a group of five hundred followers, then by Jesus' brother James and lastly by Paul himself. Paul then asks, "Am I not an apostle? have I not seen Jesus, our Lord? . . . Last of all, as to a child untimely born, he appeared also to me. For I am the least of the apostles, unfit to be called an apostle, because I persecuted the church of God. But by the grace of God I am what I am: and his grace which was bestowed upon me was not found vain." Paul made the claim that his appointment as an apostle was by God himself. He wrote of himself that he was, "A man in Christ, fourteen years ago . . . caught up in the third heaven, heard things that cannot be told, which man cannot utter . . . had set me apart before I was born . . . to reveal his Son to me in order that I might preach him among the Gentiles." To prove that he was equal to the sufferings and hardships this apostleship entailed (and he actually did endure these trials), Paul not only justified his position but sarcastically cast aspersions on his Jewish opponents in the early church by adding, "I reckon that I am not a whit behind the very chiefest apostles. . . . Are they ministers of Christ? I am a better one. . . . For neither did I receive [the gospel] from man, but it came to me through revelation." In effect, upon the basis of his own personal mystical experience that the greatest and most important act of faith is the belief in the Christ risen from the dead, Paul maintained that he was not only one of the apostles but the greatest of them. In fact, Paul declared himself to be *the* Apostle.

In Paul we find a Jew who rebelled against the early forms of Christianity as much as, or even more than, he rebelled against Judaism. Paul opposed the Judaizers of Christianity, who advocated keeping all Jewish observances as did Jesus himself. Christianity did carry over the Jewish

Passover into the celebration of Easter, the Jewish
Shavuoth into Pentecost and the Jewish Sabbath into Sun-
day worship. Why did not Christianity retain the Jewish
Day of Atonement, the Yom Kippur? The answer under-
lines the difference between Paul's Christianity and Judaism. Paul insisted that one could find atonement only by
having Christ the Lord in oneself, whereas Judaism said
that man must first make atonement for himself through
thought and deed, and that only then would God forgive.
This is the theme of the Jewish Day of Atonement, and
this is why it is no longer found in Christianity. Paul
quarreled more with those Jews in the early Christian
movement than with those Jews who never accepted Jesus
as the Messiah.

Paul did not merely replace discipline by the Law of
Moses with self-discipline through faith in Christ. His
belligerent disdain for the Laws of Moses was almost
anarchistic. Paul told his Galatian converts, "Christ
redeemed us from the curse of the law . . . upon the Gentiles might come the blessing of Abraham in Christ Jesus;
that we might receive the promise of the Spirit through
faith." To his Roman converts Paul wrote, "We reckon . . .
that a man is justified by faith apart from the works of the
law." Of course, Paul did not mean that faith gave the
convert license to practice wrong deeds. To his Corinthian
converts he wrote, "And now abideth faith, hope and
charity, these three; but the greatest of these is charity."
By charity Paul did not mean almsgiving but the attitude
of love. He said, "And though I bestow all my goods to feed
the poor, and though I give my body to be burned, and
have not charity, it profiteth me nothing. Charity suffereth
long, and is kind: charity envieth not; charity vaunteth not
itself, is not puffed up." Paul's substitution of faith in
Jesus Christ, the Lord risen from the dead, for the Mosaic

Laws is succinctly put in this sentence: "For in Jesus Christ neither circumcision availeth anything, nor uncircumcision; but faith working though love." As a nonconforming, individualistic libertarian, bordering on the anarchistic, Paul declared to his converts, "Stand fast therefore in the liberty wherewith Christ has made us free, and be not entangled again with the yoke of bondage."

Paul is the founder of Christianity insofar as with him began the breaking away of the Jewish followers of Jesus as Messiah from Judaism. The debates between Paul and Peter on whether converts to the Messiahship of Jesus were to maintain the Mosaic Laws, particularly that requiring circumcision, dramatize one of the significant "ifs" of history. Had Peter's argument prevailed, then Christianity would have become another sect in Judaism, differing from other forms of Judaism only insofar as its members believed that Jesus was the Messiah. In that event Christians today would have been observing all the Jewish laws as did Peter himself. Instead, Christianity became a separate religion because Paul would not submit to Peter's point of view.

Paul became the founder of a new religion, Christianity, for individuals, but not the founder of an organized church. The Christian church has its own legal and institutional structure based on canon law. Christianity used the radical revolutionary, nonconforming individualism of Paul in order to secede from Judaism. However, for the authority to build an organized church based on new laws for a new religion, Christianity turned from Paul to Peter.

There is an ironic contradiction wherever a church is called the "Church of Peter and Paul," because of the opposition, sometimes bitter, between these two apostles. The contradictions between two gospel biographies of Jesus—those of Mark and Matthew—can be understood only on the basis of this opposition. In Mark we have a life of Jesus which supports Paul; in Matthew we have a life of Jesus which supports Peter.

Mark, an early non-Jewish convert, favored the Pauline view that all one need do to be saved was to accept Jesus as Christ the Lord. Therefore, the picture of Peter in the Gospel of Mark is hardly flattering. Mark admits that Peter was the first to recognize Jesus in his lifetime as the Messiah, but suggests that Peter never understood just what this meant, since Peter compares Jesus to Moses and Elijah. Jesus predicts that Peter will deny him, and demotes him by saying that "the first shall be last." Peter falls asleep at Gethsemane where Jesus is arrested, and when the cock crows three times in the morning Peter, in order to protect himself, denies he ever knew Jesus. Jesus even calls Peter "Satan": "Get thee behind me, Satan." All the orthodox Palestinian Jewish disciples of Jesus in the Gospel of Mark are portrayed as a cowardly lot.

Matthew, who was a Jewish convert to Christianity, favored the Petrine view of Jesus. In Matthew Jesus preaches to the Jews albeit "to the lost sheep" among them and he is also a new kind of Jewish lawgiver. In Matthew Jesus says, "Think not that I am come to destroy the law." Because he emphasizes the Jewishness of Jesus, Matthew's description of Peter differs radically from Mark's. Peter is supposed to be the very first follower who recognized Jesus as the Messiah, and therefore upon Peter Jesus is supposed to have given a special blessing, as follows: "Thou art Peter, and upon this rock will I build my church. . . . And I will give unto thee the keys of the kingdom of heaven; and whatsoever thou shalt bind on earth shall be bound in heaven; and whatsoever thou shalt loose on earth shall be loosed in heaven." In Matthew Peter is the chief disciple and apostle. Peter is supposed to organize a church and develop its legal structure because the better laws of Jesus supplant the outmoded laws of Moses. Through Peter, to counteract Paul's lawlessness, Jesus becomes a new legislator; and thus Paul's position about the abolition of all law is neutralized.

We should now understand why the Catholic Church turned not to Paul but to Peter as the basic authority for its legal organization. No institutionalized church could be based upon the chaotic individualism of Paul. Paul could never accept any man, no matter what his hierarchical position, as an authority. The process of neutralizing Paul's anti-legalism went on in the early days of the church. In order to counteract the real Paul, this process included ascribing to Paul one of the books of the New Testament which in view of his nature he could never have written. This is the Epistle to the Hebrews, whose ascription to Paul most scholars regard as spurious precisely because this book justifies the newly organized Christian church with its own set of canon laws and its ecclesiastical hierarchy. In that letter Paul is supposed to have said, "Obey them that have the rule over you and submit yourselves." This refers to the early Christian priesthood. Paul, the anarchistic individualist, never could have recommended such obedience.

The churches which Paul himself founded all over the Greek world could never have been organized on this ecclesiastical basis. They were more like little communist groups. Paul said to them that "if any will not work, neither let him eat." The members of Paul's small Christian groups were supposed to be related to one another in a common love and mutual cooperation. When Paul was in their presence these new converted groups were influenced by the tremendous power of his personality. However, it is apparent that when Paul left them to return to his home city or to Jerusalem it was not so easy for these converts to maintain the high moral position of loving one another.

It seems that his least successful group was the one in Corinth. There the new Greek Christians did not readily give up their Hellenic sensual pleasures. Paul was always troubled by their backsliding, and particularly by the difficulties which the bachelors and widows presented on issues concerning morality and sexual conduct which were disturbing the communal life of this group of loving Christians. Therefore to the Corinthians, Paul made his famous statement, "It is good for a man not to touch a woman. . . . I say therefore to the unmarried and widows, it is good for them if they abide even as I [Paul was a bachelor]. But if they have not continency, let them marry: for it is better to marry than to burn." In this connection there appears, in the eleventh chapter of I Corinthians, Paul's annoying anti-feminine conviction, namely that women were created for men and not men for women.

It seems that Paul was more successful with the Greek converts in the city of Philippi, who apparently became his favorites. Paul warned the Philippians against selfishness and egotism exhorting them to do "nothing through strife and vainglory; but in humility let each esteem the others better than himself. . . . Do all things without murmurings and disputings: that ye may become blameless and harmless, the sons of God without blemish in the midst of a crooked and perverse nation [i.e., the Greeks], among whom ye shine as lights in the world." In one of his most magnificent statements, again to the Philippians, Paul defined the behavior appropriate to the believer in the risen God and the attitude needed for mutual cooperation. "Finally, brethren," wrote Paul, "whatsoever things are true, whatsoever things are honest, whatsoever things are just, whatsoever things are pure, whatsoever things are lovely, whatsoever things are of good report; if there be any virtue, and if there be any praise, think on these things."

It was through Paul that Christianity broke away from Judaism. Ironically, this same mystical Greek-Jewish genius initiated those forces within Christianity from which all the later rebellions against its orthodox authority stemmed. The image of this unreconstructed Jewish individualist remained forever in the Christian movement as the inspiration for protests against the established church. In the history of Christianity one force used Paul's theology about the dying and the risen god of Greek mythology to establish an organized church based on canon law and ecclesiastical authority. Another force used the emphasis upon salvation through individual faith which Paul had derived from his Jewish Mosaic background to protest against that same church. The Catholic church attached Paul to Peter to establish its authority for the new religion. Protestantism divorced Paul from Peter to justify the Reformation. It was Paul's letter to the Galatians that Martin Luther used to initiate the Protestant revolution. Paul thus did change the world, not only as the founder of Christianity, but at the same time as the catalyst of change within Christianity.

The Jewish contemporaries of Paul could accept him even less than they could accept Peter. Paul's theology, rooted in Greek Dionysiac mysticism, was entirely foreign to the Jews. His communalistic asceticism, while not removed from the world, was no more popular among Jews than were the Jewish Essenes with their monastic isolation. Paul's derogation of the sexual, and his depreciation of women, ran counter to the Jewish tradition which sanctified the sexual relation. Above all, Paul's pessimism about man's ability to change himself denied Judaism's basic psychology of optimism about man. Indeed, it was Paul's pessimism about this world that accounted for the rise and fall of his popularity among Christians. When Western society was optimistic it refuted Paul; when it was pessimistic it revived his views. Nineteenth-century Christians, with their Victorian emphasis on progress and man's capacity to change his world, found Paul's pessimism unattractive. Twentieth-century existentialist Christian thinkers, depressed by the evidence of human evil in the genocide of the atomic age, have revived the Pauline theology of the inherent sinfulness of man, who remains irredeemable except through the dying and risen God.

Although through Paul's thinking Christianity divorced itself from the religion of Judaism, wherever Paul went he carried with him the Biblical culture of the Jews. When Paul preached, the present canonized gospel of Christianity was not in existence. Paul seldom quoted the words of Jesus. However, familiar with the books of the Old Testament, Paul frequently quoted the pronouncements of Moses. Indeed, because of this Jew's zealous effort to abrogate the Laws of Moses, there are more references in Paul's letters to what Moses said than in the Gospels. Thus, again ironically, it came about that through Paul the Old Testament came to be incorporated in the Bible of Christianity as the indispensable foundation of the New Testament. It was Paul who familiarized the non-Jewish Christian world with the basic Jewish origins of Christianity. It was Paul who made the name of Moses almost as significant to Christianity as the name of Jesus. His effort to create a religion without law would have left the Christian Church in chaos as an unorganized society of small communal cells. To give Christianity an organized structure and a social and moral law, the Church had to restore Moses to a position of importance alongside Jesus. The Ten Commandments of Sinai were united with the Sermon on the Mount. For the world cannot depend on love without law, even as it cannot survive on law without love.

IV: Karl Marx

Communism surprised itself when it achieved its first successful revolution in the backward country of Russia. Starting in the chaos of a colossal military defeat and in a largely illiterate, unindustrialized peasants' farming land, Lenin's *coup d'état* of 1917 set in motion the Communist revolution of the twentieth century. In less than forty years the force of this revolutionary movement put under its control one-third of the world's population, occupying over one-fourth of the world's territory, and made of the Soviet Union the only rival to the United States of America in advanced scientific industrialization and nuclear power. This fantastic achievement was based on a rigid adherence to the idea of one man—Karl Marx, who died just before the turn of this century. The Marxian idea came to be accepted as an economic religion, as an infallible scientific analysis of history and society. It contained a formula for the prediction of social behavior, and also a strategy for achieving political and economic power.

The two men who applied the Marxian formula and strategy with the greatest success in the twentieth century have been Lenin in Russia and Mao Tse-tung in China. The two agricultural land masses where Marxian ideas have flourished were the very last places where their originator had thought they could be successfully applied. Yet today when the Russian or the Chinese Communist party holds a great celebration, a huge poster picture of Karl Marx is displayed in parades alongside the portrait of Lenin or of Mao. The world is familiar today with these poster portraits of Karl Marx. He looks small, almost squat in stature. He has long black hair with streaks of gray, and a thick, bushy black beard. Heavy black eyebrows project over dark and apparently short-sighted eyes. He wears an old-fashioned black suit with a Prince Albert coat. The picture of a dark man in black clothing is true to reality; for his intimates—his father and his wife—commenting on the darkness of his complexion, gave him the nickname "The Moor."

In 1845, when he was only twenty-seven years old and a political exile in Brussels, Karl Marx founded the Communist Party. This party was to put into action his strategy aimed toward the ultimate goal of freeing the workers of the world. The first Communist Party consisted of seventeen members. They were Germans, and most of them were not workers but middle-class intellectuals, poets and writers. A hundred years later, workers rising to power through the exploitation of Marxist ideas by the Communist parties of Russia and China came to rule hundreds of millions of peasants and workers. The war of ideas today and the concern about the ideological weapons used in this warfare, are in great measure the result of the work of Karl Marx—who proved that a word can be stronger than a sword and an idea more powerful than an army. It is impossible to comprehend the present-day ideological struggle between communism and democracy without a thorough knowledge of what Karl Marx believed.

For a number of reasons, however, it is difficult to arrive at a sound and objective knowledge of the thinking of Karl Marx. During the Red scares and witch hunts after the First World War, and again during the McCarthy hysteria after the Second World War, the average American ran the risk of being accused of treason by simply discussing Marxian ideas. Americans were frightened of the influence of these ideas. Like forbidden fruit, the suppression of Marxian thinking made it more attractive. In secrecy it is easier to accept Marxian ideas as infallible; in open debate, they may be seen to be questionable. Only now is it becoming permissible to subject Marx in the classroom to study and objective criticism. It required a sensational public event, the Scopes trial, to bring the discussion of Darwinism into the open in America some years ago. It is a pity that the study of Marxian political economic theory did not evoke a similar trial, for Americans might have been better prepared intellectually to meet the ideological war which now confronts them.

There is a second reason why it is difficult to appreciate what Karl Marx thought. It is not easy for anyone to be objective in a study of his thought. There is a prejudice against him. There is a semantic reaction to the very name Karl Marx, almost as though it were a pseudonym of the devil. In fact, most things Americans hold sacred Marx blasted as hypocritical and false. Furthermore, whatever he wrote, Marx never wrote solely as a scientist (if, indeed, politics and economics are sciences at all). He always wrote as a polemicist, criticizing and bitterly attacking everyone and every institution. Therefore, the reader of Marx must always be careful to separate his theory from his propaganda. One must be equally careful when reading what others have written about Marx. There are probably more books, in dozens of languages, about Marx than about that other mental giant of the nineteenth century, Darwin. There are probably more books written about Marx than about Freud or Einstein. The writers of these books on Marx are either vehemently against his theories or enthusiastically for them. Both protagonist and antagonist leave the reader with analyses that are not objective or dispassionate.

Finally, it is not easy to read Karl Marx himself. He was heavy-handed when he wrote about theory. However, he was brilliant as a propagandist. His short *Communist Manifesto* is known to tens of millions around the world, while his classic book *Das Kapital* is rough going even for the most scholarly. Yet what Karl Marx was like as a person is not divulged by his propaganda or by his theories. His personality is best revealed by the hundreds of letters he wrote privately to his socialist friends—few though they were—and particularly to his socialist collaborator, Frederick Engels. For some years his European socialist followers concealed the full contents of these voluminous letters, which do put Karl Marx as a person in a bad light. Strangely enough, after the First World War the Marx-Engels Institute in Moscow did publish these letters in full—probably because the Communists have a different code about what is morally just and decent. They do not consider Marx's attitudes and language, as revealed in his letters, unjust or indecent.

Marx believed his unique contribution to be his economic interpretation of history. Therefore, Marx would have been the first to state that anyone who wanted to understand his life, as well as his thinking, must recall the entire environment in which Marx was born, lived and died. According to him, men do not make history but circumstances — particularly economic circumstances — make men what they are. Individual personality or individual will has little to do with human history; history is governed by laws like the laws that govern nature, which man cannot alter. It will be pointed out that this theory is the chief weakness and error in Marx's thinking, and that even Marx's own life and the success of his idea is a refutation of Marxist theory. Nonetheless, that there is a close relation between environment and character is undeniable. Therefore a brief examination of the first fifty years of the nineteenth century in Europe is in order.

Marx was born on May 5, 1818, in the German Rhineland city of Trier, noted for its wines. Though he died in London sixty-five years later, in 1883, Marx had arrived at the main structure of his theories by 1849, when at the age of thirty-one he became a political exile in London. There he lived the last thirty-four years of his life, mainly in isolation, prefecting the theories he had already defined.

What happened in Europe from 1818 to 1849 which helps to explain Marx's complex ideas? Three years before his birth, Napoleon had finally been defeated. The regimes of the monarchs, which had been supported on the last legs of feudalism and which had been overthrown by the French Revolution, were restored all over Europe, including France. Nonetheless, wherever Napoleon's invasion had penetrated, the French revolutionary principles of Liberty, Equality and Fraternity, representing the people against the nobility, had left their mark. This was especially true in Germany, where Marx was born. The King of Prussia energetically tried to restore the old aristocratic land-owning regime. The more progressive elements in early nineteenth-century Germany included not only the intellectuals influenced by France but also the bourgeois middle and upper classes of the cities, particularly in west Germany. Committed to industrial capitalism and its assumption that success depended upon independent initiative, they were imbued with liberal and democratic ideas.

The German landed aristocracy recognized that this

democratic spirit was benefiting by the growing industrialism of Germany. To maintain its privileges, this aristocracy proceeded to curtail the rise of new trade by the imposition of tariffs. This move antagonized the industrialized liberal democrats of the cities. German police power was increased to censor all liberal thought. Therefore, many German intellectuals—even poets and musicians like Heine and Wagner—went into voluntary exile, in Paris or Switzerland, where they conducted vigorous protest propaganda against the reactionary regime in Germany.

In the days of the French Revolution the conflict was mainly between the peasants and the aristocrats of an agricultural economy. In the nineteenth century the conflict was between the landed aristocrats and the city folk who were the new rich manufacturers. Their industrial products demanded free trade. Another part of the conflict of the nineteenth century was the rise in the number of industrial workers congregated in these cities. Their wages were low, their hours long, their working conditions poor. Factories even employed little children and exploited them. The old guild handicraftsmen, seeing their livelihoods disappear and their work displaced, were in some instances inspired to riot. They tried to destroy the machine factories, particularly in England. Conditions among the newly industrialized city workers stimulated their unrest.

The conflict between the liberal, industrialized cities and the reactionary landed aristocrats particularly affected the Jews who lived in the cities. The Jews had every reason to be grateful for the French Revolution, and even for Napoleon. These French libertarian forces had broken down the ghetto barriers and opened the doors of trade and professions to the Jews. In the early 1800's the Jews enthusiastically entered into the newly liberated world by breaking away from orthodox Judaism. However, with

the restoration of the old regimes after the defeat of
Napoleon, the bars against Jews were put up again. The
few emancipated Jews either retraced their steps back to
the ghetto or altered their names and religion and started
new lives as German patriots and members of a Christian
church.

The case of Hirschel Levi was typical of this generation
of emancipated German Jews. His father had been Rabbi
of Trier, and his brother succeeded him in the same position. The Levi family, in fact, had been noted for its rabbis
for centuries. The family included the famous Joseph
Gerson of Cracow and Rabbi Katzenellenbogen of Padua,
both of whom lived in the 1500's. Hirschel Levi's wife also
came from a rabbinic family which had settled in Holland.
Taking advantage of the new enlightenment of the period,
Hirschel Levi received a secular education and became a
lawyer. He accepted the philosophy of reason and humanity of the liberals of his day. His legal practice was moder-
ately successful; he detached himself from his family and
changed his name to Heinrich Marx. As a non-religious
freethinker, Hirschel Levi decided to adjust by conversion
when the anti-Jewish laws were re-established in 1816.
Trier was a Catholic community, but Levi chose the
Protestant Lutheran Church because he was an ardent
admirer of the neighboring Lutheran state of Prussia,
whose founder, Frederick the Great, stood for enlightened
practical progress.

Under the pressure to convert, some Jews became devout
Christians while others rebelled against all religion. Sensitive and intelligent Jews like Heine in Germany and
Disraeli in England were obsessed all their lives with the
problem of their peculiar conflicting status. In their
ambivalent position, they alternately mocked and defended
the Jewish religion of their fathers, or they were suspicious

of a lurking condescension behind their apparent accept-ance by their Christian friends. However, Heinrich Marx was a timid and accommodating person. He became a pas-sionate Prussian patriot. Only once, at a public dinner, the lawyer Heinrich Marx did suggest some reform. When it came to the attention of the police, he retracted his state-ment immediately. The submissive and cowardly attitude of the father was never forgotten by his son Karl, who was sixteen years old when this retraction took place.

When his children were ready for school, Heinrich Marx had all eight of them baptized at one time. Karl, the second child, was then six years of age. His mother, who never could understand the whole business, at first resisted but later accepted conversion. Karl had little to do with his mother, who spoke a broken Dutch-German, and even less to do with his sisters and brothers. The entire family, even the educated father, found it difficult to communicate with Karl, who had a sharp intelligence but was obstinate and had a domineering temper. His father, who in contrast was a compromiser, was always gently lecturing Karl to govern and adapt himself to the new world; for he optimistically believed that reason would eventually triumph and equal-ity be forthcoming for all.

Karl Marx had few young friends when he went to the local high school, where his main interests were literary. His chief friend was an older man, the royal Counselor von Westphalen, who lived on the same street in Trier. An educated, liberal German of the philosophical school of Goethe, he was attracted by the keen mind of the young Jewish lad. Von Westphalen, who introduced Karl to Shakespeare, strengthened Karl's belief in himself by befriending him. Karl fell in love with Jenny, von West-phalen's daughter. She returned his love, and just after he entered the University of Bonn they became engaged. At the time she was twenty-two and Karl was eighteen.

As a college student Karl Marx's ambition was to become a poet. He wrote two unpublished books, *Love I* and *Love II*, and dedicated them to Jenny. He enjoyed the typical riotous student life of those days, and was always asking his father for more money. He was arrested once for drunkenness, and even fought the typical German student duel. In order to separate him from Jenny, in 1836 his father encouraged Karl to transfer to the University of Berlin. Berlin then was the center of the Prussian bureaucracy, but it was also a meeting place for discontented radical intellectuals. At the University of Berlin Karl Marx finally realized he would never make a poet, and became absorbed in the dominant philosophy of his time, the philosophy of Hegel.

Hegel had been head of the philosophy department at the University of Berlin, and had been dead only five years when Marx, at the age of eighteen, became a student there. To understand Marx, one must understand Hegel. Even though his writings are pedantic and frequently obtuse, Hegel became the leading thinker in Germany after the defeat of the French Revolution, as a reaction against French ideas. The application of reason and the observing of facts in order to overcome ignorance and superstition had been the dominant philosophy of the French revolutionary thinkers. They held that man was capable of using reason in order to find the Good. The privileged classes, they argued, must not obstruct the education and enlightenment of men for the purpose of applying their scientific skills to the progress of society. The outstanding spokesmen of this French rationalism were, of course, Voltaire and Rousseau. They believed that men could change and develop new qualities of behavior if they were given certain new material conditions.

The British industrialist Robert Owen became an ardent

follower of this French philosophy. He put into practice the theory that proper reasoning could alter and improve conduct. He owned cotton mills at Lanark in Scotland. He became the first manufacturer to limit the hours of work, and to provide health insurance and cooperative savings banks for his workers. Owen not only increased his productivity but also raised the standard of living of these workers, and at the same time trebled his own fortune. The experiment of Owen in Lanark was the first successful effort at peaceful cooperation between labor and capital, and provided a classic example of the practice of French rationalism.

German national pride had been hurt by the Napoleonic invasion. The German philosophers were stimulated to think in opposition to French rationalism. In the natural sciences one law does apply. The law of gravity had been the same in the days of the Caesars as it was in the days of the kings of Prussia. Nature repeats itself, but civilization never repeats itself. This is true, the German philosophers contended, because each age differs in the history of man; for each age inherits something new from its predecessor. Historians had once described an age as a separate entity, having nothing to do with the previous or succeeding ages. Hegel contended that this separatism was erroneous, since all ages were interrelated with each other by a dynamic law of historical motion. Hegel declared that there existed an absolute Idea or Spirit moving through each historical period. This Idea produced the music, the poetry and even the government of any particular period, and therefore these expressions of man held much in common. Historians must therefore regard all the factors of history as part of the moving spirit of that age.

The dominating spirit of each age differed from that of any other age because it was a result of a conflict between the old and the new. The previous age and its successor, the new age, were in conflict with each other because each was only a partial fulfillment of its own inherent idea. Each was therefore a partial falsehood. Therefore every historic period carried within it the seed of its own destruction. The old thesis was in contest with its antithesis, and as a result, by a process of synthesis, produced the new age. This process Hegel described as *dialectical.* By the dialectical law of history, Hegel meant that the dialogue or argument between the old and the new, succeeding period resulted in a movement toward greater perfection in society.

Hegelianism became the official creed of the anti-French European intellectual. This abstruse metaphysical idea became popular because it fitted the reaction against French libertarianism with its doctrine that all men were brothers. Hegelianism supported the new, separate nationalisms that were growing up in Europe. Hegel contended that in each nation there was a peculiar genius which grew out of necessity. The development of the idea of nationalism was supposed to be incarnate in a nation. It could not vanish overnight by the efforts of individual reformers. The attempt to destroy a national tradition, instead of modifying it, opposed the law of history and therefore was irrational. Because he did not recognize the inevitability of the historic position of nationalism, the individual reformer must fail. Because he was sensitive to the Spirit of his age, the philosopher saw the relation of the individual to that age. The only method to bring about a better society was by the process of analyzing one's environment and one's relation to it. This was called Hegelian criticism. Attempting to change society by physical violence was merely to return to the brute, and was not a sign of progress. Progress could be accomplished only under the

influence of those who were adequately sensitive to the
Spirit of the age.

Why was this complex Hegelian system of thought so
popular? It appeared to solve the great problem that
troubled all European thinkers in the days of Karl Marx.
That problem was: Why had the French Revolution failed?
Why had the greatest human effort to secure liberty, equal-
ity and fraternity for all, even though the violent seizure of
power had been successful, failed utterly to secure this end?
Bitterly disillusioned by that failure, many intellectuals
fell into cynical apathy. They concluded that man was
impotent before the powers of evil. Mankind was totally
unable to improve its lot by its own efforts. Hegel provided
a new answer to the problem. According to his analysis a
process existed in history which was inevitable, and therefore any attempt to change society by violence must fail.

To this theory of the inevitability of the dialectical process of history Karl Marx became a convert. In Berlin he
joined a new group called the Young Hegelians. The old
Hegelians held that what was real was rational—in other
words, that any institution that existed at any moment by
the mere fact of its existence proved its own excellence,
since it was the result of a previous cultural conflict. On this
reasoning the old Hegelians justified the Prussian state as
good, and argued that therefore it was futile to change it,
since the decision had already been made by history. The
radical Young Hegelians held that man's reasoning power
was just as real as the institutions about him. Many of these
institutions were chaotic, irrational and therefore evil. The
intellectual should lift himself above the existing institutions, and should criticize them in order to bring progress
nearer the truly real. Such intellectual criticism would
heighten the conflict between the past and the present and
thus help to bring on the future. Criticism therefore

became the duty of the philosopher, according to the Young Hegelians. They believed they should promote revolutionary conflict by the only weapons they had, namely, by intellectual warfare. They should not appeal to the mob, the lowest level of the Spirit of an age, for that would be irrational. Only a revolution in ideas could bring about a revolution in practice.

The Young Hegelians at the University of Berlin boldly began to criticize the institutions of their time. Since political pamphleteering against the Prussian state was forbidden, the Young Hegelians first directed their attack against orthodoxy in religion. Karl Marx was studying law at the University of Berlin, but despite the warnings of his father he plunged into the hot debate on the campus regarding Hegel and religion. Bruno Bauer, a professor at the university, had denied the historical existence of Jesus. With him Marx, who now decided to become a professor, planned a violent atheistic campaign. They concocted an anonymous attack on the deceased Hegel himself. They invented a fictitious Lutheran minister and had him charge that Hegel's idea of the Spirit in history naturally denied the existence of God. The hoax was exposed. Bauer was dismissed. Marx continued as a student but did not attend classes. He became more deeply involved in this battle of words over what Hegel said and what Hegel did not say.

Had it not been for the sudden death of his father, Marx might have continued to live in this fantasy world of words. His father left funds barely sufficient for the widow and the younger children. The Bauer hoax closed Marx's academic hopes. Then twenty-four years of age, Marx had to look for an occupation. He found an admirer in Moses Hess, a Jewish writer from Cologne who combined an ardent traditional loyalty to Judaism with an idealistic humanism. Hess preached that economics was more important than politics, and that any effort to reform the world would be impossible so long as property, both private and national, impeded justice for the worker. Hess declared his ideal to be a new international society based on a collectivist economy. Hess had an uncanny enthusiasm for the 24-year-old Marx. Hess wrote then, "He is the greatest . . . and will give medieval religion and politics their *coup de grâce*." Later Hess left Marxism to become one of the first Zionist nationalists, and the author of the book *Jerusalem*.

Moses Hess induced some liberal, democratically minded industrialists in Cologne to finance a liberal journal, which was to contain articles against the reactionary Berlin government and in sympathy with the rising middle class. It was called the *Rheinische Zeitung*. Hess appointed Marx editor. Marx changed it from a mildly liberal paper to a vehemently radical one. He attacked Prussian censorship and the landowning class. The paper became famous throughout Germany. However, Marx began to expose the conditions of the wine-growing peasants and also to attack the Russian Czarist government—an ally of Prussia—and when the Czar protested, the journal was suppressed and Marx was again unemployed.

Marx deepened his thinking during this period of unemployment by pursuing the activity he loved best—reading books. He was always a voracious reader. At this time he came under the influence of a critic of Hegel named Feuerbach, who held that when Hegel said that any age was moved by the Spirit of that age he was actually saying nothing. It would be as reasonable to say that God made that age. It would be less absurd to attribute an age to the work of individual genius. The moving force of history, said Feuerbach, was not a spiritual but a material force. The spiritual aspects of an age were only the result of unsuccessful efforts to escape from the material distresses of that age. "Man is what he eats," said Feuerbach. The material was what moved history, and any other ideology—such as religion—is only a compensation for real misery, a superstructure to conceal economic failure. Up until this time the young idealist Marx had remained a Hegelian in his opposition to violent revolution; but he now came to believe that Hegel was wrong in not being able to see that the moving force was materialism rather than an abstract idea.

Disliking the Bohemian life of his frustrated fellow radicals, and seeing no future for himself in Germany, Marx accepted an invitation to go to Paris and help a German socialist exile edit a new journal called *The German-French Yearbook*. When Marx arrived in Paris in 1843, he took Jenny von Westphalen with him; for after seven years' courtship they had finally married, in spite of the opposition of her family. Jenny's forebears included not only Teutonic but also Scottish nobility. The marriage joined Karl, a descendant of the Rabbi of Padua, with Jenny, a descendant of the Scottish Duke of Argyle. Jenny was loyal to her husband all through his lifetime. She admired and trusted him, and was entirely dominated by him. As we shall see, she suffered with him throughout his career.

When Marx arrived in Paris at the age of twenty-five, he was thought of by his contemporaries as a radical journalist who had been forced to leave Germany because he advocated democratic reforms. Two years later, he had become notorious as an enemy of all reformist liberalism. He came to be known to the police of many lands as an uncompromising revolutionary, the notorious leader of a subversive movement with international dangers. The two years Karl Marx spent in Paris from 1843–45 were the most decisive years of his life, and determined the shape of his influence on history.

During these years Paris had become a place of asylum for liberal poets, painters, musicians and thinkers. Paris had won for itself the reputation of the city of light because there these men could freely protest the old order of tyrants, the church, the army and the Philistine masses. Every year brought new exiles from those lands in which the monarchies had been restored after the defeat of the French Revolution. They came from Italy, Poland, Hungary, Germany and especially from Russia. There existed an international camaraderie of revolutionists. Karl Marx did not make heroes out of the romantic idealists of revolutions that had failed. He was of that unemotional temperament that distrusts heroics. He had chosen Paris because it offered a job, and also because it would give him a better opportunity to find the answer to the question—why did the French Revolution fail. History, he believed, must contain discoverable laws. By obeying these laws, one could avoid the errors of a French Revolution to make the next revolution successful.

With characteristic thoroughness, Marx began to study the facts of the French Revolution itself. Finding no satisfactory answer in Hegel's mystical dialectics concerning the Spirit of the Age, Marx turned to the realistic political writers of France. From Saint-Simon, the intellectual spokesman of the rising French middle class, Marx learned that history was simply a conflict between economic classes. According to the analysis of Saint-Simon, the banker, the industrialist and the scientist had already supplanted the power of the priest, soldier and landowner. He therefore advocated the abolition of the law of inheritance, although he insisted on continuing private property as a necessity. From Saint-Simon's opponent, Fourier, Marx learned that the industrial process tended to produce monopolies. The rich monopolists would put the smaller traders out of business. Over-production would result, and it in turn would lead to war between the rival capitalists for world markets. This would force the lowering of wages and therefore lead to more poverty. Since he opposed all governmental bureaucracies, Fourier did not advocate that the state should intervene to control monopolies. He had a rather fanciful program for counteracting the laissez-faire policy of capitalism. Fourier proposed that the whole earth be divided into small phalanxes consisting of 816 citizens each. Within each phalanx there was to be a self-governing cooperative with property held in common. As part of his eccentric plan Fourier conceived of one central electric plant providing electrical power to all these phalanxes. Incidentally, the idea of such colonies holding property in common inspired the Fourierist movement which developed the city of Oneida, New York. Still another radical French writer, Proudhon, declared that "property is theft" and competition for property the greatest evil. However, Proudhon was also against the intervention of the state, but advocated the organization of the people into small trades, workers' and consumers' unions. Karl Marx, after studying all these French writers on economic and political theory, bitterly attacked them for not being able to see that the entire system had to be destroyed. To prove his own theories, Marx then designed his philosophy of Dialectical Materialism.

Dialectical materialism is both an analysis of society and a political strategy. The theory is most extensively developed in a bizarre collection of essays entitled *German Ideology*, which Marx wrote in 1846. Marx agreed with Hegel that there were laws of growth and change which could be traced in history. However, if the study of history was to be scientific it must contain something that could be inspected. One could hardly inspect what Hegel called the Spirit of history. Marx drew a simple conclusion, namely that history was made in a social environment. As ice becomes water, or water steam under pressure, so social environment changed under social pressure. In society this pressure was economics. Social conflict was always a clash between economically determined groups. The individual himself was conditioned by his economic role, whether he was aware of it or not. In one of his most quoted statements Marx concluded, "It is not the consciousness of men that determines their existence, but on the contrary, their social existence determines their consciousness."

At a certain stage in history the material forces of production would conflict with property relations in a society within which these forces had been at work. The result would be social revolution. "No social order ever disappears before all the productive forces, for which there is room in it, have developed; and the new higher relations of production never appear before the conditions of their existence have matured in the womb of the old society." Accordingly, Marx concluded that the revolutionists must be patient and await history, which would itself bring about the inevitable revolution.

On the basis of this economic determination of history, Marx developed his own psychology of human behavior. What an individual would do could be predicted by discovering whether he was a part of or was outside of the ruling economic class. His personal emotions were irrelevant to his behavior. It was wrong to say human nature was unalterable, because economic changes would change human behavior. Since one must behave in accordance with the demands of the economic environment, one would act first and only later give reasons for the action. When a man had convinced himself that his actions were based on reason he was only rationalizing an inescapable condition. Moral codes and religious organizations, according to Marx, were just such rationalizations. They were only superstructures erected upon the economic foundations in order to make the latter acceptable to the masses. "Religion is the opiate of the people," said Marx; but any socialist who thought he could bring about the revolution by removing religion Marx ridiculed as mad and neurotic. Not by altering the superstructure, but only by radically changing the material foundation, could the revolution be brought about.

Marx ridiculed the mild socialists who opposed violence and hoped to bring about change through influencing moral sentiments. They were only fiddling with the super-structure. He saw them as sentimentalists holding on to an outworn fallacy—for men never willingly gave up their possessions and power. This sentimentality Marx called stupid and cowardly utopianism. Since men were guided by material interests, the question of morality—of good and evil—had nothing to do with the case. It was to the interest of the bourgeois to maintain the status quo; it was to the interest of the proletariat to alter it. If the proletariat accepted slogans that hold good for the bourgeois—Justice, Liberty, Principle—they were merely being hypnotized, but could not act in their own interest. Therefore, socialists who talked about liberty and justice were more dangerous enemies of the proletariat than the bourgeois, who were open enemies the proletariat could learn to distrust.

So long as one class controlled the industrial system, the workers must be made to understand that human liberty would be impossible. Inventions might abolish scarcity, but an artificial scarcity would be created by the monopo-listic struggle within the capitalist system. The remedy was not the democratic establishment of equality between the classes but the disappearance of the class struggle itself. Marx was convinced that he had found the key to the failure of the French Revolution. It had only altered political forms and entrenched the middle class. That was what its task had been in that stage of history. It had to be the replacement of the feudal lords by the bourgeois. Now in the industrial age only one class remained submerged, namely the propertyless proletariat. According to the dialectical process of history each lower class must supplant the higher class. Thus, it was inevitable that the lower working class would free itself from the upper classes. The bourgeois would fight, but their cause was hopeless because just as they had defeated the feudal lords, so the working masses would defeat them. These masses would fight for freedom not because they had chosen to do so but because the process of history would force them to do so. They would be fighting a foe already doomed to decay. Thus the working classes would be fighting not merely for themselves, but indeed for the survival of humanity. The victory of the proletariat would end the process of the class struggle. Their victory would abolish the state itself —which heretofore had been merely the instrument of one class over another. The victory of the working classes would bring about the classless society.

The victory of the working classes was already determined by history, whether the individuals of that class willed it or not. Nevertheless, how soon that victory came, and how efficient it was to be, depended on the degree of understanding possessed by the masses and their leaders concerning this process. They must understand that there could never be any compromise with capitalism, even if temporary alliances were made with it to defeat a common enemy. Such capitalist allies would always turn against the worker in the end. The duty of the philosopher of the revolution, declared Marx, was to educate the masses concerning the dialectical, materialist determination of their destiny. Their leaders must pay no attention to the outworn moralities of the old order. They must not even believe that they themselves had free will. They must only know the direction which the world process must inevitably take and identify themselves with it. Those who failed to do so prepared their own destruction. When Khrushchev recently declared that the Soviet Union would "bury" American capitalism he was appealing to the Marxian metaphysical basis of Communist doctrine. Whether or not all the dialectics of Karl Marx finally prove to be false, the theories he arrived at before 1848 unquestionably introduced a new approach to the social question of the world. The scientific study of economic relations and their bearing on life began with Marx's theories. Undoubtedly the father of modern economics and sociology is Karl Marx.

Marx had arrived at his basic conclusions at the age of twenty-seven. Communism, he concluded, could be achieved only by an armed rising of the proletariat. The rest of his life was dedicated to the organization and the disciplining of the leaders of the working class for this task. His personal history became inseparable from the general history of socialism at the middle half of the nineteenth century. Since according to his theories his task was a scientific undertaking and not an expression of himself, the facts of his personal life were unimportant to him. He felt that his personal fate had no more bearing upon the subject of his interest than the personal life of Darwin had upon his study of biology. The world in his day might applaud individual romantic rebels like Byron, or be fascinated by revolutionary romantics like Garibaldi in Italy, Bakunin in Russia or Lassalle in Germany, but Marx himself was immune to all this emotional intensity. For him, to indulge in emotions in the war of ideas was unpardonable. He could not be preoccupied with his own soul while he was on the battlefield of history. This detachment accounts for the boorishness of his relations with all other people.

In view of his theory it was logical for Marx to turn away from the socialist intellectuals of his day, and to appeal to the actual workers to support his Communist League. Expelled from Paris at the request of Prussia because of his attacks on the latter's tyrannical government, Marx moved to Brussels. A branch of Marx's Communist League, made up of German workers residing in London, commissioned Marx to compose a statement of his beliefs. A few weeks before the outbreak of the Paris Revolution of 1848 he submitted *The Manifesto of the Communist Party*. This is a document of dramatic power. It opened with the menacing words: "A specter is wandering over Europe today—the specter of Communism. All the forces of Europe have united to exorcise it—the Pope, the Czar, the French radicals, the German police spies." In this manifesto Marx popularized his doctrine of the class struggle. The bourgeois who had overthrown feudalism would in turn enslave the workers as hired labor or negotiable commodities exploited by religious and political slogans. As a result of overproduction there would be frequent economic crises, in which the capitalists would try to destroy their own products as a sign of the bankruptcy of their system. They could not destroy the proletariat, whom they needed in order to produce. The workers would become internationalized since capitalism was international. The solution of the future would not be an imaginary utopia but the international abolition of private property. In this process the concepts of liberty, religion, morality and culture would be destroyed because they were only bourgeois illusions. The culture of capitalism was merely mechanical. Only the classless society would produce a free culture. The revolution would nationalize land, credits, transport; increase taxes, intensify production, establish compulsory work and free education for all. Any other socialist scheme would merely protect the bourgeois. Only the Communists were the self-conscious vanguard who would fulfill historic destiny. The Manifesto openly declared that its aim could be achieved only when the entire social order was overthrown by the force of arms. It ended: "The workers have nothing to lose but their chains: They have a world to win. Workers of all lands, unite!"

As an instrument of destructive propaganda the Communist Manifesto has no equal. There were childish weaknesses in it, such as Marx's statement that in the capitalist system the family would deteriorate because of the pleasure its leaders took in seducing one another's wives. However, its effect on succeeding generations was unparalleled, even though its immediate effect was only to get Karl Marx expelled from Brussels. The next day the revolution broke out in Paris, and Marx was invited to return by a radical member of the new French government. German radicals in Paris formed a legion to invade Germany and bring the new revolution into their homeland. On the basis of his theories Marx objected to this as a rash act, since the time was not ripe for the overthrow of capitalism. However, he did return to Cologne to revive the old newspaper. His strategy then was the joining of the workers with the bourgeois, and even advocating that Germany should go to war against Russia in the hope that the war's débacle would hasten the overthrow of capitalism. The 1848 Revolution was not, according to Marx, a test of his theories, because the workers then would not

follow their radical leaders, but instead joined the democratic forces of the bourgeois. Marx now concluded that
the stupidity of the masses was a greater obstacle to the
progress of history than capitalism. When he called upon
the workers to refuse to pay taxes to Germany, his paper
was closed by the government. His last issue was printed
in red ink. Marx was arrested and tried. He made his
trial the occasion for a lengthy speech in which he analyzed
the conditions of Germany. He was acquitted, after the
foreman had thanked him for his unusually interesting
lecture. He was again exiled to Paris, but with the return
of the French royalty he once more had to leave. His
socialist friends raised some money, and in August 1849
he left for London, where his friend Engels—who had
participated in the abortive German legion's invasion of
Germany—joined him. Thus began the long collaboration
between Marx and Engels in London.

Marx had little to do with the other emigrés, who lived
in London in hopeless stagnation. He limited his contacts
to a small group of followers. After militant radicalism
collapsed in the 1850's and was replaced by the growing
prosperity of industrialism, there was no choice left to
Marx but the pursuit of scholarship. He was contemptuous
of the English socialist liberals, who were chiefly interested
in trade unionism and the improvement of working conditions. In the daytime he could be seen in the British
Museum, where he was the first to use government reports
in the study of economics; and in the evenings he saw
only a few German exiles, with whom he discussed the
possibilities of reviving and reconstructing his Communist
League.

Throughout the thirty-four years that Marx lived in
London, and until his death, he suffered abject poverty.
Many times he literally went hungry. He lived in one

hovel after another in the slums of Soho. He had money
for neither food nor medicine. Once he pawned his only
suit and stayed in bed in order to pay for a few potatoes.
His embittered feelings found outlet in his writings. He
saw himself as the victim of plots. He suffered from diseases
of the liver, and from boils. "I am plagued like Job though
not so Godfearing," he once wrote. He became a chain
smoker to serve as anodyne to his pain. During these years
three of his children died of malnutrition. For one of them
he had no money even to purchase a coffin. His own condition made Marx hate poverty more passionately even than
he hated slavery. Accordingly, he began to revive his
strategy for the inevitable Communist Revolution. Since
the failure of the Paris revolution in 1848, and the alliance
of the French workers with the democratic forces, Marx
advanced the strategy of the *coup d'état* by a small body
of trained revolutionaries. They were to seize power and
act in the name of the masses. The masses had been too
long in bondage to be ready for self-government or to
understand the necessity of liquidating their opponents.
Until the masses were ready for the classless society, there
would have to be set up a dictatorship of the proletariat.
This dictatorship would not make alliances with the
middle class; it would seize power and educate the masses.
This interlude Marx defined as "a state of permanent
revolution." During this period the leadership must be
based upon "the purity of the elite in the Party." The
Communist elite would not follow the example of the
socialist and participate in parliamentary procedures or
trade unions. They would strike when the time was ripe.
Those who did not follow this theory, Karl Marx insisted,
should be purged from his Party.

The German socialist movement provided the nucleus
for Marx's new militant Communist Party. Another Jew,

Ferdinand Lassalle, a noted and brilliant lawyer born in Silesia, became the real organizer of the German Socialist Democratic Party. The strategy of Lassalle was to form an alliance with the middle class and to negotiate with Bismarck in order to liberalize the Prussian monarchy. Marx's determination to purge Lassalle from the Party became unnecessary when Lassalle was killed in a duel over a casual love affair. Although other exiled revolutionaries lost their courage with the death of Lassalle, Marx was convinced of the inevitability of his doctrine. The ripeness of time, not the popularity of a socialist orator and not even the masses, could be relied upon for the revolution. However, with the phenomenal growth of industry in the 1850's, faith in liberalism and science grew and interest in the Communist Revolution temporarily died down.

During this period of the decline of interest in Communism, Marx found some relief for his poverty by writing articles for the New York *Tribune*. This paper was then the leading spokesman for the ideas of progress. It opposed slavery and the European aristocracy. For ten years Marx sent weekly dispatches, which even today make interesting reading. In one article he made his celebrated generalization that "economic slump leads to successful revolution." Always on the alert for a major economic crisis, Marx would write articles about world markets, bankruptcy, bad harvests—commonplace subjects of news articles today. An article on India written in 1853 was prophetic. In it Marx agreed that the English were in India not to help the Indian masses but for their own economic interests, but that nonetheless England was unconsciously the historical instrument which would cause the social revolution of Asia. Typical of his *Tribune* articles was his vitriolic attack on the hypocrisy of the

Duchess of Sutherland. She had espoused the cause of the Negro slaves in America, but at the same time was expelling the tenants on her own English estate in order to make room for a deer-hunting preserve.

Two things occurred in 1865 to restore fame to Karl Marx. He founded the First Workers' International, and he published his most famous book, *Das Kapital*. Though unknown in England, Marx became famous abroad. He and Engels became the center of the propaganda to weed out their doctrinaire opponents to the communist ideology. The German workers in London had appointed Marx to be their delegate at a meeting attended by trade unionists from France and England, held in London in 1863 in connection with an exhibition of modern industry. Marx gave the inaugural address at this meeting, and wrote the constitution for the First Workers' International. In it he called for a political action which was against reformism, and insisted that the workers should take over the ownership of production and abolish private property. English workers could protest English capitalists helping the Southern states in the Civil War, or the worker might gain control of existing Parliament; but in any event the eventual goal was the communist revolution. Branches of the International spread, but Marx, through his friend Engels, continued to control the organization from London, fighting all those in the Party who favored collaboration with other non-communist liberal groups. His most famous personal fight was against the Russian revolutionist Bakunin.

In view of the character of the successful communist regime in the present century, Bakunin's attack on Marx makes interesting reading. When Marx insisted that undisputed power be put in the hands of a small controlling committee of the Party, Bakunin declared, "We believe

power corrupts those who will it as much as those who are
forced to obey it." Concerning Marx's unemotional, doctrinaire analysis, Bakunin wrote: "Intellectuals, positivists,
doctrinaires, all those who put science before life . . .
defend the idea of the state and its authority as being the
only possible salvation of society — quite logically, since
from their false premise that thought comes before life,
that only abstract theory can form the starting point of
social practice . . . they draw the inevitable conclusion that
since such theoretical knowledge is at present possessed by
very few, these too must be put in control of social life . . .
not a free association of popular bodies working in accordance with the needs and instincts of the people, but a centralized dictatorial power concentrated in the hands of this
academic minority, as if they really expressed the popular
will. . . . The difference between such revolutionary dictatorship and the monarch state is only one of external
trappings. In substance both are a tyranny of the minority
over the majority in the name of the people—in the name
of the stupidity of the many and the superior wisdom of
the few . . . enslavement of the masses, to destroy the
present order only to erect their own rigid dictatorship on
its ruins." In a bitter intellectual battle Marx succeeded
in purging Bakunin from the Party.

The fame of Karl Marx spread under the influence of
his control of the First International. The German socialists objected to the Prussian War against France in 1870,
and against the annexation of French territory which
brought about the jailing of some of their members in
the German Parliament. However, after the conclusion of
the French defeat, the workers' revolt in Paris, which led
to the establishment of the famous Paris Commune of
1870, was short-lived. Marx had defended the terrorism of
this workingmen's French revolution, and thus came to be

known as "the Red terrorist Dr. Marx." The association of his International with the Red terror in Paris led to the dissolution of the movement. However, before Marx abandoned the First International he was influential through it in creating the British Labour Party, the single contribution he was to make to his adopted country, England. On the other hand, when German socialists began in his name to adopt a new program of compromise, Marx complained bitterly that he was being misinterpreted, blurting out "I'm not a Marxist!" in his attack on this socialistic compromise. Although his strategy thus failed during his lifetime, his formula for the revolution survived.

Marx completed his formula for the revolution in the greatest book he wrote: *Das Kapital,* published in 1867. In it he set out to discover natural laws which could be shown to govern the history of classes. The value of a thing, Marx concluded, was determined by the number of hours of human labor required to produce it. When production resulted in more than the worker needed for himself, surplus value was created. This became the profits of the owner. However, only one class really produced value—namely, the workers, who produced more wealth than they enjoyed. The state, religion and law concealed this fact from them. In order to make their workers more efficient for the sake of greater profits, the owners had centralized production into monopolies and concentrated the workers in one place. Without any planned economy, periodic crises would arise in the competitive business. These would lead to wars on an unprecedented scale. As a result, the decreasing number of capitalists would be overthrown by the increasing number of workers. The state would disappear. A new community would arise, in which the world's goods would be distributed rationally but not equally. The economic policy would be, "To everyone according to his need, from everyone according to his capacity."

Das Kapital became the intellectual foundation of international socialism. Marx preferred the word *socialism* to that of *communism*. In the name of *Das Kapital*, revolutions were made and new social orders proposed. It was blindly worshiped or hated by millions who had never read a line of it. It set the standard for economic and socio-political research. It inspired a whole army of interpreters. The volume of the commentaries on *Das Kapital*, in any number of languages, outgrew that of the text itself. Believing he was creating a new social science comparable to the natural sciences, Marx offered to dedicate this book to Darwin, for whom he had the greatest admiration. Darwin, however, politely declined the honor. Marx intended *Das Kapital* to be his greatest contribution, and with single-minded stoicism he sacrificed fifteen years of poverty to it. In the remaining sixteen years of his life he published very little that was new.

Marx's own confidence in the proximity of world revolution declined as the successful revolutions he had predicted for his own day in *Das Kapital* failed to materialize. However, his long-term predictions turned out to be more successful. His prediction concerning capitalism erred; instead of centralization, in his day there was a growth of small investors. On the other hand, when Prussia annexed Alsace, Marx predicted that this event would throw France into the arms of Russia and bring about the first great world war. Thereafter, *Das Kapital* won a new reputation and was translated in French, English, Russian and Italian. His old opponents had died, leaving him the supreme intellectual authority of the international socialism.

As Marx grew older his impatience and irritability

increased. He broke off relations with his oldest friends. Only Engels, who settled a small annuity on him, remained true. When he lost his job with the New York *Tribune,* he tried to become a bookkeeping clerk in a railway office. He was rejected, not because of his menacing appearance and tattered clothes, but for another, ironic reason: this man whose words changed the world could not get a job because his handwriting was illegible.

Younger socialist pilgrims, notably Russian readers of *Das Kapital,* came to visit Marx in London. It was again ironic that this book should have had its greatest success in Russia. Because the Czarist censors pronounced *Das Kapital* "so difficult it would be unlikely to have any readers," it was permitted to be published in Russian. Marx's theories were not adopted by the Russian workers and peasants, who could not read, but by the middle-class Russian intellectuals who in that period were mystically identifying themselves with the Russian peasants as Tolstoy had done. Well-to-do young men from Moscow and Petersburg tried to live with the Russian peasants. Russian radicals read the *Communist Manifesto* and *Das Kapital* much as French intellectuals in the previous century had read Rousseau. It was greatly to his own surprise that Marx found his most ardent disciples in Russia, since it was against that country that he had written so critically for the past thirty-four years. The Russian disciples asked him whether the revolution would take place by bypassing the necessity of industrialization. Could one cheat the Marxian dialectic and leap from a peasant agricultural state into the socialist revolution? In order to answer the question Marx began to learn Russian, and in six months he had mastered it sufficiently to read works smuggled in to him. He concluded that the social revolution could take place in agricultural Russia only if a proletarian revolution were to take place throughout Europe. If capitalism continued in Europe among Russia's nearest neighbors, for its own economic defense the social revolution in Russia would be forced to industrialize along the lines of the West. The present-day debate as to whether Russian or even Chinese communism can coexist alongside Western capitalism is still carried on within the framework of Marx's original interpretation.

His friends describe Marx in his old age as a shabby but unbowed old man. He would behave like an angry prophet when he attacked unjust social conditions, but then would revert to the calm of a philosopher as he explained the future. He continued to work and to read all day long—reading Shakespeare in English, Pushkin in Russian and Balzac in French. He had a passion for books, and before he died he even took up the study of the Turkish language in order to become acquainted with the problems of the Near East. His joys were still with his own family—his daughters, whom he nicknamed Quee Quee, Quo Quo and Tootsie, and who called him "The Moor." His wife died of cancer. One daughter committed suicide. Two years after that tragedy, Marx died seated in an armchair in his study.

Eight persons went to the cemetery for the burial of Karl Marx. His friend Engels gave the funeral oration, in which he said that Karl Marx, who had fought to overthrow capitalist society, was "the most hated and the most calumniated man of his time," but that nevertheless "he died beloved, revered, and mourned by millions of revolutionary fellow workers from the mines of Siberia to the coasts of California." His death passed unnoticed by the newspapers.

The eight who attended the funeral of this man are a startling contrast to the hundreds of millions whose lives were altered by his ideas. The paradox reveals the nature of Marx's attitude toward himself. He refused to examine or to place great importance upon himself. He declared that personal emotions had no part in the historic social struggle. His rejection of himself went so far as to include the notion that even his own ideas would not appreciably affect events, since those events were already and inescapably predetermined by economics.

Psychologists associate the rejection of self with one who fails to identify himself with any other person. Marx could never be close to an individual, nor to the masses he sought to set free. He was close only to an idea, which he ironically said was itself only a picture of events and not the maker of them. His inability to identify himself with another person began with his relations with his own father. Heinrich Marx was weak and timid. In order to adjust to his era he eliminated himself. To be accepted as a Prussian patriot, he not only suppressed his Jewishness but surrendered every other sign of individuality. Against his father's weakness, Karl Marx reacted violently. His disgust with his father's cowardly conversion led him to hate all religion, and especially the religion his father had betrayed.

When he was twenty-six years of age, Karl Marx wrote one of the most vehemently anti-Semitic essays ever penned. In the 1840's a well-intentioned liberal German writer had observed that the Jews were lagging behind in becoming emancipated. To speed up the process, he suggested the Jews should be baptized. Karl Marx replied bitterly and angrily. The Jews, he declared, were not a race, nor did they have a religion. The Jews were purely an economic group forced into usury by their neighbors. Renouncing his father's conversion entirely, he declared that baptism would be only substituting yet another absurd religious shackle for the Jews' former religious enslavement. Jews would be emancipated only when all of Europe was emancipated from capitalism. The vehemence of the language with which Marx expressed his hate for Jews is the best proof of his own painful struggle with the fact that he himself was a Jew. In his essay on the Jews Marx did not write, he exploded—shouting, "What is the cult of Jews? Bargaining. What is their worldly God? Money." In his private letters to Frederick Engels he invariably attacked Jews. "The Jews of Poland are the smeariest," he wrote. In his extreme jealousy of Ferdinand Lassalle, the German socialist, orator and leader, he described him as "that Jewish nigger." In his scorn for the Jews of London he wrote, "Barnsgate is full of Jews and fleas."

Marx carried this hate of himself as a Jew into his hatred for others, including his socialist colleagues. Having no trust in his father, who had betrayed himself, the son never was able to trust anyone else. His attacks on socialists who differed — especially on those who believed society could be reformed without revolution—were savage. These trusters in the good will of men must, he said, be purged —or, in the words he himself used, "demolished" and "annihilated." Marx was wholly insensitive to the feelings of other people.

But above everything else he hated, Marx hated poverty. Because he had experienced so much poverty in his own life, he hated poverty more than he hated slavery. For the sake of removing poverty, he arrived at a strategy that would keep his fellow human beings enslaved by a dictatorship until poverty was removed. Individual feelings did not count—only economics was important.

In the rejection of self, of emotion and of the individual we have the fundamental reason why Marxism had its outstanding failure in the very place where it was supposed to have achieved its greatest success, namely in the United States of America. According to the Marxian formula of dialectical materialism, socialism must inevitably have developed first in the most advanced industrialized nation. Marx simply refused to recognize that a people could reach a democratic development which placed its primary emphasis on the dignity of the individual. Fanatics who envision an authoritarian fate, whether religious or political, can see no alternatives, for they do not admit of the flexibility and the adaptability of human life. As Clinton Rossiter has pointed out, Marx could not see the fresh uniqueness of the American experiment. He foretold the doom of liberal democracy. Yet even in its most desperate periods of depression or of war, America has always been hostile to political radicalism, and never turned to Marxism. Marx's ideas never have taken root in America.

Despite Marx's insistence that only economics counts, ideas do affect history. His own idea did. The conflict between democracy and communism today is far more acute because of the existence of ideas. The conflict is not merely an adjustment to economic realities; it is a conflict between two ideologies. To paraphrase Clinton Rossiter, the difference between Marxist and anti-Marxist is also the difference between those who believe that you can condition and manipulate human nature by controlling environment and those who believe there are fundamental decencies in human nature that cannot be controlled; between those who trust the dictatorship of an elite and those who fear to grant unlimited power to any man; between those who support a rigidly materialistic interpretation of life and those who believe in an idealistically pragmatic approach to life; between those whose temperament supports a dogmatic, violent and amoral leadership obsessed with the sins of capitalism and those who are at once more easy-going, more moral and more willing to grant that no group has a monopoly on righteousness or truth; between those who are fanatical in their insistence upon an apocalyptic doom and those who are disposed to believe that mankind may eventually live in peace; between those who believe that government is only for the people and those who believe government is also by the people.

While much of the difference today between Western democracy and Eastern communism is derived from Marx himself, it is a mistake to charge Marx with responsibility for the present excesses of Russian and Chinese communism, just as it is a mistake to charge Jesus with the responsibility for a Torquemada of the Inquisition. It will be recalled that in the 1870's, when the early Russian disciples of Marx asked him whether Russia could skip what Marx thought to be the necessary prerequisite for the socialist revolution—namely the industrialization of their country—Marx replied that it could do so only if the rest of Europe had first become proletarianized. The Russian communists defied Marx's theory of history. The Bolsheviks did not wait, but through ruthless political terrorism tried to impose a planned industrial economy on a backward country whose people were unready and unwilling to accept it. While Marx himself was cold in his reaction toward men and in his analysis of their behavior, he was never so contemptuous of men as a Stalin or a Mao, who without conscience or compunction could engineer crimes against men in the name of Marx. In fact, even though he charged the socialist reformers of his day with the foolishness of utopianism, Marx himself was naïve enough to believe in men's capacity for self-control to the extent of suggesting that they could do without the government of a state altogether. The dogma of the "withering away of the state" is still the most embarrassing of all Marxian doctrines to the monolithic states of Khrushchev and Mao. As Sidney Hook has rightly pointed out, "To make Marx the historical scapegoat of contemporary communist totalitarianism is too easy. It tends to make us overlook the failure of the free cultures to solve the problems which gave the despotisms of this century their chance."

If the West is to meet the challenge of the East's terrifying distortions of Marxian ideas, it must become more thoroughly conversant with and sensitive to those findings by the founder of economics and sociology that are real and applicable. To Karl Marx the world owes its present-day consciousness of the importance of the effects of economics on life; of the relation of productivity to the future; of the significance of conflict between economic classes; of the challenge of an industrial system to the psychological security of the individual; of the fact that poverty is not heaven-ordained but can be eradicated. However, economic interpretations of life will not suffice to lead the way to success in the struggle between Western democracy and Eastern communism, and especially in the struggle to attract the uncommitted peoples of the world. Men want not only economic security and freedom from poverty; they also want freedom for themselves as individuals. That man does not live by bread alone is not merely a religious slogan. It may surprise the reader to learn that Marx himself wrote of the working class that it "regards its courage, self-confidence, independence and sense of personal dignity as more necessary than its daily bread." It remains the task of the West to prove to the working classes of the world that in this Marx was right—that they should prefer a free society to a closed society, and an open mind to a closed mind.

Finally, Marx could not have conceived in his day the possibility of the total annihilation of the human race by the atomic bomb. Had he known this, would he have been so certain in his predictions about the inevitability of a war to the death between opposing economic forces? No man-made theory is perfect. Perfection is for fanatics, and our nuclear age can neither afford nor endure fanaticism. Western democracy is not perfect. It can improve; it must be open to change. Eastern communism is not perfect. To survive, it too will have to make changes. Could not these changes include the possibility of peace?

V: Sigmund Freud

Every age has its particular image of what a man is. Twentieth-century man has a more conscious image of himself than did his predecessors. He is more keenly aware that what he thinks he is becomes a powerful determining factor in what he believes, builds or buys. If he thinks he is a nobody he may become destructive; if he thinks he is a somebody he may become constructive. According to the proverb, "As a man thinketh in his heart so is he." Yet this is not altogether true, for the image a person has of himself may be false; a man may not be what he seemeth. There may be no connection between the real person and either the image he has of himself or the image others have of him. In fact, because our age is a psychological one, it has been able to devise techniques to manipulate persons and manufacture images of them which are only empty masks.

The Greeks had a word for such a mask—*persona*. Personality can be the superficial mask which conceals the real person. Each then becomes two people—the real self and the self-image. In this case, can one ever really know himself—an accomplishment which the Delphi oracle held to be the highest virtue? Are the image and the real person completely separate?

The human mind is unhappy with the unrelated. The development of human thought is a persistent attempt to connect things which seem separate. The Greek naturalists observed the radical differences between such things as air and water; yet, they insisted that each of these seemingly unrelated materials was only an elaboration of some common stuff of life. The Hebrew religionists could not tolerate many gods each responsible for some special virtue or fate. They held that all virtues and all destinies stem from a single, primary divine power. The mind is not content with the disconnected. There must be a continuing relation between one thing and another. This mode of thinking might be called the Principle of Continuity. It is a mode of thought which distinguishes civilized man from primitive man. Primitive man is unable to establish connections between one phenomenon of life and another.

The civilized Greek idea of nature and the Hebrew idea of God both advanced the view that beginning with a common origin, life is a continuation of one form into another form, and that thus all things are interrelated even though they appear different or, indeed, contradictory. Yet in modern society this classical idea has only recently been popularly accepted. One hundred years ago, the average person saw little connection between man and animals. Indeed, he saw no relation between savage primitive man and his civilized modern brother. The average person was unaware of the close relation between the rational and the irrational, between reason and madness, between dreams and reality, between the mind of a child and the mind of an adult. When the modern world finally accepted the relation between man and animals and the interrelation between the divisions within man himself there arose a new image of man—one whose effect has been revolutionary.

How can the image one has of man instigate revolutions? If an objective scientific study should prove that man is so closely related to the animals that he is more animal than human, and it should also be proved that although superficially man appears good he is basically evil, such an image of man would have a revolutionary effect on government. Rather than foolishly play at democracy it would be wiser for government to become dictatorial in order to control the bestial, amoral man. The new image would also affect educational policies. To keep the human animal at war with itself within the law it would be better to train him to conform and not permit him the chaos of self-expression. If a person's inner feelings were proved to be more real than his external aspect, then a revolution would also take place in literature, art and music. These art forms would then become more significant when, instead of expressing the concrete, they expressed the abstract. If it were proved that life is so interrelated that there can be no separation of the body from the soul, there would ensue a revolution in religion, particularly regarding its concept of immortality.

The new scientific image of man has indeed been the basis of a revolution of the twentieth century in government, in education, in the arts and in religion. This twentieth-century image of man has challenged what man has always cherished—the image of himself as he likes to think he is. Thus we have also witnessed a powerful counter-revolutionary resistance to the new scientific image of man. The result has been the intellectual civil warfare of the twentieth century. The two intellectual insurgents, the two master minds chiefly responsible for the present-day revolutionary conflict over the image of man are Charles Darwin and Sigmund Freud.

What Darwin did to change the view of man's relation to the animal kingdom, Freud did to change the view of man's inner relations within the kingdom of the self. Darwin demonstrated the organic unity and continuity extending from the simple cell through all stages of biology, including man, under the unifying principle of evolution. According to his theory, all the varying species owe their particular forms to one and the same set of circumstances, namely the biological survival of the fittest. Of course, Darwin still placed man at the summit of this evolutionary scale, and therefore man could still view his own image with a degree of satisfaction. Whether made by God or evolved by nature, man could still think of himself as the perfect finished product. It remained for Sigmund Freud to carry Darwinism further by presenting an image of man himself as an unfinished product.

Freud said that inside man a continuous struggle goes on. This is the struggle of reason against unreason, of social control against primitive, barbaric urges: a constant struggle by the adult to free himself from his own infancy, from the tentacles of his own childhood—a childhood not at all as innocent as we should like to believe. Freud gave the world a radically different concept of man. Man at his best and at his worst, both are the result of a common set of conditions. This in itself was not new, for Judaism long before had called God the creator of both good and evil. The novelty in Freud's image of man lay in its scientific explanation of the origin of the conflict within man—namely that both good and evil grow from one and the same mechanical process within the mind.

Because in the last fifty years the name of Freud has become a household word, it has become not easier but more difficult to explain what he actually said and did. A tough humanist and a profound skeptic, Freud would have been amused and shocked by the degree to which so much today is explained away as "Freudian." Alfred Kazin has correctly observed that because of the widespread revolutionary effect of his ideas, Freud's name is no longer the name of a man; it is synonymous with man's nature. People use his name to define something in human nature that they believe actually exists and therefore have to accept even when they do not want to accept it. Today when people forget a name, make a slip of the tongue, feel depressed, begin a love affair, or break off a marriage they immediately begin to wonder what the Freudian reason may be. Many who boast that they do not believe a word of Freud's writings will nonetheless use Freudian terms as though they were commonplace, telling you that they do things "unconsciously," or are looking for the "motivations" or "compensations" behind the behavior of their friends. They will insist that one must understand what makes an individual "tick" before passing moral judgment on him. Even when they intellectually damn Freud, they will nonetheless admit that they prize sexual satisfaction as the key to happiness. To have one's name in this manner, both consciously and unconsciously, identified with human nature itself indicates the greatest kind of influence a man could possibly have.

Freud did not change the world simply through having his name become an adjective to describe human nature. Through his use of the technique of psychoanalysis, Freud uncovered the hidden motivations behind human actions of which the individual is not conscious. Before Freud, when a person thought anything, he thought he knew what he was thinking, but since Freud—to quote an observation from the English magazine *Punch*, "When a man thinks a thing, the thing he thinks he thinks is not the thing he thinks he thinks, but only the thing he thinks he thinks he thinks." The concept of the "Freudian unconscious" was to have have a radical effect upon medicine, the arts, religion, education, criminal law, child-rearing and attitudes toward sex and marriage, and to produce new approaches to a variety of social and political issues. His contribution to medicine was unique insofar as he was able to drag the resisting physicians out of the nineteenth century and into the twentieth-century era of psychosomatic medicine. No less significant was his effect on literature and art; men like Thomas Mann and Picasso owe much to Freud's studies of dreams, myths and symbols. Freud's criticism of religion forced it into a soul-searching re-examination of itself. Indeed, except for the great religions, no other system of thought has been adopted by so many as a systematic interpretation of individual behavior. Although Freud denied that he was a philosopher, to those with no beliefs Freudianism has come to serve as a kind of philosophy of life.

The image of man that Freud discovered grew out of his own very painful effort to get behind the image of himself. Of course, many before Freud had been deeply introspective and had struggled to know themselves; but Freud was the first to be analyzed in the modern scientific sense. At the age of forty-one he psychoanalyzed himself. It was a most heroic feat inasmuch as he forced himself to remember not only his own dreams but also his own infant sexuality. To learn how Freud was qualified to become the originator of psychoanalysis, and to understand not only his medical but also his philosophical and psychological ideas—particularly as those ideas were related to Freud's Jewishness—it is necessary to review the history of Freud the man. He remained a loyal and proud Jew albeit an avowed agnostic; and his ideas can be better understood as they are related to this fact.

The story of the man has been woven together with his ideas in a 1900-page, three-volume biography by the late Ernest Jones, one of Freud's first trainees in the practice of psychoanalysis. A Canadian psychoanalyst who practiced in London, Dr. Jones was a devoted lifelong follower of

Freud, and personally saved him from the Nazis in 1938. The weakness of his biography lies in Dr. Jones' effort to detail his own personal relations with Freud and his colleagues. For an understanding of Freud's life it must be supplemented by Freud's autobiography, written when he was sixty-nine, and by his recently published letters. Literally thousands of his letters have been preserved, in particular those to his friend Fliess, to his disciple Ferenczi and above all to his wife. The standard edition of the *Complete Works of Sigmund Freud* consists of twenty-four volumes. It includes his first publication, *Studies in Hysteria* (1894), and his final, posthumously published *Moses and Monotheism*. In the opinion of this writer, Freud's most significant works are *Interpretation of Dreams, Three Contributions to the Theory of Sex, Psychopathology of Everyday Life, Totem and Taboo, Wit and Its Relation to the Unconscious, Civilization and Its Discontents, The Future of an Illusion* and *History of the Psychoanalytical Movement*. His writings are indeed a monumental mental production. Freud once said that the one thing that distinguished the Jew was his brain power. He directed his psychic energies not to athletics but to mental gymnastics.

Freud was born in Freiberg, Moravia, in 1856. As a young man he had a great curiosity about his family history. He believed the Freuds had settled before the fourteenth century in Cologne, Germany, from which they had fled to Galicia and Rumania. His grandfather and great-grandfather were rabbis. His father, Jacob, who lived to be eighty-one, was a wool merchant. He had two sons by a first marriage. Jacob's second wife, Amalie, was Sigmund's mother. His father was gentle and beloved—a self-taught freethinker with a sense of humor, who was always pointing a moral with a Yiddish anecdote. His mother, who lived to be ninety-five, was more temperamental, but a lively and attractive personality. She was a descendant of a famous talmudic scholar. She was sixteen when she married Jacob, a widower twice her age. Sigmund's half-brother was already married and had a son and a daughter when Sigmund was born. Thus at the time of his birth, Sigmund not only had a very young mother and a middle-aged father, but was already the uncle of a nephew who was one year older than himself. These complications in his own family relations always puzzled Freud. His unique family situation is the background of his later ideas concerning a son's jealousy of his father in competition for the love of his mother. Freud had much to analyze in his own relations with his mother. He was Amalie's favorite among her five children, thanks to the pride of the mother in her first-born. "A man who has been the indisputable favorite of his mother," wrote Freud later, "keeps for life the feeling of a conqueror, that confidence of success that often induces real success." The superstitious midwife, seeing a strange mane of black hair on his forehead, predicted greatness for the child. The young mother believed the prophecy and named him Sigmund, after a legendary Moravian hero. His maturer father was much more reserved about the new addition to the family whom his young, pretty wife was soon spoiling.

At that time Freiberg was a town of 5000, whose population was mostly Roman Catholic. The Jewish textile weavers, of which Freud's father was one, experienced considerable anti-Semitism in the community. When the new machine looms replaced handicraft in weaving, the family suffered financial reverses. The older half-brother moved to the cloth-making city of Manchester, England, where the Jewish population was increasing. When he was three, Freud's family moved to Vienna; he later remembered being frightened at the time by his first train ride.

It is from his own honest analysis of himself that Freud's biographers have obtained the facts of his life. Since Freud had come to believe that character is already formed by the age of three, he made a heroic effort to rediscover the earliest experiences in his own life. As a result, we know much about his childhood fears, hates, conflicts and awakening to sex. He learned that one could both love and hate a single person through his early experiences with his older nephew, John.

The family lived in the ghetto section of Vienna. Every Friday evening two bath porters brought in a tin tub, and all the children were bathed. Sigmund was always bathed first, while the water was hot and clean. Freud was self-taught; not until he was ten did he enter the school of Vienna. He was a brilliant student, winning all the first prizes. In order to pursue his studies undisturbed, his mother provided her favorite with a separate room in the family flat. His youngest sister had to give up studying piano, since her practice disturbed the favorite son's studies. Freud had a gift for languages. He studied Latin, Greek and French at school. He taught himself Italian and Spanish, and had a special capacity for the English language, reading Shakespeare at the age of eight. At sixteen he had the usual frustrated adolescent love affair.

At seventeen Freud entered the University of Vienna to begin the study of medicine. He chose this profession not so much because of any interest in becoming a physician as because medicine gave him the opportunity for scientific study — especially of the discoveries of Charles Darwin. Nevertheless, at the very beginning he combined his interest in science with his interest in literature. He was inspired to pursue this combination by his reading of Goethe's essay *Die Nature*. In it, Goethe described nature as a bountiful mother who allows her favorite children the privilege of exploring her secrets. To discover these secrets Freud decided on medicine instead of law. However, he never sacrificed his literary talents to the medical sciences. Incidentally, later in life, his admirers offered Freud's works for consideration for the Nobel prize not for medicine but for literature.

In view of his later sensational studies of sex, it is amusing to note that Freud's first assignment as an advanced science student was to examine the reproductive organs of the eel. Though a brilliant researcher, Freud was refused a position in this field at the medical school because he was a Jew. He forced himself to continue studying to become a physician even though he had no urge to open a practice. He studied with Professor Bruecke, who taught that every nervous disease was caused by an actual lesion in the nervous system. However, at that time there were patients suffering from three types of so-called nervous disease which the doctors laughed off as imaginary because no organic causes for them could be discovered. These three were the hysterics, who simulated paralysis; the neurasthenics, who were only weak and tired; and the neurotics, who suffered from unreal fears. He had learned from dissecting the tissues of the brain that different areas of the brain controlled taste, smell, touch, speech and bodily actions. However, no disease in the brain tissues could be discovered to account for the hysterics, the neurasthenics or the neurotics, even though half of the patients in the hospital he attended suffered from these non-organic nervous illnesses. Freud himself suffered from a fear of travel, and he had a personal as well as a professional interest in these strange, unaccounted-for illnesses.

At the medical school, Freud chose to specialize in the histology of the nervous system; but he was profoundly disappointed at the lack of progress in this field. He learned that at the famous hospital for the insane in Paris (where "Citizen" Pinel had introduced a more humane treatment of the insane), a French neurologist, Charcot, had discovered that by hypnotizing his patients he could cause them to behave in a hysterical manner. Charcot had become world-famous for his studies of nervous tics, paralyses and tremors of the body, from which he himself suffered. Charcot was the first to describe accurately such now well-known diseases as muscular dystrophy, infantile paralysis and multiple sclerosis. When Freud met him Charcot was already an old man, and was especially interested in hysteria. This was the illness in which patients appeared to be paralyzed when they tried to walk, talk, see, hear or swallow, even though there was no demonstrable physical cause for such handicaps. *Hysteria* comes from the Greek word *hystron*, meaning "womb," since it was thought that hysteria was confined to women. Charcot had proved that male patients could also be afflicted with hysteria. From Charcot, Freud learned to distinguish between real paralytics, who suffered from brain lesions, and pseudo-paralytics, who are not afflicted by any physical trauma. Because he was able to hypnotize patients and make them behave as though they were afflicted in a particular part of their bodies, Charcot concluded that there was a connection between hysteria and susceptibility to hypnosis. He did not believe that hypnotism could cure his patients, for he did not know what caused the pseudo-paralysis of hysteria. Thus, in 1886, when Freud returned to Vienna to set up his practice as a specialist in nervous diseases, he still did not know how to treat such patients. In fact, his Viennese medical colleagues scorned him for asserting with Charcot that hysteria was not confined to women.

As soon as Freud had set up his office to begin the practice of medicine, he had married Martha Bernays. Her family provided a dowry. Their marriage had by then been postponed for over five years because of his financial difficulties. Also, his wife had waited during this long engagement period because Freud wanted to advance his knowledge of nervous diseases. Freud had met her through her brother Eli, who had come to Vienna to study, and who had married Freud's sister. The Bernays family came from Hamburg and were descendants of a famous German rabbi who had been a founder of modern orthodox Judaism. Martha's sister Minna had been engaged to a brother of the composer Schönberg. Minna's fiancé had died, and she remained single. She became a member of her brother-in-law's household, and her critical mind had considerable influence on Freud himself.

Freud was thirty and Martha was twenty-five when they married. She was a superb housekeeper, and kept Freud's domestic life in order. Their married life is a refutation of that popular misconception of Freud's theories which attributes to him a license to be promiscuous. Freud was not only monogamous but uxorious. He literally doted on his wife. Theirs was a beautiful marriage, which lasted fifty-three years and whose happiness the publication of their letters confirms. This does not mean that Martha did not have to contend with Sigmund's stubbornness, beginning with his vehement opposition to an orthodox Jewish wedding ceremony, which he regarded as barbaric. They had six children, three sons and three daughters. His favorite child was Anna, who later became a brilliant psychoanalyst, expert in the analytic treatment of disturbed children. The Freud family lived on the second floor of a building where he also had his medical office. For forty-seven years Sigmund Freud lived at the same address, 19 Bergasse Street in Vienna. That address was to become the Mecca of disciples of Freudian psychoanalysis throughout the world. After the defeat of the Nazis, the restored Austrian government, in a public ceremony, placed a plaque in his memory on that building.

In the beginning of his practice as a nerve specialist, Freud could hardly make ends meet. He tutored students, translated medical works, and borrowed money from his good friends. He suffered from nasal catarrh and migraine headaches and had the typical complaints—the grumpiness and the chronic dyspepsia—of a neurasthenic. However, his wife Martha had an intuitive talent for dealing with these illnesses of her husband's—illnesses which the world has since, as a result of his influence, come to describe as psychosomatic. In his family life and social activities Freud found some relief from his unsuccessful early practice and hospital duties. He participated in the cultural life of Vienna. He was a voracious reader and liked to attend lectures. Once he listened to a lecture by Mark Twain, whom he admired. He loved the music of Mozart. Every Saturday night he played cards with his friends. On alternate Tuesdays he attended the meetings of the *B'nai B'rith* lodge in Vienna, to which in 1897 he gave a lecture on "Dreams." His hobby was collecting antiquities. In his study were statues of primitive Greek and Egyptian gods and goddesses. Significantly, in view of his later theory of ambivalence, his favorite statue was of the two-faced Roman god Janus. In a well-known photograph, the consultation room of the first modern analyst of the human psyche shows as its central feature an internationally famous piece of furniture—Freud's couch. Upon it the first trainees in psychoanalysis, and many other notable people, lay for their analysis by Freud. In this consultation room

Freud developed his new technique for treating neurologically disturbed patients.

Freud had the most profound sympathy for his first patients, who came to him complaining of pains or terrors which had no known cause and because of which they were teased by their relatives and ridiculed by their doctors. They lived in agony and needed help. The treatment for such persons in Freud's day was little short of quackery. Lying in a dark room, or going for horseback rides, or taking hot baths, or the ice-water cure, or—as one so-called specialist advised—the wearing of colored glasses, or the administering of sedatives or tonics—all were in vain. Freud tried the new method of applying electricity to his neurologically ill patients. He wrote to his friend Dr. Wilhelm Fliess, who had moved to Berlin and had turned over his practice in Vienna to Freud that none of these techniques worked, least of all the use of electricity—which, he wrote, had "no more relation to reality than some Egyptian dream book!" His letters to Fliess in those days reveal his dismay at being unable to relieve his patients.

One day, by accident, there fell into his hands a book written by one of Charcot's students, a Dr. Bernheim, who practiced in the French city of Nancy, and who described how a certain country physician, by the use of hypnotism, had cured patients whom Bernheim had not been able to help. Dr. Bernheim had then begun to prepare patients for operations in his hospital by means of hypnosis, and also used hypnosis in treating hysterics. Freud began trying hypnosis. After putting patients into a trance, he would suggest that they would feel better upon wakening. They did. However, some patients could not be hypnotized. One desperate patient Freud actually took to Nancy to be treated by Dr. Bernheim. The treatment proved to be a failure. Freud then began to doubt whether hypnotism could be applied to everybody and whether the so-called cures produced by it were anything but temporary.

One of his Viennese colleagues, Dr. Joseph Breuer, turned over a patient to Freud for hypnotic treatment, which apparently was a success. In the course of their collaboration, Breuer told Freud of a case he had had six years before, in which an intelligent girl seemed to have been cured of hysteria by hypnosis. The most significant of Breuer's observations was that when this girl talked freely about her own fantasies, the hysterical symptoms would disappear. He therefore urged her, under partial hypnosis, to talk about what was bothering her. Breuer's patient had been bedridden for five months with a paralysis of the limbs. One day she could not see properly; another day she had lost the ability to speak German and could only speak in English, which she had been taught as a child. The strangest symptom was one that occurred at a certain hour every afternoon, when she would undergo a kind of hypnoid fit in which she complained of being tormented; it was as though every day she were living over again some frightful experience. This experience was connected with her nursing of her dying father, whom she deeply loved but whose demands upon her she resented because they deprived her of the company of young men. As she brought out these painful memories her symptoms one by one disappeared, even though, according to Dr. Breuer, the cure required repeating many times the details of her experiences until her memories of them were complete. His clever patient called his method "the talking cure." For reasons which he did not wish to divulge, apparently because they would have been embarrassing to him, Breuer never published an account of the case. However, Freud sensed that Breuer had accidentally come upon the cause and probably the cure of hysteria. Breuer objected to such a conclusion as being based only on one case. Thereupon Freud decided to test the Breuer talking-out technique on his own patients.

Applying the Breuer method, Freud would urge a hypnotized patient to talk out his hidden memories, and after the patient had been awakened led him into discussing the experience. There were the cases of Miss Lucy and Miss Elizabeth. An English governess, Miss Lucy, complained of persistent colds and of being able to smell only burnt pastry. It transpired that two months before she had allowed the pastry to burn while she debated whether to open a letter from her mother, asking her to return from Vienna to England. In her discussion with Freud she admitted that she was secretly in love with her widowed employer, and therefore did not wish to leave, even though he totally ignored her. When she acknowledged to herself the futility of her attachment, Miss Lucy was cured.

The case of Miss Elizabeth was more dramatic. She had been suddenly paralyzed as she stood at her sister's deathbed. Her physicians believed this to be merely the shock of grief, but the paralysis grew worse, and a year later she still could not walk. Under Freud's treatment she admitted to having thought, at the onset of her paralysis, that she was glad her sister was dying, since she now might marry her brother-in-law. When Freud had helped her to face this shocking thought without considering herself morally depraved, Miss Elizabeth was cured. Becoming a cripple had been Miss Elizabeth's unconscious effort to run away from her guilt. Later, Freud had the extreme satisfaction of taking his wife to a Viennese ball, where he was able to point out Miss Elizabeth dancing with a young man whom she later married.

In 1893 Breuer finally agreed to join Freud in publishing an account of his only case, that of Anna O., together with Freud's own cases, in a book called *Studies in Hysteria*. Freud observed of the patients in these cases that "rather than face the feeling by which they were possessed and which might hurt their pride or sense of morality—they developed symptoms." "The hysteric," Freud wrote, "suffers mostly from hidden memories. . . . The mechanism producing hysteria is, on the one hand, an act of moral faint-heartedness, and, on the other hand, a protective process of the ego." Treating merely the physical symptoms would not work. The emotional trauma in the conscience of the individual which caused the hysteria must be treated. Freud noticed that in all these cases what the patients were afraid of facing was in some way connected with love and sex, which seemed to be forbidden to them. Breuer rejected this theory of the sexual basis of neurosis, and withdrew from his collaboration with Freud after the book was published because he was ashamed of the sexual theory and embarrassed by it as a family physician. At this point in his career Freud went on using the new method for curing neurosis absolutely alone. He felt that a discovery had been made which was as great as Pasteur's and which would revolutionize medicine.

As Freud proceeded, he found not only that some patients were not amenable to hypnosis, but also that he could get some of them to talk simply by putting his hand on their foreheads and asking them to remember. The pain of remembering forbidden thoughts was so great that as his patients lay on the couch, Freud learned to be patient until they could overcome their resistance to admitting their feelings. He suggested that his patients talk about anything that came into their minds. This he called *free association*. While his patients would talk freely, what they said was not free. Their thoughts were being determined by wishes they repressed. The cure was not to permit the patient to do what was not allowed but rather to allow the patient to become conscious of the desires he was repressing. When the patient brought into the foreground what was deeply buried in the background of his mind, the words and thoughts had to be analyzed. Using the Greek word *psyche* to mean not only the conscious process of the mind, but also these unconscious processes, Freud described his method as analysis of the psyche, or psychoanalysis.

Psychoanalysis required the patient to overcome his resistance to expressing desires he had repressed. Going back to the repressed episode and talking about his feelings in that situation was what Freud called *abreaction*. When past emotions that are considered harmful have been repressed they are in a sense dammed up. The psychic energy must burst out into some other channel. This may produce the paralysis of a limb. The cure which allows the dammed-up emotions to be given expression Freud called *catharsis*, from a Greek word which means "to let something out."

Catharsis relieves the patient of the tensions produced by repression. This talking-out also establishes a close attachment to the analyst, as Freud soon discovered. To the analyst the patient will transfer the mixed feelings he once had, and still has, toward other people who are intimate in his life—those feelings which he has been repressing or refusing to admit. Therefore, the patient may at one time hate and at another time love the analyst. The analyst becomes a kind of substitute mother, father or lover. By the process of catharsis combined with this transference, the patient relives his wishes without fear of being punished. When the patient begins to understand the true motives of his behavior, he starts to be re-educated and is on the way to being cured.

In the course of his treatment of many patients through

the technique of free association, Freud noticed that as
the patients allowed their thoughts and feelings to proceed
freely along a stream of consciousness, two subjects were
constantly being brought up—namely dreams and sexual
experiences. Freud's patients related dreams which seemed
to present a common pattern. He collected a thousand
dreams—dreams of falling, of flying and climbing, of fire
and water, of loved ones dying, of being caught in public
without clothes. Did these dreams have meaning? The
ancient Greek physician Hippocrates had diagnosed diseases from dreams of a kind that are now called "pro-
dromic," from the Greek *prodromos,* meaning "forerun-
ner." A dream of suffocating Hippocrates interpreted as a
prognosis of lung disease. A medieval Jewish physician,
Almoli, had written in Hebrew a popular book, *Pitron
Cholomoth,* on the meaning of dreams. Dreams, in short,
constituted a mystery that had fascinated men since ancient
times, but it remained for Freud to become their scientific
interpreter.

Freud observed that very little children dream of things
which have been denied them, but being still unashamed
of their desires, they openly admit the wishes behind their
dreams. On the other hand, the dreams of adults express
wishes they must suppress because these desires are not
approved by society. "Dreams are wish-fulfillments," Freud
wrote. They are motivated, he observed, primarily by sex
and aggression—drives over which control is suspended
during sleep. However, even in sleep a person may resist
desires, especially if they are presented in their crudest
form. These desires are then smuggled into dreams by
being transformed into innocuous symbols. A dream symbol is a disguise for a reprehensible wish. One may dream
of climbing a tree instead of masturbation, since the former
is permissible. Since Freud believed dreams were moti-

vated largely by sex repression, he saw such activities as riding a horse, plowing a field, firing a gun or opening a window as representing male or female genitalia and hence sexual intercourse. Dreams might also represent their opposite: being in a crowd, for example, could mean being alone. The interpretation had always to be confirmed by the dreamer in his own free association regarding the dream. One of Freud's most famous cases was that of Dora, whose dreams revealed the attachment to her father that was the source of her neurosis.

After five years of collecting and analyzing his patients' and, especially, his own dreams, Freud was ready to publish his greatest book. Violating his own privacy and using himself as a laboratory, he discovered "a psychological technique which makes it possible to interpret dreams." As Pasteur had revealed the cure of physical diseases by his analysis of hitherto unseen microbes, so Freud discovered the causes of neuroses lying hitherto unidentified in the dream. On January 2, 1900, he published *The Interpretation of Dreams*. The book did not receive one favorable review, and Freud wrote to his friend Fliess, "I am a Robinson Crusoe on a lonely island. I am reconciled to knowing that during my lifetime my work will be ignored." Thirty years later, *The Interpretation of Dreams* was acclaimed as a classic, the work of a genius, and in a third edition (1931) Freud wrote, "It contains, even according to my present judgment [Freud was then 75], the most valuable of all the discoveries it has been my good fortune to make. Insights such as this fall to one's lot but once in a lifetime."

Although *The Interpretation of Dreams* went unnoticed when first published, Freud had accomplished much for himself: through his analysis of his own dreams, he had found the cause of his own fear of travel and its cure. This fear was based on his childhood relations with his own father and mother, which confirmed his theory that infantile sexuality is the foundation of healthy or unhealthy emotional adulthood. It was during this period, in which Freud was psychoanalyzing himself and interpreting his dreams, that his father Jacob died (1897). Freud was then forty-one years old, and he wrote to his friend Fliess, "My hysteria is yielding at last." It had yielded because at last Freud understood his childhood relations with his own parents. His mother had doted on him, but his father had been reserved and critical. Nonetheless, Freud had had the satisfaction of knowing that an operation on his father's eye, shortly before the latter's last illness, had been possible only because of an eye anesthetic which Freud had himself discovered at the age of 26. He had discovered cocaine as an anesthetic, and had rashly been using it on himself as a tranquillizer during his early medical career. A friend to whom he confided his discovery had divulged the secret to another physician, who later took credit for it. Now, the father who had doubted the son's talents as a child was no longer a person to whom Freud had to prove himself. His jealous rivalry with his father had vanished, but Freud's attachment and attentiveness to his mother had never waned. Indeed, he had always felt more at ease with his mother than with his wife or his own children.

Freud struggled to find out the reason for his conflicting feelings regarding his father and mother, and it dawned upon him that as a child he had been acting out the role of Oedipus, the hero of the play of that name by the Greek dramatist Sophocles. Abandoned as a youth, Oedipus had not known his parents, but later he had unwittingly killed his father and then married the woman who unknown to him was his mother. Children do not commit patricide and incest, but they do play-act such things: A girl play-acts falling in love with her father, and a boy with his mother. These are necessary and usual childhood feelings, which later develop into the mature emotions concerning mating which serve to perpetuate the race. Freud concluded that the average healthy child eventually moves out of these loves and hates connected with its infantile competition for the favor of its parents. If it fails to do so, and becomes fixated in this oedipal stage, Freud concluded that the child becomes the victim of an Oedipus complex which prevents maturity.

The normal child moves out of the oedipal situation into various stages of gratification. If the child does not advance from one stage to the next, but remains fixated at one particular stage, its whole future adult behavior is neurotically affected. In the first stage the child concentrates on its own body, which it enjoys. Like the mythological youth Narcissus, who was enamored of his reflection in the pool and became rooted to the ground as a flower, the child finds pleasure in its own body. This stage Freud called *narcissism*. At the next stage, the child becomes attached to the first person of whom it is aware, namely its mother. Through this attachment the child learns the feeling of love; if the tendency toward attachment at this stage is denied, the child may grow up distrusting all adults unless it finds a substitute for the parent—what Freud called a surrogate parent. Later the child finds friends among its own sex, and during adolescence it begins to feel affection for those of the opposite sex. Parents who are unhappily married may prevent the child from passing from one stage to the next by holding on to the child in an unconscious effort to keep it from growing up.

Freud used the word *sexuality* in its broadest possible meaning as not being confined merely to the reproductive organs but to a variety of areas of pleasant sensation. He frequently used the Latin word *libido*, which means "desire for physical pleasure." The object of a child's pleasures changes as the child grows. The baby's first pleasure comes through the sucking by which it obtains food. This satisfaction through the mouth Freud called the oral phase. Then the baby becomes aware of the process of eliminating waste from its body, and of the connection of that process with pleasing or displeasing its mother. This is the anal phase. Finally, during adolescence, comes the genital phase, in which the sexual feeling is focused in the reproductive organs. As the person develops, different objects for love are found. First, as a baby, it loves itself; then, as a child, it loves the parent of the opposite sex; then it loves a member of its own sex and finally a member of the opposite sex. It is around the age of five that the child advances from loving the parent to loving someone outside the home. This Freud called the latency period. If the development prior to this has been arrested, neurotic patterns of behavior are the result. If the child is fixated in the oral stage, its personality may become too dependent and demanding of attention. If the child is fixated in the anal stage, it may enjoy punishing the mother and may develop hostility or a personality which enjoys hurting others. Denied the proper attention, a child may be fixed in the stage of hurting itself in order to get attention. Freud called the compulsion to hurt others *sadism*, and the tendency to allow others to hurt oneself *masochism*. Those who have failed to grow out of the period when they love a member of their own sex may develop homosexuality. Those who are fixed in the oedipal situation will look for a mother, not a wife, in marriage. Unless one properly grows out of one sexual stage and into the next, various types of neurotic disorders will develop.

It was only after his theory of sexual development was

published in a small book entitled *Three Contributions to the Theory of Sex,* that the people in Vienna began to mention the name of Freud. Few had shown any interest in his book on dreams, nor were many interested in his second book, *Psychopathology of Everyday Life,* in which Freud demonstrated how the slip of a tongue, the forgetting of a name or an object, the mispronunciation of a word, and even getting into an accident might be subtly motivated by desires one had wished to repress. These important discoveries were ignored as the public began to associate the name of Freud with sex. The Viennese public looked upon him as a salacious pornographer, and his own colleagues in psychiatry labeled him demented. Physicians asked for Freud's expulsion from the city's medical society because he inquired into the sexual life of his patients. Freud's reply was to publish more evidence in support of the theories for which the Victorian prudery of his time was unready.

Only a few adventurous souls of Vienna had the courage to accept Freud's discoveries because they dared to face themselves which these discoveries required. Those who formed Freud's first inner circle of Viennese disciples were Jews: Hans Sachs, Otto Rank, Wilhelm Stekel, Sandor Ferenczi, Alfred Adler and Max Eitigon, all of whom became pioneer contributors to the development of Freudian psychoanalysis. Then came unexpected recognition from outside Vienna. Under Dr. Eugene Bleuler and his assistant Dr. Karl Jung, the hospital for the mentally ill in Zurich had become so famous that physicians from abroad were coming there to study. Among them at this time were Karl Abraham of Berlin, Ernest Jones of London, and A. A. Brill of New York. This small group began to study together the new ideas of Freud, and soon each made a pilgrimage to Bergasse Street to meet him in person. By 1908 there were some forty persons, physicians and trained lay analysts, practicing Freud's techniques. That year, at Jung's suggestion, the first meeting of these psychoanalysts took place in Salzburg.

Freud's therapeutic techniques were slowly beginning to spread to Russia and even as far as India. To celebrate the twentieth anniversary of Clark University in Worcester, Massachusetts, its president, the psychologist Stanley Hall, invited Freud to give a course of lectures. Two famous Bostonians who attended were profoundly impressed, although one—the psychiatrist J. J. Putman—had reservations on Freud's sexual theories and the other—the psychologist William James—had reservations on Freud's interpretation of dreams. To protect psychoanalysis from charlatans and to maintain for it the highest scientific standards, Freud decided to form an International Psychoanalytic Association and to publish an official *Journal of Psychoanalysis*. Instead of a member of his original group of Viennese Jewish disciples, he chose the Swiss, Karl Jung, to be the association's president, since he wanted to remove from psychoanalysis "the danger of becoming a Jewish national affair."

Unquestionably the dominant personality, Freud was a patriarchal figure to some of his disciples, who resented his favoritism and were jealous of Jung, whom they saw becoming the "crown prince" and successor to Freud. This was especially true of Adler. Soon both Adler and Jung were rebelling against Freud, to become deviationists from his basic theory. Alfred Adler, calling his system "Individual Psychology," developed the theory of the inferiority complex, and declared that the urge to conquer was fundamental to the male ego, and that this urge included a masculine protest against the female. Adler maintained not sex but aggressessiveness was the impelling drive in human nature. Jung's defection was even more serious, since he intended to save psychoanalysis by freeing it from the sexual, which had alarmed so many. Freud declared that this was a cowardly evasion of scientific truth. Jung retained Freud's approach to the interpretation of dreams, while insisting that their basis was not sexual, but consisted of universal images from the distant past of man's history; according to his theory, this mythology was relived in the unconscious of each person and was the source of neurotic disorders. Jung's psychoanalysis, which was meant to free the person from these archetypes, he called "Analytical Psychology." Embittered by his pupils' betrayals, Freud said, "Pygmies standing on the shoulders of a giant can also claim they see a far country."

The dissenters reinforced popular opposition to Freud's psychoanalysis. The public concluded that psychoanalysis was all wrong, since former devotees like Adler and Jung had already started new schools. Freud, now fifty-eight, undertook a new campaign to defend his theories. He would attempt to popularize psychoanalysis by writing about it for the layman. He put the lectures he had been presenting over the years into a book entitled *Introductory Lectures on Psychoanalysis*. The charm and clarity of his style attracted readers, and the book was eventually translated into many languages. Nevertheless, during this period in his life Freud felt even more isolated because the First World War had separated him from his few devoted disciples. Some were drafted into the Austrian army, as were his three sons. It is surprising to note how patriotic Freud was in supporting the German side; yet as the war dragged on he became more and more depressed over the "unworthiness of human beings." His fear of dying soon prompted him to write the essays (unpublished until after his death) on *Mourning and Melancholia* and *Thoughts for the Times on War and Death*. He wrote to a friend, "The only cheerful news is the capture of Jerusalem by the English and the experiment they propose about a home for the Jews." When in 1918 the war came to an end, Freud wrote, "This war reveals our savage instincts in all their nakedness. We have let loose the evil spirits we have hidden deep inside of us, and which even after centuries have not yet been tamed."

To explain why and how the savage in us can be let loose, and to discover by what means man can succeed in taming the hate-filled, bloodthirsty savage in him became the task Freud was to pursue during the remaining twenty years of his life. His techniques involving free association, catharsis and transference, and the use in therapy of his new insights into sex and dreams, were being furthered and deepened by fellow analysts all over the world, whom his works had inspired. To each of his first faithful six, Freud gave a reproduction of the ancient Roman ring he wore, on which was engraved the head of Jove. These six were to direct the rapidly growing movement of psychoanalysis and the establishment of professional associations in many countries, and to keep the movement faithful to the ways of its creator. (Otto Rank, one of the six, later deserted, to propound the theory that neurosis came from the shock or trauma of birth and to develop his own treatment, called "Will Therapy." Although Ferenczi did not secede, he altered the Freudian technique. Holding that neurosis was an acting out of repressed feelings and that it resulted primarily from being unloved in childhood, he maintained that therapy should include the active participation of the analyst, and that the patient should be convinced of the analyst's affectional concern.)

Non-medical interest in the psychoanalytic interpretation of sociology, anthropology, religion and art had led Freud earlier to found an international journal for workers in these fields. This journal, called *Imago,* attracted articles from all over the world. Now that his movement had been well launched, Freud devoted his time (or what remained of it after his psychoanalytic practice, which now included world-famous figures as his patients) to collecting his thoughts and writing on the two great themes which the barbarism of the First World War had impelled him to study—first, the savage in man, and second, how it might be tamed.

These two themes were analyzed in three books written during the ten years following the First World War. They were *The Ego and the Id, The Future of an Illusion* and *Civilization and Its Discontents.* Having made his major scientific contributions to psychoanalysis, Freud now began to apply his creative imagination to a more speculative exploration of human behavior. How had man become as he was in the twentieth century? The answer to this question called for a psychological study of man's past history. Freud had already made two attempts to demonstrate how important the historical past of man was to an understanding of his present psyche. Here, despite his admiration of Darwin, Freud supported the Lamarckian theory that acquired characteristics are inherited. In an earlier book, entitled *Beyond the Pleasure Principle,* Freud had described the human tendency to return to more primitive stages of behavior. Freud had noticed, especially in the cruelty of war and the frequent abuse of sex for destructive purposes, that there existed in man a force for self-destruction. This Freud called the Death Instinct, as opposed to the Life Instinct with which it was in conflict. Aggression against others was a deflection of this drive to destroy oneself, in the manner of a ruler who foments a war in order to forstall a rebellion of his subjects against himself.

In another, earlier study, *Totem and Taboo*, Freud had observed that the primitive man was not as able as the civilized man to protect himself against the temptation to commit incest with his mother. Hostility to his father was not as readily reconciled by the primitive as it was by the civilized man. Therefore, to protect himself against the "horror of incest," primitive man had set up a whole system of taboos, especially against incestuous marriages. The primitive man also worshiped totem images of animals which he made to symbolize the father of the human herd. The father of the prehistoric human herd was slain by the sons in their rivalry for the females who had been denied them by the father. The sons then worshiped the totem symbol of the slain father in order to atone for their crime. Freud now joined these two theories—the primitive man's destructive aggression against himself and his guilt of parricide. Civilization, and especially religion, Freud asserted, had developed in order to assuage this guilt and to restrain the aggression of the savage in man. This combined aggression and guilt continued to work unconsciously in modern man.

In *The Ego and the Id*, Freud explored more deeply this unconscious past. Now he concluded that the unconscious contained more than the actual childhood feelings his patients had repressed and then revealed in their dreams and free association. In man's unconscious there dwelt feelings to which the savage man had been subject millions of years ago. In fact, these unconscious elements were present in both the consciousness and the conscience of modern man. This led Freud to introduce his famous three-part division of the human psyche—the id, the ego and the superego. We are conscious, he concluded, only of the trivial manifestations of each of these divisions, and are unaware of their most important operations. The first division, of which we are the least aware, consists of the primitive, libidinal, instinctual drives, mainly sexual, which seek outside objects for gratification. In the savage, these drives for self-gratification will lead him to kill for food or to obtain a mate. This collection of drives Freud labeled the *id*, from the Latin impersonal pronoun "it." Savage man then began to have an awareness of himself, of an "I," and developed a sense of the real world about him. This made him realize that certain instincts would have to be controlled in order to better his chances of survival. This awareness of self and of reality Freud called the *ego*. In advancing toward a less savage society, man developed certain patterns of behavior, which were then transmitted to the next generation. These habits of behavior, super-imposed from without, Freud called the *superego*. As the savage passed through the stages of a more civilized society, in his superego were accumulated the controlling ideals of that society. The savage in every child is controlled when that child identifies itself with the ideal superego of its parents. What is called conscience is the result of the end-less unconscious struggle of the person—the ego—against society's restraining ideals—the superego—for control of the savage instincts—the id—in each man. When the savage instincts find no outlet on the outside they turn inward. The ego represses these savage instincts at the bidding of the superego; but at the same time the ego tries to over-come the sense of guilt derived from the superego. Even in the superego there is a feeling of guilt when the individ-ual is not able to meet the highest ideals of civilized society; this guilt is appeased by seeking punishment. Therefore, the unconscious is both moral and immoral.

According to this Freudian analysis, a healthy person is one whose ego is able to harmonize his instinct with his conscience. A person overpowered by instinct may develop into a psychopathic delinquent. One in whom conscience is so strong that it weighs one down with imaginary guilt feelings may become neurotic. When a person totally ignores exterior moral requirements he is a psychotic. Freud's cure for these disorders of the ego was not an unbridled release of instincts. On the contrary, as his famous epigram, "Where id was, ego should be" suggests, he insisted upon the proper control of instinct. However, he tied up the control of instinct with sex as the most abused of all instinctive drives, and this led him to say also, "Where there is normal sex life, there can be no neurosis."

It is true that when civilization represses normal sex life, it produces neurotic individuals. However, civilization itself was won at the expense of repressing the most primitive desires. It began when individuals banded together to resist the "brute force" of another individual, especially as that individual tried to gratify his sexual impulses. That savage individual was made to feel that his animal aggression against another person in order to satisfy himself was wrong. He was made to feel guilty, and this guilt was a way of internalizing his aggression—directing it against himself rather than against others. This is the origin of conscience. "This sense of guilt," Freud wrote, "is the most important problem in the evolution of culture. . . . The price of progress in civilization is paid by forfeiting happiness through heightening of the sense of guilt." On the other hand, civilization can reach a point of no return, in that it no longer offers acceptable compensation for repressing self-gratification. Indeed, it may make ethical demands that are so unrealistically high as to be impossible to fulfill, so that the frustrations will cause even greater misery than that caused by aggression. Then the primitive will break out of the restraints of culture and become a menace to civilization. These conclusions outlined by Freud in *Civilization and Its Discontents,* published in 1929, were to receive terrifying confirmation in the ascendancy of Hitler four years later.

Freud was pessimistic about group life, although he was more optimistic that psychotherapy could help the individual develop a mature balance between self-gratification and self-control. In the behavior of a group he found much that was irrational and represented a return to the primitive. The mere intensification of group life, he believed, would not necessarily preserve or advance civilization. Group life did not alter individual differences in power and influence, which were exploited by aggressive men for their own purposes. Leaders within a group exploited primitive fears. Freud exposed the naïveté of Marx in thinking that the economic man could build a mechanical utopia without regard to these interior human equations. When a communist told him that the Bolshevik revolution would result in some years of misery and chaos but would then be followed by universal peace and prosperity, Freud replied, "I believe the first half." He saw that the abolition of private property could not resolve the inner conflicts of man. It is no wonder that Russian Communists have labeled Freudianism a reactionary tool of the bourgeoisie. Social changes may take place, but, said Freud, "Difficulties inherent in the very nature of culture will not yield to any efforts at reform."

These "difficulties inherent in the very nature of culture" Freud came more and more to associate with the rise of religion. Religion he saw as the major force which civilization had developed in order to repress the savage instinct in man. Freud himself did not believe in a supernatural being. He felt that he had no emotional need for a God, particularly after psychoanalyzing himself and feeling that he had overcome his own childhood wish for the death of his father in his rivalry with the latter over his mother. To Freud, religion was a reaction to this primordial Oedipus complex. "God is psychologically nothing other than a magnified father; we are shown every day how young people can lose their religious faith as soon as the father's authority collapses. We must recognize the root of religious need as lying in the parental complex." Freud combined his clinical observation of the child's relation to his father with his anthropological theory about the behavior of the prehistoric human herd. The members of the earliest human herd enacted overtly the pattern which the infant enacts covertly. Not being civilized, the primitive savage actually murdered his father. The fear and guilt which this act entailed would have destroyed any chance for mankind to move out of barbarism were it not for man's discovery of a wonderful way to make expiation. This way of atonement was found in the mind's creation of an illusion—God, the Father who never really died. God's protection and love for his children may always be assured by certain ritualistic behavior which will guarantee his favor.

Freud observed that certain of his neurotic patients performed acts that were irrational, such as repeatedly washing their hands, and that they were obsessed by such rituals through a compulsion to atone for guilts deep in their unconscious. Freud put religious rituals into the same category of obsessional neurosis, and held that the "illusion" of religion might "save individuals from neurosis" but could do little more than that. He expressed the belief that this "illusion" would have no "future" if mankind could mature out of its infantile fear of and dependence upon a universal Father. He acknowledged that ethical controls were necessary for civilization, but argued that these would be more effective without religious support. "Experience teaches us," Freud wrote, "that the world is not a nursery. The ethical commands to which religion seeks to lend its weight require some other foundation instead, since human society cannot do without them and it is dangerous to link up obedience to them with religious belief." This was the explosive theme of Freud's book, *The Future of an Illusion*.

The public attack on Freud was now greater because of his religious theories than it had been because of his sexual theory. The shocked traditionalists condemned him outright. On the other hand, the liberal religionists saw in Freud's psychology of religion a new and needed warning against man's infantile tendency to use religion as a quick and sure way of resolving unfulfilled wishes. Freud had always insisted that he had used the word *illusion* in its specific psychological sense, and not as the equivalent of "error." When wish-fulfillment was the prominent factor in motivation, one had an illusion, and this illusion might or might not be contrary to fact. In other words, Freud did not prove or disprove the existence of a God; he only proved that man's need for a belief in the existence of a God had behind it powerful primitive origins, in addition to the persistence into adulthood of a helpless child's reliance on a Father, and that therefore these religious beliefs could be accounted for whether or not there really was a God. These religious beliefs do strengthen ethics, but at the same time, Freud believed, they made for immature rigidity in a person.

In view of his disbelief in a supernatural being, it is surprising to find that Freud had nonetheless a continuing interest in the occult. His skepticism about the existence of a God contrasts with his credulity about the possibility of the existence of thought in space. He visited mediums to attempt communication with the dead; he explored clair-voyance, astrology, mental telepathy, extrasensory percep-tion and thought transference, and even tried to predict his own death by means of numerology. Of course, Freud examined these "supernatural" phenomena critically. Most of them he regarded as projections of unconscious wishes retranslated into mental processes. Nevertheless, his inter-est in psychical research was a constant source of embarrass-ment to his more skeptical colleagues and disciples. If one could believe in thoughts floating through the air, they argued, one could also believe in God. If thoughts could be transferred through space, psychoanalysis itself might be revolutionized. One might be able to be psychoanalyzed without actually visiting the analyst. Freud defended him-self against these jokes at his expense by simply insisting that telepathy was his private affair, "like my Jewishness and my passion for smoking," and adding, "Telepathy is in essence alien to psychoanalysis."

Freud's interest in religion, as well as in psychical research, demonstrates the wide range of his bold mind. If his conclusions in regard to these interests shocked society, he would nonetheless pursue the search for truth as he saw it. He was now past seventy, and was still adding to the structure of his theory of man's psyche which he had begun to build thirty years before. He still lived at 19 Bergasse Street, in the more genteel Jewish ghetto section of Vienna. His family of six children had now grown up. All were married except Anna, who remained by her father's side to the end and carried the mantle of his genius. His three sons engaged in other professions. He expe-rienced the loss of a daughter and of a four-year-old grand-child of whose death his friends said that it was the only time they had known Freud to shed tears. The death of his mother at ninety-three gave him the opportunity to bury with her those childhood wishes which, as revealed to him in his own analysis, had started Freud on the way to his great discovery. His own fatal illness was finally made known to him. He was an inveterate smoker of twenty cigars a day, and whether this had anything to do with his illness or not, a scar left on his jaw as a result of a childhood accident had now become cancerous. During the last years of his life he underwent thirty-three operations on his jaw, and wore a removable artificial mouthpiece which impeded his speech.

Freud stoically accepted his personal suffering even as in the early years of his career he had accepted his lonely ostracism. In fact, he had shown the same stoical reserve in regard to his new world-wide fame. Famous people came for analysis. Those whom he could not take he referred to his disciples. Two who came to him remained his undying friends and were involved in his rescue from the Nazis. They were W. C. Bullitt, the United States Ambassador to France, and Princess Marie Bonaparte, the sister-in-law of the King of Greece and a descendant of Napoleon. Princess Marie in particular became Freud's devoted disciple. She was only one of the many disciples who appeared from all over the world. Exponents of his views that unhealthy emotions affect the body became pioneers in the development of psychosomatic medicine. Freudian terms—Oedipus complex, libido, fixation, repression, inhibition, transference, narcissism, Freudian slip, id, ego, superego, and so on—became a part of the language. His insights into factors which condition the emotions of children brought about radical changes in education, in child guidance and in the attitude toward juvenile delinquency. The Hearst newspapers offered Freud $25,000 to come to Chicago to testify in the famous Leopold-Loeb case. Because of Freud's insight into the relationships between man and woman

Samuel Goldwyn offered him $100,000 to serve as consultant for a picture on Cleopatra. All these commercial exploitations Freud of course declined. The more serious influence of his ideas in the non-medical field was recognized in his own lifetime. Painters like Picasso and Salvador Dali were illustrating these hidden symbols of man's unconscious life; writers, for example James Joyce in his *Ulysses,* were developing the stream-of-consciousness style of writing; the playwright Eugene O'Neill dramatized the Freudian concept of the attachment of a child to a father or a mother in his plays *Strange Interlude* and *Mourning Becomes Electra.* On Freud's seventy-fifth birthday, even psychiatrists who were noted enemies of his theories gave public recognition to his genius. He received the Goethe prize, the highest literary award that Germany could give. Even the Czech government celebrated the occasion of his seventy-fifth birthday by placing a plaque on the house in Freiberg where he had been born.

On the occasion of Freud's eightieth birthday, a special postoffice had to be set up on Bergasse Street to receive the mail that began arriving from all over the world. The outstanding German writer of the twentieth century, Thomas Mann, gave the principal address at the celebration on May 6, 1936. In that address Mann said, "As physician and psychologist, as philosopher and artist, this courageous seer and healer has for two generations been a guide to hidden and undreamed-of-regions of the human soul. . . . In all spheres of human science, in the study of literature and art, in the evolution of religion and prehistory, mythology, folklore and pedagogics, and last, not least, in poetry itself, his achievement has left a deep mark; and, we feel sure, if any deed of our race remains unforgotten, it will be his deed of penetrating into the depths of the human mind." A copy of Mann's address was signed by

Romain Rolland, H. G. Wells, Virginia Woolf, Stefan Zweig, and nearly two hundred other writers and artists, and was personally delivered to Freud by Thomas Mann. Yet, with all this admiration, Freud never misconstrued his fame as being a full acceptance of his theories, for as he had once said, "One cannot exaggerate the inner resistance against accepting unconscious tendencies."

Two of these unconscious tendencies came together at the close of Freud's life. The resistance of Freud himself made him unable fully to accept the one; the resistance of the world made it unable to accept the other. For unconscious reasons, Freud resisted accepting fully the implications of his being a Jew; for unconscious reasons, civilization resisted accepting fully the implications of his theory concerning the return of society to the primitive—notably that the barometer of this regression was anti-Semitism. Freud concerned himself with the fact that he was a Jew not only in his analysis of himself but also in his struggle to free the psychoanalytic movement from being labeled a "Jewish affair." However, it was not until the last ten years of his life, which coincided with the success of Nazism and the beginning of its horrifying program for annihilating the Jews, that Freud undertook a thoroughgoing analysis of the causes of anti-Semitism, and of his ambivalence about being a Jew himself. The product of this combined effort was his last book, *Moses and Monotheism.*

The Nazis had taken over Austria in 1938. Freud's books had already been burned in Nazi Germany, and that event prompted Freud to make this wry observation, "What progress we are making; in the Middle Ages they would have burned *me;* nowadays they are content with burning my books." One year later the Nazis would have also burned his body, just as they sent to the gas ovens his four elderly sisters, who declined to leave Vienna with him. Storm Troopers occupied his home, confiscated his possessions, money and books, and arrested his beloved daughter Anna. The humiliation, the beatings and the nightmare of the concentration camp had begun for the Jews of Vienna. Freud thought he had no choice but to hold out to the end; but through the influence of Ambassador Bullitt, the United States government persuaded Hitler to allow Freud, now eighty-two years old, to leave with his family. Princess Marie Bonaparte paid the Nazis a large ransom. Dr. Ernest Jones arranged for his diplomatic clearance and provided a home and a public welcome in London. While his fellow Jews in Europe were about to experience the worst persecution in their long history of suffering, the dying Freud completed *Moses and Monotheism* in London.

Sections of *Moses and Monotheism* had already been published in the journal *Imago,* and important Jewish leaders began to plead with Freud not to publish the book, since it would only further demoralize the Jews in their hour of greatest trial. They took this position because Freud had set forth in his book the conclusion that the greatest of all Jews, Moses, had not been a Jew at all, but an Egyptian. This notion had been advanced some years before by an anti-Semitic German biblical scholar named Sellin. Freud had always admitted that he was weakest in his knowledge of the Bible; but the reason why he should have taken the opinion of a discredited anti-Semitic German exegete and disclaim Moses as a Jew is related to Freud's personal struggle with his own Jewishness. Freud's unfounded theories about Moses are much more a portrayal of his own attitude toward his Jewishness than they are a portrayal of Moses.

Before his self-analysis, there is little doubt that Freud

suffered from Jewish self-hate. He was convinced of a
theory which he called the "family romance"—namely, that
a child frequently entertains the fantasy that it is a foster
child born of unknown parents superior to his real parents
who, as he imagines, have merely adopted him. Ernest
Jones says Freud was "obsessed" by this idea, which he
used to explain the character not only of Moses but also
of Leonardo da Vinci and of Shakespeare. When he was
forty-four Freud interpreted his own dreams as wish-fulfillments based on his desire to conquer his feeling of inferiority because he was a Jew. In one dream he assumed the
role of a bigoted Minister of Education. In real life this
minister had refused Freud a position in the medical school
because he was a Jew. In that role, Freud dreamed of treating two Jewish colleagues badly. In other words, to compensate for his frustration by a real enemy who is the
stronger, the Jew may become an aggressor against a fellow
Jew whose enmity is imaginary but is vulnerable. Freud's
self-analysis led him out of this trap of self-punishment. He
then turned, in his *Wit and Witticism*, to the examination
of Jewish jokes as a form of relief from frustration and a
safe redress of grievance. Humor, according to his view, is
only one side of the coin, the other side of which is tragedy.

His next step involved his liberation from the fear of his
father. When Freud was a lad of ten, his father had related
to him a story of his own cowardice back in Freiberg, where
he had been assaulted by an anti-Semite. Ever after, the
Semitic Carthaginian general Hannibal had been a fantasy
hero for Freud because Hannibal's father, in contrast with
his own, had made his son swear to take vengeance on the
Roman persecutors of Carthage. Freud, then in his forties,
decided that the best defense as a Jew was a courageous
offense—a fearless challenging of every prejudice, even of
those which enjoyed the protection of Christianity; and

this is one of the reasons he advanced his notion that psychoanalysis could only have been discovered by a Jew.

Freud was even more convinced of the special Jewish affinity for psychoanalysis when his Swiss disciple Karl Jung, who was the son of a Christian pastor, defected and substituted his mythological archetypes for Freud's basic premise concerning infantile sexuality. Trying to conciliate Jung and to retain his loyalty, Freud said, "We Jews, if we want to cooperate with other people, have to develop a little masochism and be prepared to endure a certain amount of injustice." Jung nevertheless broke with Freud, and later even accepted an appointment from the Nazis. Freud concluded that it was easier for a Jew than for a Christian to break through the unconscious inner resistance to psychoanalysis. From Freud's Jewish background, and also from his theory of religion, may be deduced the two reasons why Freud thought it easier for a Jew to accept psychoanalysis.

Since according to the psychoanalytic point of view there are no accidents, Freud's interest in the occult and in such subjects as numerology was not accidental. This interest stemmed indirectly from Jewish mysticism, with which Freud was personally acquainted. Freud's family, as well as that of the Bernays, his in-laws, not only had a rabbinic background but were steeped in the current Jewish mystical movement known as Hassidism. A mystical revolt against legalistic orthodox rabbinism, Hassidism was based on the Cabbala, an esoteric interpretation of Judaism. Freud records discussing the Cabbala with one of his closest followers. Like himself, these followers were recently emancipated from the Jewish ghetto. Breuer was the son of a Hassidic rabbi, and Freud's most intimate friend, Fliess, grew up with Jewish mysticism. In his *Interpretation of Dreams* Freud refers to a mystical Jewish physician of the sixteenth century, Solomon Almoli, who in his popular book *The Solution of Dreams* sought to train his readers how to interpret dreams. Drawing on his knowledge of the Talmud, Almoli identified sexual symbolism, wish-fulfillment and word play as elements of the dream, in a way that is a remarkable parallel with modern psychoanalytical theory.

The similarities between psychoanalysis and the *Zohar*, the classic collection of Jewish mysticism written and compiled in the Middle Ages, are so startling that they appear to be more than accidental. Counterparts of Freudian theory are found in the *Zohar*, where the divine act of creation is given an erotic character, and where sex relations are treated as avenues to salvation. Even Freud's apparent originality regarding the Oedipus complex is reflected in the *Zohar's* mystical-erotic idea of man having intimate relations with the female partner of the Father God, called the Shekinah. Freud's use of free association in analysis finds striking similarity in the thirteenth-century cabbalist Samuel Abulafia, who used a skipping from one concept to another in order, as Abulafia said, "to unseal the soul, to untie the knots which bind it." On his seventieth birthday, in expressing his gratitude to the members of the *B'nai B'rith* Lodge in Vienna for their understanding friendship, Freud made the following reference to this Jewish mystical background: "There remained other things to make the attraction of Judaism and Jews irresistible—many dark emotional forces, all the more potent for being so hard to group in words, as well as the clear consciousness of our inner identity, the intimacy that comes from the same psychic structure." The origins of modern science can be seen, in the case of Newton, to be related to theological speculations. The origins of modern psychoanalysis can be seen in Freud's effort to separate and abandon the supernatural elements in Jewish mysticism, and to use its insight for his discoveries. Even if one discredits the Jewish mystical origins of Freud's thinking, or differs with Professor David Bakan, who has called psychoanalysis a scientific secularization of the Cabbala, the fact remains that Judaism was less shocked by Freud's theories than was Christianity. Not handicapped by the Pauline-Christian derogation of sex, Freud could view civilization as a sublimation of sexual energy—a theory long ago implied by the Talmudic rabbis in their well-known saying that were it not for the *Yetzer Ra*—the sexual instinct—men would not build homes.

The second reason for Freud's belief that the Jews had a peculiar affinity for psychoanalysis is to be found in his analysis of Judaism and Christianity along psychological lines. The difference between these two related religions, according to Freud, lay in the difference between the image of Moses and the image of Jesus as seen in terms of the basic Oedipus complex. In Christianity, God demands the death of His son to atone for mankind's guilt of parricide. There is a "return to the repressed" of the primitive man in the central symbols of Christianity. Christ on the Cross and the communion feast of his body compel the Christian worshiper to identify himself with the slain son. This revives unconsciously in the Christian the guilt of the prehistoric crime of parricide. In Judaism, Freud asserted, although the Israelites murdered Moses, nonetheless they were able to atone for their guilt by circumcision, which Freud erroneously regarded Moses himself as having introduced. In Paul's pagan, primitive fantasy about Jesus, there is a son who the father insists must die; but in the first Jew, Abraham, there is a father whose God tells him not to slay his son; Abraham only circumcises the boy. Even in the light of his own formula, had Freud more fully understood the Abraham-Isaac story as it is found in the Bible, he would not have invented the preposterous murder of Moses, which is not found there, nor would he have gone to the extreme of calling Moses an Egyptian simply because of his name; for if the president of a Union of Orthodox Rabbis can have a Yankee name like Adams, no doubt a Jew could have had an Egyptian name like Moses. However, Freud did maintain that by making circumcision not a hygienic measure but a religious one, the sign of a covenant with God the Father, the Jews had achieved a brilliant peaceful resolution of the prehistoric herd conflict between the father and the son. The sign of circumcision proved to the son that his father accepted him and that he need no longer have any fear of his father's castrating him in retaliation. Furthermore, Freud insisted that circumcision, the physical mark of difference between Christian and Jew, symbolized the powerful unconscious origin of anti-Semitism. Anti-Semitism, as defined by Freud, is envy and hate for the son who has been successful in making peace with his Father, and whom none now can destroy since it is his Father's will that he shall live.

Freud attributed the uniqueness of Judaism to the greatness of one man, Moses, who freed Israel not merely from slavery in Egypt, but also from the fantasy fears of guilt-ridden primitive man. Freud thought of himself as the liberator of modern man from enslavement to the unconscious, so that in the continuing struggle between the life instinct and the self-destructive instinct man might be enabled better to confront the reality of this world and to direct it toward healthier goals. The evidence strongly suggests that, as the discoverer of a new law of dynamics for the freedom of the mind, Freud actually identified himself with the Moses he so profoundly admired.

The genius of Freud was to open up more problems than he solved about the nature of man. To him the sign of maturity was not the absence of problems but the realistic facing of problems, no matter how deeply one was obliged to probe in order to uncover the unconscious layers of the past in each individual and in the past of the whole human race. He offered no panacea for achieving peace of mind. On the contrary, he was a disturber of the mind. Therefore in the beginning a state of belligerency existed between twentieth-century attitudes and Freud's theories on medical science, on social history and on religion. The present phase is an effort to arrive at a peaceful coexistence with Freudian ideas and even, to a smaller degree, an effort at active cooperation.

The great progress in present-day psychosomatic medicine is the fruit of the seeds Freud had sown, although the increasing use of drugs—chemotherapy—in treating serious neurotic and psychotic disorders has been challenging Freudian verbal psychotherapy. Although the sexual causes of neurotic behavior are still a primary consideration in modern psychoanalysis, the unconscious aspects of the non-repressed, the non-sexual ego in man are being actively explored by the school of "Ego Psychology."

Although literature and art have been influenced by Freud's emphasis on the unconscious truth revealed in the stream of consciousness, literature and art are now known to be worse than second-rate if they merely reproduce a psychoanalytic case history. Plays and movies concerned merely with sex are not serious portrayals of character. Freud himself would hold no brief for those who simply confuse their urges with art, who always blame their parents in a crisis, or who worship their analysts as gods. Certainly a rebel himself, Freud would not approve the tendency to regard anyone who criticizes the status quo as sick and neurotic rather than as a person making a valid protest. Since he declared that psychoanalysis was a technique and not a total philosophy of life, Freud would also not approve the delusion that to be a psychoanalyst automatically qualifies one as an authority whose opinion on any subject is to be accepted.

Even in his critical attitude towards religion, Freud would have welcomed a joint undertaking to explore its depths further and to rescue religious morality from irrational piety. To the first clergyman to become one of his disciples, Oskar Pfister, he wrote: "In itself, psychoanalysis is neither religious nor the opposite, but an important instrument which can serve the clergy as well as the laity, when it is used only to free suffering people. I have been very struck at realizing how I had never thought of the extraordinary help the psychoanalytic method can be in pastoral work, probably because wicked heretics like myself are far away from that circle." Freud even granted that probably healthy "religious piety stifles neurosis," but added that because people are no longer really religious, those who cannot endure their suffering must needs turn to psychoanalysis to master their "obdurate instincts." Worried about the long time it took for a patient to be freed from his transference to his analyst without any guarantee of relapse, Freud wrote to the clergyman Pfister: "It is easier for you in this respect than for us physicians because you sublimate the transference on to religion and ethics, and that is not easy with seriously ill people."

Measured by the degree of its penetration into popular thinking, the greatest effect of the Freudian revolution upon the image of man has been a new awareness of childhood as the most important stage in personal development. There is a new emphasis on tender love as the most satisfactory therapeutic agent in the establishing as well as the healing of human relationships. Though Freud admitted he did not really understand women, his studies have given women a new sense of their own dignity. Indeed, what explains Freud's popularity in America in contrast with his condemnation in Russia is Freud's insistence that the individual's mature fulfillment, satisfaction and happiness are primary to civilization, and that the communist experiment was based on a naïve optimism in supposing that it could solve the inner conflicts of man simply by the production of material things.

These inner conflicts in man involve sexuality, but Freud is completely misinterpreted by those who would use his theories to justify sexual license and immorality. On the contrary, Freud insisted that the mature man accepts limitations and that civilization requires a degree of repression. Freud warned mankind that unless the right, mature and rational kind of self-discipline brought about a more rapid advance in culture than heretofore, men resenting the sacrifice of their savage instincts to the demands of society would wonder whether civilization was worth the price. The Nazis' mad return to barbarism proved how right Freud was. Man becomes civilized by a rational, conscious awareness of and control over the irrational. Freud hoped man could do this before it was too late.

Freud tried to change the image of man in the twentieth century in order to make man ready for the twenty-first century. He believed that the only kind of change in life which means anything is not the mere elaboration of machines, but a change in people's thinking, a change in their deepest convictions, a change which makes them see life and the world in a different way.

VI: Albert Einstein

"When I behold Thy heavens, the work of Thy fingers, the moon and the stars which Thou hast established; what is man that Thou art mindful of him?" So wrote the Hebrew poet of Psalm 8. He must have composed his lines after looking up into the heavens at night, for he does not mention the sun. On the other hand, Psalm 19 reads: "The heavens declare the glory of God . . . In them hath He set a tent for the sun, which is as a bridegroom coming out of his chamber, and rejoiceth as a strong man to run his course. His going forth is from the end of the heaven, and his circuit unto the ends of it; and there is nothing hid from the heat thereof." Unlike the quiet, subdued evening meditation of Psalm 8, Psalm 19 is a vigorous daytime song. It praises the sun by comparing it to a happy, virile bridegroom.

When any person makes any observation, be it artistic or scientific, to understand what has been said, it is always relevant to know the location of the observer. The writer of Psalm 8 viewed the heavens at night; the writer of Psalm 19 viewed them during the day. Any idea held by a person has a relation to where that person stands. The expression "where that person stands" is used here both literally and figuratively.

Nothing has so inspired man to thought as has the sight of the sky—which "day unto day uttereth speech, and night unto night revealeth knowledge." Man has searched for the answer to the riddle of the universe which the heavens place before his eyes. In every age, only strong men have had the courage to confront that impenetrable mystery. The author of the Book of Job described the strength such a man must have simply to be able to ask the question: "Gird up thy loins like a man; for I will demand of thee, and declare thou unto Me. Where wast thou when I laid the foundations of the earth? Declare, if thou hast understanding. Who determined the measures thereof, if thou knowest? . . . Whereupon were the foundations thereof fastened? Or who laid the cornerstone thereof, when the morning stars sang together . . .? Where is the way to the dwelling of light? . . . Canst thou bind the chains of the Pleiades, or loose the bands of Orion? . . . Knowest thou the ordinances of the heavens?"

Modern as well as ancient man has tried to explain the laws by which the universe is run. The differences in the results of their respective efforts are also related to location —to where each thought he was standing when he made his observations. The Hebrews asked the questions, but the Greeks were the first to attempt rational answers. It is probable that the ancient Hebrews sought no answers because by a leap of faith they intuitively arrived at what they thought was the answer in their one God, the single originator and director of the heavens as well as of the earth. In contrast, the Greeks had many gods, each controlling the actions of a separate planet. However, a sound Greek thinker was puzzled as to why, if the behavior of earth, moon, sun and stars was dependent on the whims of these self-willed, unpredictable and capricious Greek gods, the planets nevertheless appeared to move in such an orderly, cooperative fashion. The planets did not behave like the gods on Olympus who were incessantly quarreling with each other.

About the time that the Psalmist and the author of the Book of Job were asking the questions, Pythagoras was advancing .an answer. He was the founder of a Greek religious, mystical and ascetic brotherhood. Pythagoras thought arithmetic was good for other purposes than mere commerce. He turned to numbers to explain life and the universe. Pythagoras observed that in order to sound an octave, one of the two strings on a musical instrument had to be twice the length of the other. From this he deduced that the nature of anything might be known if you knew its position in a series of numbers. Pythagoras suggested that the whole cosmos was arranged like a musical scale, and that the planets corresponded to a series of numbers. He represented number one with one dot, two with two dots, and so on. Placing these dots in series, Pythagoras was able to form triangles and squares; and thus he became the inventor of geometry. Pythagoras was the first man known to have held that the earth was round and the universe a sphere. However, he believed the earth was the center and that around it revolved the seven known planets like seven notes on a musical scale. From this Pythagoras poetically described the harmony of the heavens as "the music of the spheres."

Twenty-five hundred years ago, the theory of Pythagoras was a revolutionary change. The mythological world in which each planet was ruled by a capricious god was changed into a universe operating according to definite geometric patterns and mathematical relations. Two hundred years later another Greek, Euclid, elaborated on these geometric figures by proving all bodies had three dimensions—length, breadth and width. These bodies, as described in Euclid's famous textbook, moved in straight lines, and wherever those lines were parallel they could never meet. In the second century of the common era, an Alexandrian Greek, Ptolemy, popularized these theories.

For fifteen hundred years men accepted the Greek idea that the earth was the center of the universe, but they forgot Pythagoras' idea that the earth was a sphere. During the time of Columbus the idea that the earth was flat was finally abandoned; but not until the sixteenth and seventeenth centuries were the Greek ideas of the centrality of the earth disproved. Then Copernicus proved that the earth circled about the sun. Kepler demonstrated how the planets orbited, not in circles but in ellipses, attracted by what he called the magnetic spirit of the sun. For continuing these deductions, Galileo would have forfeited his life to the Inquisition had he not recanted. The greatest of the observers was Newton. In the eighteenth century Newton proved that the planets, including the earth, rotated about the sun. Pulled toward it by the force of gravity, all the planets moved around the sun in a fixed order. Newton conceived of the universe as being bathed in a substance he called "ether." Through this ether, which occupied all of space, particles of matter pulled at each other. According to Newton, light rays were also made up of minute, corpuscular particles pulling at each other as they speeded through "space-ether" at 186,000 miles per second.

Such were the laws of the universe as conceived by observing man up until the year 1905. These laws added up to a brilliant achievement of the human mind, a body of knowledge arrived at by complex calculations and apparently confirmed by the then existing telescopic observations. They pictured a universe in which huge masses measured by three dimensions of width, length and height, moved in space according to an orderly, fixed time schedule. Like light, these bodies moved also in straight lines, or would have done so indefinitely were it not for the pull of the sun which caused them to orbit around it. All the planets thus had an absolute size and moved through an absolute space, in an absolute direction, according to an absolute time—a magnificent logical design of the absolutely determined. Its designers, the giant intellects in mathematics, physics and astronomy, left out only one simple factor. They had failed to take into account where they themselves were standing when they made their calculations.

Thoughtful scientists at the end of the nineteenth century did not seriously question the monumental discoveries of Newton and his predecessors. His laws were good, day in and day out, for the most cautious scientist. With further refinements upon the laws of Copernicus and Newton, especially in the telescopic study of light, conditions on the planets Venus and Mars, thousands of millions of miles way, became better known to modern man than the other side of their own little earth had been known to the Greeks. For the daily life of the average man it was sufficient (and still is) to rely on Newton's law of gravity. However, suddenly some seemingly minor and unimportant exceptions were being observed at the turn of the twentieth century. These exceptions were three in number.

The first was that the planet Mercury was misbehaving. According to Newton's laws, Mercury should swing clear around the sun once in about 220,000 years. Mercury was a delinquent, guilty of speeding. It was swinging around in 200,000 years, or faster than the legal celestial speed limit by forty-three minutes per hundred years. This would scarcely have disturbed earthly traffic courts; but it was a puzzle to pure thought.

The second unsolved puzzle concerned the speed of light. If light were aided by the drift of the ether that was supposed to be in space, then light should have traveled faster in the direction of the drift. Light should have traveled faster from west to east, in the direction of the earth's rotation, and slower in the opposite direction, against the ether drift, just as a boat travels faster downstream than upstream. In 1887 a Jew, Albert Michelson, the first American winner of a Nobel prize invented in Chicago an instrument for measuring which was one of the most precise ever devised by man—with an accuracy down to one ten-millionth. With his interferometer Michelson picked up light beams from the opposite sides of one red star in the constellation Orion, and calculated its diameter to be 250 million miles, or three hundred times larger in diameter than our own sun. If it were substituted for our sun, this star would extend a third of the way across our sky. Michelson also tried to measure the speed of light, to determine whether it would go faster eastward than westward, as it should have done according to the laws. He thought his instrument had failed, through being unable to catch the enormous speed of light, because it showed that there was no difference in either direction. The light sped as fast in one direction as it did in the other—against the logic of the Newtonian laws as they were then known.

The third puzzle entered the picture with the new discoveries of electricity made by Faraday in the nineteenth century. Newton had said, "God in the beginning formed matter in solid, hard, impenetrable movable particles . . . so very hard as never to wear or break in pieces, no ordinary power being able to divide what God himself made one." At the end of the nineteenth century and the beginning of the twentieth, Newton's unbreakable particle was broken by epoch-making discoveries made by a succession of great scientists and Nobel prize winners. With their discoveries of the X-ray, radium and radioactivity, with the development of highly complex instruments for measuring and photographing the inside of the atom, and finally by smashing the atom with extremely high-voltage machines, these scientists completely revolutionized the concept of the nature of matter that had been held for centuries, as far back as the Greeks. The Greeks had given to the smallest unit of matter, which they thought to be indivisible and unbreakable, the name *atomos*, which was their word for "indivisible." Now, for the first time, the atom was found not to be indivisible—and not solid at all.

Each atom was discovered to have a tiny solar system all its own. Each atom has a center around which electrically charged smaller particles revolve like planets. Atoms may even be classified according to whether they have one such tiny planet in their orbit (as in the hydrogen atom) or as many as ninety-two such planets (as in the uranium atom). Indeed, an atom can even be weighed to determine whether it has more or fewer isotopes than one with the same constitution. Now, the old classical physics had declared that the size or weight of a thing did not change when it moved. For all practical purposes this is still true. We do not see any change in the size or weight of an automobile when it moves. But the new electromagnetic and atomic science showed that electrons were changing their mass and size as they changed their speed. This was the third puzzle.

An elite among intellectuals, the physicists and astronomers of the twentieth century, tried to solve all three of these puzzles. Some examined the movements of the planets, some the movement of light, others the movement of electrons. None questioned, however, the *accepted* general laws of nature that had been handed down from the past, even though they were aware of the contradictions between Newton's mechanical explanations of gravity and the new electromagnetic phenomena. The scientific world was ripe for a new look at the nature of the universe and of the behavior of matter. It was ready for a mind that would not be satisfied with making little adjustments to account for the growing number of flaws in all the past theories. The world was ready for a new intellectual genius who, like Newton, Copernicus and Pythagoras, would not be afraid to question the basic assumptions so long accepted—a genius who could reshuffle the pieces in the puzzle and put them together again.

A shy, humble scientist offered the first phase of a new answer to the riddle of the universe in thirty pages handwritten on letter-sized paper. On June 30, 1905 he placed his manuscript (which would have been a priceless original, but which was discarded by the author after its publication) on the desk of the editor of a leading journal of physics. The paper bore the title, "Toward the Electrodynamics of Moving Bodies." The author merely told the editor that he hoped it would be found worthy of publication. The author was completely unknown. He was a Jew named Albert Einstein. He was twenty-six years old. When he left the editor's office he took to his bed for fourteen days, ill with fatigue after what is possibly the most extraordinary achievement by any human mind. This paper was the last of four that Einstein had written in 1905. Each one was original. (In the first paper he described a method for measuring molecules; in the second he explained the photoelectric effect, the principle underlying the photo tube, which has made possible the world-wide communications of the twentieth century — the long-distance telephone, talking motion pictures, radio, television and the electron microscope; in the third he presented a kinetic theory of heat.) Einstein had stood where no other man had stood before.

A very small group of the world's leading scientists recognized the revolutionary implications of young Einstein's four essays. Soon they began to look upon his additional findings during the next ten years, comprising Einstein's Special and General Theories of Relativity, as the greatest achievement of the human mind. Einstein had succeeded in synthesizing and resolving the contradictions of modern science. He soon came to be admired in a small circle of scientists as the greatest intellect the human race had thus far produced.

The world at large did not know for another fourteen years what a revolution in thought this Einstein had initiated. Even then, the Einstein Theory of Relativity remained an awesome mystery to the average person. Not until forty years later, in 1945, did the human race fully comprehend what this Jew, Einstein, had done. By one equation in his original essay of 1905, $E=MC^2$ or, energy is equal to matter multiplied by the square of the velocity of light—Einstein had indeed changed the world. The world would never be the same after the bombing of Hiroshima in 1945 had been made possible by Einstein's theories.

Einstein changed the entire question of how man should look at and think about his world. By this alteration in thought he unchained a power imprisoned in nature so mighty that man may use it for his salvation or his total annihilation. Einstein changed the world by asking himself that simple question which all his predecessors had ignored—where does the observer stand when he observes anything? Is he on the outside when he watches what takes place in the heavens? The answer seemed perfectly simple to Einstein. That answer was no.

Man, the observer, is part of what is being observed. Even when watching the stars, man must include in his findings the fact that he is standing on an earth which is itself in constant motion. Indeed, even the smallest object, which to the human eye seems to be standing still, is in constant motion. Therefore, any description of a thing which gives only its length, breadth and width is incomplete. One must always take into consideration a fourth dimension—motion. Movement from one place to another can only be measured by time. Even space moves, and therefore one must now speak of "space-time." Even time is not the same everywhere, but changes with the differing speed of the motion of each planet. As long as man relied only on his own senses, his eyes could not see this universal motion and these differences in time. It was a mistake to abstract theories from experimental observations which did not take into account the limitations of the human senses. Philosophers had said this; but Einstein was the first theoretical scientist to take the philosophers seriously. When he put into his mathematical equations the observer as well as the signals by which things become known to the observer, Einstein had the basis for solving all three of the puzzles. Only through the precise, impersonal language of mathematics could man escape personal and subjective conclusions and arrive at laws correct for all times and places, whether for man on earth, or for beings on Mars.

Physicists were astonished. Einstein's deductions explained, first, the delinquency of the planet Mercury; second, they showed that light could not go faster or slower because its speed was the only constant thing in the universe, and that, furthermore, light could travel in curved as well as straight lines; third, his deductions showed that the so-called stationary matter and moving electrical energy, instead of being distinct and separate, are so linked together that they are related forms of the same thing—that they are, indeed, interchangeable.

What all this meant in a practical sense was remotely guessed by a few. Even understanding Einstein's ideas theoretically called for a unique ability in deciphering his mathematical symbols. Indeed, once his theory became known to the world in the 1920's, popular interest was increased by the exaggerated notion that nobody else knew what Einstein was talking about. It was jokingly doubted whether even Einstein could explain it. Yet no one in the succeeding years worked as hard as Einstein did himself to make clear to the common man the meaning, in terms of life and death, of this new atomic age, which is so properly called the age of Einstein.

Einstein even resorted to jokes to make his theory better known: "When a nice girl sits on your lap for an hour you think it's only a minute, but when you sit on a hot stove for a minute you think it is an hour—that's relativity." Another story told by Einstein to explain how all things are related to each other is the one in which a thirsty blind man is offered a drink of milk. He asks, "What is milk?" and the answer he receives is, "A white liquid."

He replies, "Liquid I know, but what is white?"

"White is like the feathers of a swan," is the answer.

"Feathers I know, but what is a swan?" the blind man asks.

"A swan is a bird with a crooked neck."

"Neck I know," replies the blind man, "but what is crooked?"

To explain "crooked," his friend bends the blind man's arm. "Oh," exclaims the blind man, "now I know what milk is."

The immortality of Einstein rests on three factors. It rests first on his scientific achievement, which is and will remain the foundation of his greatness. However, his fame also rests on the change in world outlook that he brought to this century. He made "Relativity" a household word. Third, his fame rests upon his international humanitarianism and wise counsel, which in his later years made the name Einstein beloved and better known even than Relativity. The world came to know Einstein not so much as a universe-maker whose theories the average man could never hope to decipher, but as the twentieth century's first world citizen, one of the outstanding spiritual leaders of his time, whose every word and act became a symbol of the future and of the needs of that future.

No one could have guessed from his childhood that the boy Albert Einstein would surpass the great Kepler who had lived 250 years before in Ulm, South Germany, where Albert was born on March 14, 1879. Albert's kindly, optimistic, easy-going father even consulted a doctor about his son's slowness in learning to talk. Yet when the boy was four, the father was alarmed at the boy's passionate curiosity. He had given his son a compass, and Albert wanted to know why the dancing magnetic needle always turned north no matter in what position it was held. This secret power of the compass fascinated him, and he would rather watch it than play with toy soldiers. His uncle taught him algebra by saying, "When you don't know what a thing is you call it X, and then go right ahead and look for it." The game of solving the puzzles of numbers became Albert Einstein's undying passion. Learning by rote in school bored him—especially under the militarized martinets in the Catholic school he attended in Munich, where his family had moved. He frequently played truant to roam the woods.

Early, the bushy-haired boy with soulful eyes showed

signs of the sensitiveness, the indifference to social conventions, and the intense love of solitude which characterized his whole life. Certain events in his childhood helped to fashion this pattern of isolation. A teacher once displayed a nail which he said had been used by the Jews to crucify Jesus. The anti-Semitism it let loose in the class at the Catholic school in Munich left a deep scar which Einstein never forgot. His boyhood coincided with the rise, under Kaiser Wilhelm II, of the German militarism that culminated in the First World War. The goose-stepping soldiers parading with their steel bayonets filled young Albert with such terror that when he was only nine he pleaded with his parents to save him from being drafted into this terrifying war machine.

Albert enjoyed a happy Jewish family life, which counteracted his distress over German militarism and anti-Semitism. He rejoiced in his father's humor, which he fortunately inherited. From his loving mother he received not only the encouragement to believe in himself but also his second love in life, music. Einstein began the study of violin at the age of six. Like Pythagoras, he was inspired by mathematics and music with an adoration for the harmony in the universe that was akin to religious awe. Although his father was a freethinker, he taught Albert Judaism at home. However, like Spinoza, the boy identified God with nature. He would compose brief songs in praise of the God of nature as he roamed the woods.

Carrying out an old Jewish tradition, once a week the Einstein family invited a Russian Jewish student in Munich to share a home-cooked meal with them. For five years this east European Jewish student was a weekly visitor. Recognizing Albert's genius for mathematics, he encouraged him. He was soon surpassed by the boy who, by the age of fourteen, had read advanced books in mathematics and physics.

Business reverses compelled the family to move to Italy, but Albert was left behind to finish school. Lonely and bored by the dull discipline of the school, he ran away and joined his family. Later his father sent him to Switzerland to become an engineer. However, Albert became absorbed in the study of light and chose theoretical physics and teaching as a career—only to discover that anti-Semitism prevented him from finding a job as a teacher.

Penniless and unemployed, with his sole possessions, one baggy suit and a violin, Einstein finally appeared in Bern, Switzerland. Through a friend he got a job examining patent applications at the Swiss patent office, at a small salary, the equivalent of $600 a year. It was a routine job, but he liked it because it left him time to think. When the supervisor was not looking, Einstein would scribble his figures on a pad of paper. He did not need a laboratory, telescope or instruments. All Einstein needed was his head, a pen and paper. Secure in his modest job, he married a university classmate and fellow intellectual, a Serbian Catholic. They lived frugally. After seeing his wife darn his socks, Einstein gave up wearing socks altogether so as not to burden her. With his wife and two sons he lived in a tenement flat, where in 1905 he wrote the draft of that fourth paper, which was to shake the foundations of the world.

A few of the greatest scientists recognized the scientific importance of that one essay and communicated with the unknown clerk. After four years, the significance of this paper finally reached his own university in Zurich. The university offered Einstein a professorship, for which he had to qualify by first giving satisfactory free lectures. His first class comprised two persons, both of them his personal friends. As his fame grew, Einstein lectured at many European universities. By 1914, on the recommendation of the leading European scientists he was made director of the Kaiser Wilhelm Institute for Theoretical Physics in Berlin. This position left him free to devote himself to his studies. He was only thirty-four. By 1915 the fundamental structure of the Einsteinian universe had been established. The rest of his life, Einstein refined his theory, ever seeking a single law that would embrace the harmony of the universe.

In the meantime, his personal life was not without its problems. This intellectual visionary was dreamy and absent-minded. He had little regard for practical things and wanted only his privacy in order to think. By mutual consent he and his wife were divorced, and she settled with their two sons in Switzerland. Fortunately, he found an understanding companion in his second cousin, Elsa, who had also been divorced. She was as modest and unassuming as Einstein himself. Throughout their marriage, until she died in 1936, she protected the genius who was her husband. With Elsa's two daughters by her previous marriage, the Einsteins lived on the top floor of a middle-class apartment in West Berlin.

In an attic room fifteen feet square, filled with books and containing a large Bible, a picture of Newton and a piano, Einstein retreated from the First World War into the four-dimensional cosmic world through which his mind could navigate in tranquillity. While Germany was being defeated, this pacifist German Jew won alone a victory of the mind which was to restore the reputation for science and culture that Germany had lost through its militarism. Einstein's discoveries regained for Germany a place of respect among the nations.

During the First World War he had witnessed in Berlin

the brutality of the German militarism and the futility of war. This activated his long-standing tendency toward pacifism. He also saw the beginnings of Nazi anti-Semitism. This converted him to the Zionism he had formerly opposed. However, before his world leadership in behalf of disarmament and peace and of the Jewish people would be recognized, the dramatic event occurred which was to usher in the second phase of his career, and establish him in the world as the popular hero of Relativity.

Up until 1919 the world had known nothing of Einstein, but he had set a small circle of scientists agog by a bold statement he had made in a paper in 1915. In that paper he had written: "Watch the behavior of starlight as it passes near the sun at the next eclipse for verification of my hypothesis." Some British astronomers were determined to put Einstein to the test. The next eclipse was to occur on May 29, 1919. They made careful preparations to photograph this eclipse. At the very moment the Versailles Treaty was being concluded, sealing the defeat of the German army, these English astronomers sailed to the south Atlantic and set up their high-powered telescopic equipment near the Equator. By sheer mathematical calculation, Einstein had predicted that a ray of light reflected from a certain star, millions and millions of miles away from the area of the sun, would bend as it passed the sun. He had even figured that its curve would be 1.745 seconds of an arc. To the breathless astonishment of the British astronomers, what Einstein had calculated in his attic room was confirmed in the vast reaches of the universe. He was correct to the smallest degree. So certain was Einstein that when the dumbfounded but admiring astronomers sent him the photos, he remarked, "As if there had been any doubt!" When the report of the expedition was made known, the excitement at the meeting of the Royal Society in London was tumultuous. The news released to the press flashed headlines around the world:

REVOLUTION IN PHYSICS—
NEWTON'S LAW OF GRAVITY OVERTHROWN

The unknown Einstein was catapulted overnight into the position of a world hero. At the age of forty he became a living legend.

The deductions were sensational. Before Einstein, it had been thought that light traveled only in straight lines. Now, it was indisputable that light traveled in curves. Before Einstein it had been solely the pull of the sun's gravity which was believed to orbit the planets around it. Gravity was still there, but now it pulled not the planets but the space around the sun. Gravity formed a hollow or a curve in the space around the sun, creating valleys and hills in the heavens. By a kind of law of cosmic laziness, the planets picked the path of least resistance and traveled in the curvatures or the valleys. This was the reason, said Einstein, that planets did not travel in circles but in ellipses. Furthermore, gravity itself could not account for movement. Any mass which does exert the pull of gravity is also moving itself. The degree of its gravitational pull is related to the degree of its own motion.

Newton's famous apple had fallen straight down from its tree not only because of the pull of the earth's center of gravity, but also because the earth rotates at a certain speed. If that speed could be increased, the apple would fall not to the ground but parallel to it. If the earth went around very fast, the apple would fall upward, along a perpendicular path into the sky. An inch, a pound or even the movement of a clock is not the same everywhere. An inch could be shorter or longer, a pound lighter or heavier, a watch faster or slower depending on the speed of the motion of the place in which an inch was measured, a pound weighed, or a clock timed. The only thing which never changed was the speed of light. By joining matter and gravity to space, motion and time, Einstein had arrived at a single primary law to explain all natural events in the universe. This law of relativity was as true for sentient beings, if any, on Mars as for men on earth.

Everyone now knew that Einstein had done something, but few knew exactly what it was. In the ten years following the sensation of 1919, more than five thousand books, in dozens of languages, were published to simplify Relativity, or the relatedness of all phenomena to each other. The face of Einstein, his dark brown eyes with their faraway look, his head capped with graying hair that waved like a lion's mane, became as well known as that of any Hollywood star. Indeed, he himself turned down an offer of $40,000 a week for an appearance in a movie. The short figure, tending toward pudginess, dressed in a baggy unpressed suit, might be seen by huge audiences at leading universities which had invited Einstein to address them. He was the first German to overcome anti-German feeling after the First World War, and to be favorably received in London and Paris. Police had to control rioting mobs attempting to get into the lecture halls. In America fifty dollars was offered for one admission ticket.

In the 1920's Einstein made a tour of the world and was welcomed like a triumphant hero in India and Japan. Baskets filled with mail from all parts of the world arrived every day at his home in Berlin. The high and the lowly sought answers to all sorts of questions, from advice to the lovelorn to equally complex problems in science and metaphysics. He received letters from a girl who offered herself as his private disciple in "cosmic meditation," along with offers from inventors with a plan to make every person rich. Babies were named after him, and a cigar came out labeled "Relativity." Everywhere he walked, Einstein was lionized.

The mystery of Einstein's popularity in the 1920's was explained as postwar mass psychology. Mankind had endured the first of the agonizing global wars and witnessed the terrifying destructiveness of the new weapons of science. In Einstein the world found a genius, for whom science consisted of pure thought in the pursuit of truth. Furthermore, this giant of science was shy, humble and modest. He avoided the pomp of kings and queens who invited him to their palaces. He was a cosmic genius with the heart of a child. Here was not only a great man but a kind, simple, selflessly good man. Einstein became a kind of scientific saint, whom the world expected to heal all its postwar wounds.

But envy, fear and hate were not slow to raise their heads. Einstein, the rebel, was accused of being a charlatan, a menace to science, to religion, even to motherhood and the price of wheat. Einstein confined his theories to nature. His enemies foolishly carried over his theories into metaphysics. In their rash ignorance they concluded that relativity meant there was no such thing as absolute truth, justice or God. Einstein himself objected to this loose use of the word Relativity. It became popular to use Relativity as an excuse for immoral behavior. Because one might relate any human act to some other circumstance, one was relieved of personal responsibility for one's behavior. Einstein replied that Relativity in physics was not applicable to morals. "I do not think," he said, "that the so called 'relativistic' point of view is correct—not even when dealing with the more subtle moral decisions." Nevertheless, a cardinal in Boston publicly denounced Einstein's theory as "false, atheistic and immoral." To a superpatriotic American woman's group protesting the visit of this pacifist to America, Einstein gave one of his most delightful and disarming responses: "Never yet have I experienced from the fair sex such energetic rejection of all advances; or if I have, never from so many at once." As the debates raged in philosophic and theological circles, Einstein played his violin and kept his good humor even when he differed with his fellow scientists.

The scientists applauded Einstein's analysis of the little universe in the invisible atom. However, even scientists never really accepted his theory about the larger universe. Indeed, as Einstein continued through his life to search for that will-of-the-wisp, the single law which governs all nature, he found himself isolated from his fellow physicists. Insofar as the atom is concerned, Einstein agreed that radiation from atomic energy does not pass in a continuous stream. According to one theory, radiation was given off in separate small packages of quantities (quanta). The physicist Planck was the author of this quantum theory The quantum physicists also held not only that the particles or waves involved were separate, but also that it was not possible to predict their behavior. According to the quantum theory, there could be no cause and effect in the universe. All was uncertain and unpredictable. Einstein opposed this view.

Behind Einstein's lifelong search for a Unified Field Theory lay the schism that had persisted in human thought throughout the ages. In Einstein there converged the conflict of monism *versus* dualism, continuity *versus* discontinuity, cause *versus* chance. Einstein insisted that there would yet be found a way of demonstrating that atomic particles and electrical waves were related to each other in a continuing way. Einstein believed the universe was governed by cause and effect, in which any individual event could be predicted. It may have been his emotional loyalty to Judaism, with its insistence on the related oneness of all, that would not permit him to be satisfied with anything else. Everything from the smallest to the largest had a cause. Einstein put his view in these non-scientific but no less significant terms: "I cannot believe that God plays dice with the cosmos; God is subtle but he is not malicious."

The committee which in 1921 awarded Einstein the Nobel prize tried to circumvent the dispute about Einstein among his fellow scientists as well as among laymen. The citation made no reference to the theory of relativity. Einstein was given the Nobel prize for his theoretical analysis of the photoelectric effect. Einstein was not deceived by the omission of any reference to his theory of relativity. With the foresight and humor so characteristic of him, Einstein said in a press interview after the award that he could think of two future practical discoveries which might threaten mankind with annihilation—the discovery of atomic energy and the discovery of how to read other people's thoughts.

The first prediction came true. Einstein would have preferred that a way to read men's thoughts might have come about first, for concurrent with the fame of Einstein appeared the growth of Nazism—the most evil distortion of the human mind in all of man's history. Einstein was one of the first to realize the true nature of Nazism, and only since its overthrow has the world come to know how necessary for survival it is to know how men think. The crisis of the twentieth century is telescoped in the contrast between Einstein, the humanitarian Jew, lover of peace and truth, and Hitler, the authoritarian fanatic, the anti-Semitic exponent of war, falsehood and hate. Einstein and Hitler never met, but their paths crossed at the very crossroads of our times. Not until it was too late did the world know or want to believe what was in Hitler's mind. It did know, but paid little heed, to what Einstein thought about Fascism, Nazism, anti-Semitism and war.

Even before he had become world-famous, Einstein demonstrated his fearlessness when he refused to add his name to those of eighty-three leaders in science and art in Germany who had signed a manifesto justifying Germany's war action in 1914. Instead, Einstein denounced militarism. The fanatical German nationalists never forgave him. When he did become a world figure after the First World War, Einstein contributed the luster of his name to the ill-fated Weimar Republic by renewing his German citizenship. Because of his support of the Weimar Republic, Einstein became a target of the Nazis. His Jewish friend Walter Rathenau, the German Weimar Republic's Foreign Minister, was assassinated by the young Nazis in 1922. In his eulogy of Rathenau, Einstein warned the German people: "I would never have thought that hatred, blindness and ingratitude could go to such extremes. But I should like to say to those who have guided the ethical training of the German people in the last fifty years, "By their fruits shall ye know them.' " Einstein was prophetic in his 1922 analysis of German secular and religious anti-Semitism.

In his wish to strengthen the tottering German republic, Einstein would not leave Germany although his own life was threatened. Now regarded as the first citizen of the world and as an ambassador of good will, it was Einstein who brought the premiers of France and Germany together—a meeting that resulted in the Locarno Peace Pact of 1925. It was Einstein who rallied support among intellectuals for the League of Nations. He was an important member of this group up until his severe heart attack in 1928. Einstein's world leadership not only in science but in the cause of peace was honored all over the world in the celebration of his fiftieth birthday in 1929. This, too, was opposed by the Nazis, who made an embarrassing fiasco out of Berlin's desire to make Einstein the gift of a house on a lakeside where he might enjoy his only sport —sailing.

The last twenty-five years of his life, now that he was a world figure, constituted the third phase of Einstein's life —one devoted to a deliberate effort to change men's thinking. The thinking of the human race would have to change if the human race were to survive in a world so profoundly changed by the work of Einstein's own mind. On every available occasion Einstein spoke out on three things: disarmament and a new, supernational world organization for peace; the new role that religion must now play in behalf of uniting humanity against the threat of disaster; and the protection and the preservation of the Jewish people, whose treatment and destiny he declared to be a barometer of what would happen to all mankind. A summary of Einstein's views on each of the three world problems follows. This summary is based on direct quotations from Einstein's addresses and articles.

Einstein was a realistic pacifist. He advocated the refusal to give military service as a necessary gesture to counteract the tendency of governments to resort to organized violence. He believed this could work only if at least 50,000 conscientious objectors in each of the great States refused to fight. He knew that Hitlerism had to be stopped, but this did not blind him as it did others to the totalitarian dangers of the Communist Russian ally. Nevertheless, he believed that fears about the Soviet Union did not warrant an unlimited reliance on the rearmament of an unrepentant German people. He predicted that the rearmament of Germany would repeat the follies of the First World War. Furthermore, no one denounced the arrogant stubbornness and the ideological blindness of the Soviets more than did Einstein. He was attacked by the Soviet scientists for his attitude. Still, he held that the West was not wholly innocent of aggravating Soviet distrust. Einstein warned both East and West that neither could win the next war. Neither side could prevent war by petty piecemeal disarmament. War could not be prevented even if both sides adopted the same economic system. "The discovery of the nuclear chain reaction need not bring about the destruction of mankind any more than did the discovery of matches"—but mankind was doomed unless both sides agreed to a world government having an international police force to safeguard the peace. No other issue or goal so engaged Einstein's passionate support.

Because only idealism could prevent a war of annihilation, Einstein felt that "unless the cause of peace based on law gathered behind it the forces and zeal of a religion it could hardly hope to succeed." "The atomic scientists," he said, "have become convinced that they can not arouse the American people to the truths of the atomic era by logic alone. There must be added that deep power of emotion which is a basic ingredient of religion." "Religion without science is blind; but," said Einstein, "science without religion is lame."

Now, what did Einstein mean by religion? He did not mean a religion of superstition or of fear. Einstein did not have a definite notion of a personal God. He used the term "cosmic religious feeling," by which he meant a rapturous wonder at the harmony of natural law which reveals an intelligence of such superiority that, compared with it, all the systematic thinking and acting of human beings is an utterly insignificant reflection. "Mere thinking," said this greatest intellect of the scientific age, "cannot give us a sense of the ultimate and fundamental ends." "To make clear these fundamental ends and valuations and to set them fast in the emotional life of the individual" seemed to Einstein "precisely the most important function which religion has to perform on the social life of man." "And if one asks whence derives the authority of such fundamental ends, since they cannot be stated and justified merely by reason," one could only answer, said Einstein, that "they exist in a healthy society as powerful traditions which act upon the conduct and aspirations and judgments of the individual. They are there, that is, as something living without its being necessary to find justification for their existence." "They come into being not through demonstration," said this scientist philosopher, "but through revelation, through the medium of powerful personalities." Nevertheless, he added, "there is not room in this for the divinization of a nation, of a class, let alone of an individual," even though "the ancients knew something which we have forgotten"—namely that "all means prove a blunt instrument if they have not behind them a living spirit."

The highest expression of this living spirit he held to be the Jewish-Christian religious tradition. Einstein wrote, "If one purges Judaism of the Prophets and Christianity as Jesus taught it of all subsequent additions, especially those of the priests, one is left with a teaching capable of curing all the social ills of humanity." This religious teaching opposes "ruthless striving for success at the expense of one's fellow men." Religion opposes the "competitive spirit that prevails even in schools, destroying all feelings of human fraternity and cooperation, and that conceives of achievement not as derived from the love of production and thoughtful work, but as springing from personal ambition or fear of rejection." Unfortunately, "there are pessimists who hold that such a state of affairs is necessarily inherent in human nature." "It is those who propound such views," said Einstein, "that are the enemies of true religion, for they imply that religious teachings are utopian ideals and unsuited to afford guidance in human affairs. Such a defeatist view is wholly unwarranted."

Einstein believed, then, that purified of superstition, religion performed the function of sustaining sympathetic feeling, ethical value and the emotional springs of moral action. "In this sense," he declared, "religion forms an important part of education, where it receives far too little consideration and that little not sufficiently systematic. The frightful dilemma of the political world situation has much to do with this sin of omission on the part of our civilization"—because "the man who regards his own life and that of his fellow creatures as meaningless is not merely unhappy but hardly fit for life."

Einstein was forever grateful that it was the religious genius "incarnate in the Jewish people" which gave to the world this "affirmative attitude to the life of all creation." He defined Judaism as "making the life of every living thing nobler and more beautiful," because it declared that "life is sacred, that is to say, it is the supreme value, to which all other values are subordinate—a reverence for everything spiritual." Einstein was profoundly moved by the Jewish tradition, in which was expressed "a sort of intoxicating joy and amazement at the beauty and the grandeur of the world." Einstein compared this feeling to poetry, music and even science which "in its pure form" also manifests "the fundamental principle of the sanctification of life."

Two other characteristics of the Jew impressed and influenced Einstein. They were the Jew's keen respect for intellectual pursuits, and his deep feeling for social justice. Einstein held these Jewish qualities to be responsible for the leading role that the Jews, in disproportionate numbers, had played in developing humane solutions to man's economic problems. While Freud used psychological terms to express pride in his Jewishness, Einstein appropriately couched his pride in an astronomical referent, exclaiming, "The pursuit of knowledge for its own sake, an almost fanatical love of justice and the desire for personal independence—these are the features of the Jewish tradition which make me *thank my stars* [Italics mine] that I belong to it."

Throughout his life Einstein urged his fellow Jews to gain for themselves this sense of belonging to the Jewish community. To him "a baptized Jew was a pathetic creature" and the "moral danger of the Jew who has lost touch with his own people . . . a contemptible and joyless egoism." He was convinced that even the ghetto Jew was better off than an assimilated Jew. "Our forefathers," he wrote, "in those days were pretty poor specimens intellectually and physically, but socially speaking they enjoyed an enviable spiritual equilibrium." He admitted that in his own case it was anti-Semitism which strengthened a Jew's self-consciousness, but he came to the conclusion that "the existence and destiny of our people depends less on external factors than on ourselves. . . . We must learn once more to glory in our ancestors and our history and once again take upon ourselves as a nation, cultural tasks of a sort calculated to strengthen our sense of community."

It was not nationalism so much as this cultural sense of community that inspired Einstein's loyalty to Zionism and the new state of Israel. Einstein was more of an Achad Ha'am-cultural than he was a Herzlian-political Zionist. He had hoped that Israel would develop like the Switzerland he had loved in his youth, where three different nationalities and languages—French, German and Italian—exist peacefully under a single Swiss citizenship. This was the ideal he hoped for between Arab and Jew in Israel. "I am afraid," he said, "of the inner damage Judaism will sustain, especially from the development of a narrow nationalism within our nation, against which we have already had to fight strongly even without a Jewish state." Yet he insisted that "it is possible to be a good citizen anywhere and at the same time a faithful Jew who loves his people and honors his fathers."

Einstein advanced the conviction that the Jew's strengthening of his identification with Jews would help the whole world. He proclaimed that "the atomic age, which can itself survive only by a revival of spiritual values, needs the Jew to continue to demonstrate to the world the survival quality of these values. . . ." "In the past," Einstein observed, "we were persecuted despite the fact that we were the people of the Book. Today, however, it is just because we are the people of the Book that we are persecuted. . . . Those who are raging today against the ideals of reason and individual liberty and are trying to establish a spiritless state of slavery of brute force rightly see in us their irreconcilable foes." Thus, addressing himself to Jews, Einstein concluded, "It is our duty to remain faithful to the moral traditions which have enabled us to survive for thousands of years."

Criticized on all sides for his view on these three problems—on disarmament and world government, on religion and on the Jews—at the beginning of this phase of his life Einstein made his famous remark, "If my theories prove correct, the Germans will call me German and the French will call me a Jew; but if they prove incorrect, the French will call me a German and the Germans will call me a Jew." Just before Hitler took power, Einstein made a world-wide appeal to intellectuals to join him in an effort to prevent the next war. He even made a public appeal to Sigmund Freud, as one who, he felt, knew more than anyone else about controlling the barbaric, murderous instincts in men. It was indirectly as a result of the Nazis that Einstein also became a conscious Jew, having been converted to Zionism by a fellow scientist, Chaim Weizmann. It was in behalf of the cause of Zionism that Einstein made his first triumphant visit to America.

It was during Einstein's third visit to America to lecture on science that Hitler came into power. The German Embassy in Washington tried to get Einstein to return to his home in Berlin in order to give the new regime the mark of respectability. Einstein not only refused to go back but warned the world of the impending dangers of Hitlerism. He accepted a position at the Princeton Institute for Advanced Studies, where he worked for twenty-two years, until his death in 1955. He was the most famous citizen of Princeton. His neighbors finally got used to his eccentricities. Well-dressed Ivy Leaguers would see him dressed in baggy pants and a sweater, walking down the street licking an ice cream cone, or walking in the rain in bedroom slippers. Einstein once said that these were intellectually the happiest years of his life; for he loved the freedom of inquiry that inspired Americans, and he eventually became an American citizen.

From 1933 to 1939, in order to help Jewish refugees, scientists and children to escape before it was too late, Einstein did things which were the most difficult for his nature to do. He pleaded for funds, auctioned a manuscript and even played the violin in public to help the United Jewish Appeal. He raised his voice in defense of the Jew; he raised his voice in behalf of disarmament and world peace; he raised his voice to inspire religion to take a lead in the crusade for human dignity and peace. His voice was like a cry in the wilderness. Because he could not succeed, Einstein was compelled to face a greater crisis of conscience and conviction than any man before him had had to face.

Einstein was a lifelong absolute pacifist, who loved mankind and abhorred war. Now, he had to make the choice between acquiescing to the return of barbarism and the tragedy of fighting against it. Some refugee physicists had discussed with him recent discoveries which made it likely that the energy in the atom could be released explosively. These discoveries were known in Germany, and were being developed in the very Kaiser Wilhelm Institute which Einstein had once directed. What would happen if Hitler were to use what Einstein had made possible? Pacifism had to be viewed from a new approach, just as Einstein had once viewed the universe from a new approach in order to fit the facts. On August 2, 1939 Einstein broke with a lifetime of pacifist belief as only he could have done. He wrote, in a now famous letter to President Roosevelt, that in his view the information meant that an atomic bomb could be made, and that it must be feared that the Germans would try to make it. A letter so fantastic that it might have come from a Jules Verne would have been believed only if it came from an Einstein. Roosevelt immediately set in motion the expenditure of over two billion dollars to make the first atomic bomb. Using a quantity of uranium less than two-fifths the size of a dime, that bomb made an explosion greater and more destructive than 20,000 tons of TNT. By one of the strangest ironies of history, it was Einstein, the outstanding pacifist of his age, who initiated the move that led the United States to make the A-bomb.

The idealist who at twenty-six had equated mass with energy now, at sixty, saw that equation threaten the world.

He had made the only choice a man of conscience could have made; but later he said, "Had I been positive the Nazis would not be able to do it I would not have lifted a finger." When a reporter hurried to Saranac Lake, where he was sailing, to give Einstein the news of Hiroshima, his only statement to the world was, "Ach! mankind is not ready for it."

The one man ready for the atomic age was Einstein. He was the first to have a vision of its power for good or for evil. Einstein knew the world could not become ready for it merely by higher learning, even though in his last years he devoted much time to the support of the Hebrew University, the Weizmann Institute and the Albert Einstein Medical Center. He knew the world could not become ready for it merely by political leadership, and he refused the honor of becoming President of Israel after Weizmann's death. Learning and wise statesmanship were needed, but the world would need even more the kind of person Einstein was. He was a person endlessly good-humored and happy with human beings. He was as patient with adults as he was with children, even with the many strangers who sneaked up to his front porch in Princeton, and had themselves photographed by their wives as if they were just coming out of the great man's house. It was only with arrogant authority and ignorant intolerance that he was impatient. For him the key to the future of the world lay in the minds of men. His fight for freedom of thought was not just an abstract defense of thinking, even though his own intellectual beliefs—including his religious beliefs, which were not those of a conformist—were those of one who enjoyed having such freedom. His fight for freedom came rather from a deep empathy with those who suffer. He prized the integrity and sanctity of individual personality more highly than human science in general. He loved his own people. Men all over the world knew that if their cause was just they could turn to him for help. The illustrious name of Einstein led the lists of the great who signed petitions, from those protesting the miscarriage of justice in the Sacco-Vanzetti case to those advocating world disarmament.

Einstein, then, is the exemplar of that humanity the world needs to make itself ready for the age of Einstein. Yet, even an Einstein had to change himself to meet the world he had himself changed.

In the introduction we noted certain remarkable parallels between Jesus and Freud, between Paul and Marx and between Moses and Einstein. Moses stood on the majestic heights of Sinai where he was alone with his God—Whom, nevertheless, he was not allowed to see face to face. Einstein liked most to be alone on the peak of his scientific Sinai, seeking his one God—that single unifying law of the universe which likewise ever eluded him. Because he felt the mystery of creation to be "the highest wisdom and the most radiant beauty," Einstein did say of himself, "I belong to the ranks of the devoutly religious men." Moses descended from the clouds about Sinai to bring down to the Jewish people, and through them to the world, the moral laws by which men may live in freedom and not die enslaved. Einstein likewise came down from the rarefied abstractions where he contemplated the perfections of the heavens. He left his ivory tower that he might modestly and understandingly deal with the imperfections of man. Like Moses, Einstein accepted fully his responsibility to take up the burdens of a suffering Jewish people, and by his commitment to Jewish ideals to help all suffering men to liberate themselves for a fuller, better and freer life.

Time may or may not prove Einstein to be the greatest Jewish figure since Moses; but time will certainly prove that mankind must live by the moral laws of Moses in order to survive the atomic space age which the mind of Einstein initiated. An opportunity has now been given to make life on this little planet more fruitful for all. As man chooses, atomic energy may be fruitful for all, or it may be the end of all. Einstein made dramatically real the words with which Moses, the first of the six Jews who changed the world, warned that world: "This day . . . I have set before thee life and death, the blessing and the curse; therefore choose life." How can man make the right choice? The answer is clear. The answer is the whole life lived by the Jew who made the choice possible. The answer is Einstein himself. He matched greatness of mind with greatness of soul, and thus showed man how to match ability with morality and competence with a conscience.